T0317409

Howard Barker Interviews 1980–2010

Howard Barker Interviews 1980–2010

Conversations in Catastrophe

Edited by Mark Brown

intellect Bristol, UK / Chicago, USA

First published in the UK in 2011 by
Intellect, The Mill, Parnall Road, Fishponds, Bristol, BS16 3JG, UK

First published in the USA in 2011 by
Intellect, The University of Chicago Press, 1427 E. 60th Street,
Chicago, IL 60637, USA

Copyright © 2011 Intellect Ltd

All rights reserved. No part of this publication may be reproduced,
stored in a retrieval system, or transmitted, in any form or by
any means, electronic, mechanical, photocopying, recording, or
otherwise, without written permission.

A catalogue record for this book is available from the
British Library.

Cover portrait of Howard Barker by Victoria Wicks.

Cover designer: Holly Rose
Copy-editor: Macmillan
Typesetting: Mac Style, Beverley, E. Yorkshire

ISBN 978-1-84150-398-1

Printed and bound by Gutenberg Press, Malta.

The publication of this book was supported by
The Carnegie Trust for the Universities of Scotland.

For Jill Hallam
without whom…

In memoriam:

Paulo Eduardo Carvalho
7 July 1964–20 May 2010

Theatre critic, scholar,
Portuguese translator of Barker,
mentor and friend

Contents

Acknowledgements

A collection such as this requires the goodwill and support of a number people, and there are a number to thank. Firstly, of course, my thanks to all of the interviewers for agreeing generously to the publication of their work in this volume, and, in many cases, for providing me with material which it would otherwise have been difficult, if not impossible, for me to locate.

An enormous debt of gratitude is owed to Chris Corner, General Manager of The Wrestling School, for his immense and invaluable contribution, in terms of locating and supplying a wealth of images and information. A great debt, too, to the leading Barker scholar David Ian Rabey (Aberystwyth University) for his tremendous support and advice throughout the project.

For various forms of assistance, my thanks to Elisabeth Angel-Perez (Paris-Sorbonne, France); Michelle Brodie; Nicole Brodie; Anthony Cook (Purdue University, USA); Donald Fraser; David Goldie (University of Strathclyde); Jill Hallam; Hugh Hodgart (Royal Scottish Academy of Music and Drama); George Hunka (Theatre Minima, USA); Kay Jamieson (Brink Productions, Australia); Sonia Legge; Gerrard McArthur (associate artist, The Wrestling School); Catarina Neves; and Simon Trussler (Rose Bruford College).

Thanks to my editors at Intellect, in particular Jelena Stanovnik, who was both supportive and patient in seeing the project through to its completion.

I would also like to thank Victoria Wicks – whose performance in Barker's *The Fence in its Thousandth Year* remains a highlight of my theatre-going career – for the generous permission to use her superb portrait photograph of Barker on the cover of this book.

Finally, my enduring gratitude is owed to Howard Barker himself for giving this project – from its genesis to its conclusion – the most generous moral and practical support.

Introduction

Howard Barker can, and should, be considered a classical author, such is the imaginative originality, intellectual and spiritual ambition, and the sheer poetic brilliance of his Theatre of Catastrophe. Moreover, his highly distinctive *oeuvre* (characterized, as it is, by a profound regard for tragedy) has been accompanied by his own powerful theatre theory (encapsulated, in particular, in his books *Arguments for a Theatre* and *Death, The One and the Art of Theatre*).

Barker is a divisive figure. The response to his work by the English or, at least, the London theatre and critical establishment has made him an internal exile in England. However, his theatre also generates great loyalty among many theatre-goers and theatre practitioners (not least actors), and has given rise to an entire academic discipline of Barker Studies, both within the UK and internationally (indeed, interviews conducted by many of the leading lights in this discipline appear in this volume).

I hope and believe that this collection of Barker's interviews will prove to be a substantial and unique addition to the growing body of literature related to his work as a dramatist, theatre theorist, poet and painter. Beginning in 1980 (a decade after the first staged production of Barker's work,[1] and the year in which the *Theatre Quarterly* interviewed him as a key figure amongst the "new theatre voices of the seventies") and culminating some 30 years later, these interviews provide a fascinating, chronological insight into the development of Barker's thought.

The distinctiveness of these interviews as a reservoir of Barker's theory is enhanced by the particular qualities which attach to ideas expressed in conversation (rather than in essays or other critical writings). On the three occasions on which I have interviewed Barker, I have been struck by both his sharp intelligence and his intellectual certainty; of the many people I have interviewed as a theatre critic and arts journalist, only the late, great dramatist Harold Pinter and the wonderful actress Fiona Shaw compare with him in these regards. Moreover, Barker has a remarkable capacity to formulate ideas seemingly instantaneously and to express them with style, wit and clarity; making his interviews a gift to the editor of a volume such as this.

Due to the nature of interviews, the material in this volume also has an autobiographical aspect; indeed, it is one which sets this book apart, even from the artistic autobiography contained within the Barker/Eduardo Houth book *A Style and its Origins*. No matter how assiduously the interviews adhere to Barker's art and artistic processes, they inevitably provide us with insights into Barker as a human being. There is, I think, something rather beautiful in the gentle excavation of Barker the man which some of these interviews contain. In these days of increasingly blunt prurience in our hyper-commercial mass media, it is a pleasure to gain subtle windows into the personality of an artist through his discussion of his art.

Ironically, given Barker's understandable suspicion of critics, there is a strong relationship between these interviews and theatre criticism. Criticism – whether manifested in reviews of particular theatrical productions or in works of more general analysis – is unfashionably, ideological. It codifies and classifies, it takes pugilistic stances, both in defence and attack, precisely in order that the art of theatre itself has the freedom not to do so. Side-taking – whether philosophical, political, moral or cultural contestation – is the vocation of the activist, the politician, the theologian, the ideologue and the critic. Any attempt to impose a prescription which requires the artist to fulfil such a role is inimical to the freedom of the artist. What we have in much of this book is Barker as ideological defender of his Theatre of Catastrophe, as critical observer of a culture which is hostile to his drama, and, often, as generously engaged analyser of his own work, in conversation with those who seek, paradoxically, to find language and concepts to analyse a body of work which is inherently resistant to analysis.

We see in these conversations some major changes in direction; for instance in Barker's relationship with a self-consciously instructional or satirical, typically left-wing drama, from which he has already begun to become dislocated in 1980, and with which he finds himself in a mutually, and increasingly, antagonistic relationship in the decades which follow. More significantly, however, we also find continuous threads in his artistic thought, particularly as regards his deep respect for the timeless power of tragedy and the theatre's enduring need of metaphor and ambiguity, despite the prevailing culture's hostility towards them. Time and again, in a rich and diverse array of artistic contexts, Barker returns to the seminal and enduring connection between sexual desire and death which, he insists, lies at the heart of tragedy, and which forms the fundamental basis of the Theatre of Catastrophe.

As we move chronologically through the interviews, Barker's separation from what he calls "the theatre" in England (as distinct from "the art of theatre"[2]) becomes increasingly pronounced; a reflection both of the London establishment's growing hostility towards him, and his increasing artistic self-reliance (which is epitomized by the creation of his own theatre company, The Wrestling School, in 1988). However, in many of the interviews, we also find Barker explaining the singularity of his artistic vision in terms which extend well beyond a defiance of the very serious and concerted efforts which were, and are, made in England to destroy him as an artist.

Barker has long been criticized in certain quarters for the perceived individualism – even solipsism – of his artistic process; I remember with some amusement a conversation I had with a prominent theatre director (and one far less accomplished than Barker) who opined that, "Barker's problem is that he doesn't understand that theatre is a collective endeavour". Much aside from the ludicrously reductive nature of this statement (as if all theatrical creation must share a common *modus operandi*), its blithe collectivism refuses to countenance the possibility of the brilliant, self-generating artist. In his continuous, startling originality and his inspiring prolificacy, Barker is such an artist.

In this collection we find him expressing both his appreciation of the skills and loyalty of the many theatre-makers who have worked with him throughout his career, and, without contradicting that appreciation, his absolute clarity as regards the totalizing, individual vision that lies within his work. Without such a self-generating vision, Barker simply would not have the extraordinary intellectual and spiritual drive which, much more than any mere defiance of adversaries, is the real wellspring of his tremendous body of work.

Although this book is intended, first and foremost, as a unique addition to Barker's own theoretical writings, it is also, through the interviewers represented here, reflective of the growth and development of interest in Barker's theatre. By bringing together previously published (but, in some cases, difficult to obtain) interviews with previously unpublished material, this book achieves, if not comprehensiveness, certainly a thorough account of Barker's voice over 30 years.

As one moves through the book, the interviews become increasingly international; with work from the United States (1998), France (2007 and 2010) and Greece (2009) complementing contributions from a diverse group of academic and journalistic interviewers from across the UK. It is also interesting to note the increasing number of interviews which appear in the first decade of the new millennium. At one level this, no doubt, reflects the relative ease of obtaining the most recent material. However, it is, more profoundly, a reflection of the growth of Barker Studies as a discipline; it is no coincidence that many of the interviews from recent years have been conducted by young researchers and dramatists of various nationalities.

Here, then, is a book which is addressed, of course, to the growing band of Barker enthusiasts – often known, academically, as 'Barkerians' (although I prefer the implications of the Spanish, *Barkeristas*) – and to theatre practitioners and students of contemporary theatre. However, like Barker's drama itself, it is also addressed, perhaps above all, to the "impatient" theatre lover[3] who is in search of the beauty, pain and profundity of a great, contemporary tragic theatre.

Mark Brown,
Glasgow,
February 2011

The Interviews

'Energy – and the small discovery of dignity'

With Malcolm Hay and Simon Trussler (for *Theatre Quarterly*)

Theatre Quarterly (TQ)
Howard Barker (HB)

TQ: How was it that you began to write plays?

HB: It began with a trio of radio plays. When I was at Sussex University I'd written three or four bad novels. University intensified my tendency to introspection, and the novel was the obvious form for me. Someone said the dialogue was the best part of these and urged me to write for radio. My first radio play was *One Afternoon on the Sixty-Third Level of the North Face of the Pyramid of Cheops the Great,* a half-hour comedy about a slaves' strike during the building of the pyramids. I was encouraged to write a couple more. These were *Henry V,* where the king says that anyone who fights with him that day shall be his brother. A common soldier takes him up on it. He calls on him in England some years afterwards and finds he's not as welcome as he expected. The other was *Herman with Millie and Mick,* a parable about the work ethic. It's been done on radio stations all over the world. They are original, clever, young man's plays.

TQ: You weren't particularly active in the theatre while you were at university?

HB: No, not at all. I'd come from a stable working-class background – relatively prosperous and socially ambitious, with my parents who believed passionately in the idea of a 'good education' – but theatre played no part whatsoever. My school was a philistine South London grammar school, so 'O' and 'A' level texts were the only plays I was acquainted with there. But a few of us – regarded warily by teachers and the bulk of the school – used to improvise a satirical/surrealist serial every lunchtime in the back of a disused army truck.

We acted characters we despised, like Dr Barnardo, Ernest Shackleton, Kennedy, Christ, and James Bond. We had diabolical figures too, like Crippen and Hitler. We never saw ourselves as making theatre, though. So when the thing ran out of steam and died, no one thought the next thing to do would be to prepare a script. I suppose the whole flavour of what we were doing was influenced by the rising satire boom, but we were very vicious, with all the cruelty of schoolboys stuck in the particularly oppressive non-culture of a grammar school.

Following this, I wrote with one of those people a comedy series for television. We despised television for its tedium. We carried it round the corridors of BBC Light Entertainment, and were either insulted or ignored. Then I went to university and read history. I found it a shock, a vast and alien environment peopled by baying public schoolboys. I began a process of withdrawal which made me suspicious of, and ignorant of, the politicization of 1968. This was peculiar because I had very strong political instincts. I had a fundamental Stalinist education from my father who was a shop steward, and a very developed sense of class – class conflict if not class struggle.

TQ: So *Cheek* was written before *No One Was Saved*?

HB: I'm not sure which came first, actually. Once I'd shown them *Cheek*, they asked whether I had any other plays that might be suitable for a season for schools that Pam Brighton was mounting at the [Royal] Court, so I gave her *No One Was Saved*. It's possible that was written before *Cheek*. *No One Was Saved* was done for the schools programme but the run was extended because it was so successful.

TQ: Was the play a direct response to seeing Edward Bond's *Saved*?

HB: I went to see *Saved* with a friend – the same one that I'd written the satirical TV comedy series with. We'd gone on the strength of a review we'd read saying that this was life in south London epitomized. We just didn't think that that was so – we didn't understand much about what Bond was trying to do with the language of the play. That was why I wrote *Cheek,* and also why I took up the gang of youths from *Saved* and used them in *No One Was Saved*.

TQ: What relationship did the play have to the John Lennon song?

HB: That was fundamental. I was groping blindly towards some description of the parasitic relationship between art and experience. The song had a rare concern with despair and defeat – very unlike a modem pop song – but I was always suspicious of the Beatles, and Lennon in particular: all the financial manipulation and posturing with maharishis struck me firmly then as an indictment of the 1960s. So I created a fantasy in which Lennon had actually known this girl Eleanor

Rigby, who was not an old woman as I thought the song implied, and served her up as song material.

TQ: It's very clearly a despairing play – what comes over is a lack of hope. You don't allow one small gesture of optimism.

HB: That ties in with *Saved* again. When Bond and others claimed that the end of *Saved* was optimistic because of the action of mending the chair in the last scene, I never found the argument very convincing. The image of hope is dwarfed by having been given so much evidence against it. So I wasn't able or prepared to make a similar gesture in my play. The whole question of pessimism in my plays comes down to that, really – my inability to manufacture optimism out of situations that are amazingly dark.

TQ: Your characters do have a capacity to be fairly thoroughly defeated in one way or another. Laurie, in *Cheek*, is the next in line […].

HB: Yes. *Cheek* is a very personal play, almost an autobiographical play. It's as near to naturalism as I've got, although the language is clearly stretched. I regarded what happens to Laurie as a fair interpretation of experience, certainly of the lives of the people I knew in the bit of south London that I lived in. Some of the characters in that play are people I knew.

TQ: Right from the start you seem not to have had any problems with creating a dramatic structure, with organizing material into scenes.

HB: It's extraordinary you should say that. I was thrown out of a very successful agency for failing to understand the laws of structure, whatever they may be. And Michael Billington is under the impression I can't do it, either. In fact I do it well, and have got a good deal of pleasure from arranging quite complex plots, which is one aspect of it at least.

TQ: Your plots don't have a conventional structure, but they seem to create their own quite effortlessly. Was it a relatively easy process, when you first began to write plays?

HB: Yes. The earlier one goes back, the easier the writing was – I find it much harder now than I did then. It was very effortless and primitive. I'd had that earlier experience of knocking out satirical sketches. I've always had that ability. In a way it's something I've had to struggle against – the collapse into simply producing satirical characters and satirical moments.

TQ: Where does the idea for a play come from?

HB: I tend to start a play from an idea about a character rather than about an event. That's certainly characteristic of the earlier plays, and even of a play such as *The Hang of the Gaol*. I also know what tensions will exist in a play, what the general situations will be. But the motive force is almost always a character. Sometimes I may carry around an idea of a character for a long while and never find a situation or a place for him. With *The Hang of the Gaol*, for instance, I'd had the character of Jardine in my head for a long time, but I had no particular use for him. Then I read about the fire at Chelmsford Prison and I saw a link.

TQ: How directly were you involved with the productions of the early plays?

HB: Nothing like as closely as I wanted to be. By which I don't mean I was excluded. I was for a long time bedazzled and bewildered. There was the grotesque problem of seeing theatre as other people's property. It made me feel very alienated. And there was this very particular style and regime at the Royal Court which was unwelcoming. You were dealt the impression that it was a great privilege being there. I didn't know what the writer's function at rehearsals was, so I sat very quietly at the back and watched while Bill Gaskill directed the play and was thrilled by it in the event. But I very rarely spoke to the actors. It was a painful time for me, shame and pride coming in quick succession.

TQ: You seem to have been a very prolific playwright, even then.

HB: Having two productions at the [Royal Court] Theatre Upstairs in the space of six months gave me confidence in my talent, which being flung out of the agency had hurt. It was a tremendous affirmation. I remember being very disappointed not to get the Devine Prize, which I felt I'd earned. But I've never won a prize for anything, and now don't wish to, of course. I thought *Hang* should have got the Whiting Prize last year, and that's my last effort. I was certainly prolific, and offered the Court their commission very quickly. It was called *The War in Pictures*. I believed it was a good play, about a returning mercenary. Perhaps they thought I needed time to develop. Anyway, when it wasn't taken, I was at a loss where to go.

TQ: How did you become involved with the Open Space?

HB: Clive Goodwin, who was my agent, sent *Edward, the Final Days*, a satire on Edward Heath, to Charles Marowitz. It was done as a lunchtime play. That was the beginning of the association. I even became resident dramatist there. It ran at the same time as Recreation Ground produced *Faceache*, probably my most naturalistic piece, about two former inhabitants of a repressive children's home meeting in maturity and taking up exactly the same positions of exploitation towards one another. John Ashford featured them in a *Time Out* article. They were twin aspects of my writing, one brash, comic and endlessly inventive, the other dark, almost excessively painful. John has been very supportive to me every since.

   Edward was my best piece of unadulterated satire. It was good to do something that was ruptured in its chronology and manner. I wrote it quite early in the life of the Heath government, a long time before the miners' strike. At times I've felt I was wrong to relate so much of it to homosexuality, but that's only the unease of a liberal conscience. There should be no forbidden territory in theatre. I remember Jim Hiley expressing extreme anger with the homosexual in *That Good Between Us*. I examined the text and was certain there are no grounds for special pleading.

TQ: How consciously were you using those early plays to express particular viewpoints?

HB: They express particular viewpoints, but without complexity. I placed the characters in *Edward* squarely in their social context, but only as subjects of lampoon, because I hated them and was offended by them. I am still deeply offended by society, and still hate as much, but the habit is no longer iconoclastic, as it was automatically then. It is a habit that is only now beginning to recede in my work, partly because I recognize the value of iconoclasm and feel a powerful reflex for it. It occurs in *The Love of a Good Man*, well and healthily, but in an entirely richer context. Plays like *Edward*, *Skipper*, or *Reach for the Sky*, spring from an uncontrolled antagonism. They are a heaving out of the pain of an oppressed English youth. In that period I was further from any feeling of involvement with my characters than at any time before or since. I began to feel that being involved with my characters at all was a weakness.

TQ: What was your own political thinking at the time?

HB: I am never certain of the nature of my political thinking. It is easy to say you are a revolutionary socialist, but it is stale with cliché and a certain vanity. I knew that then, as now, I believed revolution necessary but unlikely. That tension is at the hub of my work.

TQ: You were never associated with any group, such as Portable Theatre, although some of your early plays – *Alpha Alpha*, for example – seem very similar to the kind of work that Portable was producing.

HB: That's true. I was never even part of their group authorships. I don't know much about Portable's origins, but I'd imagine the impulses behind their work were very similar to mine. At one time I'd perhaps have liked the chance to work with them: I envied their solidarity, they had an armour. Knowing myself better now, I don't think it was possible for me. But the connections are unavoidable, because of a common subject matter and ideological base. But they were ahead of me, putting their theatre together long before I wrote a play. I think criminality was a fairly common metaphor of the 1960s and 1970s. I've already mentioned we improvised round Crippen at school. In *Alpha Alpha* I was still in pursuit of public figures: Boothby and the sexual danger of the criminal, and the Kray twins' classic admiration for the vulgarity of ruling class modes.

TQ: Have you ever had any problems with libel? There are a large number of easily identifiable real-life models for many of your characters.

HB: I've never been prosecuted. But it is one of the reasons why Methuen stopped publishing me. There's always the danger of libel because I've so often exploited the public's contempt for its heroes and governors. Attacking images, proposing alternatives, forcing revelations, is something the theatre does very well.

TQ: There's a difference, though, between the attacks on Heath or on Sir Francis Chichester in *Skipper*, and characters like the female Home Secretary in *That Good Between Us* or the retired Labour peer in *Stripwell*.

HB: Yes, I was unable to carry on in that simple satirical mould. I've always prided myself on my ability to create characters quite rapidly, but my urge recently has been to deepen the characterization. That's what creates that slightly ambiguous response – there are characters whom you think you recognize, but they may be the wrong sex, or they may be an amalgam of several people. That Jarrow figure in *Stripwell*, for example, could be one of several people. And the female Home Secretary in *That Good Between Us* was based on Roy Jenkins. Everybody now thinks it is really meant to be Shirley Williams. Certainly, my contempt for the Labour Party is much more astringent than my contempt for the Tories.

TQ: The other ambiguity that occurs in those early plays is between the social context and the psychological context – particularly the theme of parental domination.

HB: Yes. This must be why I am not a good political writer. There is a persistent upsurge of the personal into what superficially appears to be a didactic exercise, an eruption of private will and shameful motive. The parent–child relationship is strong in *Claw, That Good*, and *Edward*, too. In *Claw* there is a struggle for possession of Noel's soul, but it is actually social values that initiate the psychology. The mother's contempt for her husband, her loathing for his sexuality, is almost entirely because of his social failure, his inability to deliver her from the misery of a poor life. Eddie's Toryism, and sensitivity to disgust, is produced by his father's insistence on the general squalor of the human animal, which litters contraceptives on his tiny lawn. It is not unjust to see Toryism as a manifestation of life-hatred. And Rhoda's politics in *That Good* are wrong – radical, the outcome of a personal disgust. She is persistently mocking her mother's sexuality, and desperate for sensation. So, yes, all the political positions are mediated by psychology but not dictated by it.

TQ: Sexual relationships in your plays tend to be governed by selfishness and opportunism.

HB: Yes, but also by social malformation. The weakening and distortion of sexuality and the mutilation of passion are identified socially. Noel's desire for Angie is heightened, not lessened, by his discovery of her origins. They share a conspiratorial passion. But she is the victim of her own material circumstances. I am saying that class is the enemy of freedom in every respect, not least sexually. It's true that any potentially vivid sexual relationship is distorted by a social relationship which frustrates or murders it. At its worst, the sexual pleasure comes from this degradation. Nattress in *Birth on a Hard Shoulder* can only enjoy sex through degradation, like Gadsby in *Alpha Alpha*. Rhoda's sexual response to Godber is anything but spontaneous, is almost an act of social defiance. Some of the characters, rather than endure this deformation, make a sort of withdrawal – Hilary in *Birth* refuses to discriminate, and Jane in *Hang of the Gaol* simply retires.

TQ: How easy has it been to exist as a full-time writer?

HB: I'm one of the few younger dramatists to survive through film writing, I think. *No One Was Saved* was filmed as *Made* with Carol White, a disastrous and painful experience which exposed to me the commercial degradation of the industry here, as far as the studios are concerned. I then scripted *Aces High*, whose theme reveals in comic clarity the absurdity of producer power in an artistic enterprise. It involved converting *Journey's End* into a flying film. Of course all the power that play possessed – and it's not a play I like – was instantly dissipated, and you were left with a lot of public schoolboys flying over Surrey. It infuriates me to see so many good English actors chucked away on bad material. I'm now doing a version of Alistair MacLean's only reasonably decent novel – *HMS Ulysses*, a truthful account of an Arctic convoy. David Puttman has integrity, so there is a possibility of achievement here. Of course, I depart from MacLean's governing notion of solidarity in crisis, but you cannot attack conventions in film as you can in theatre. Everything is a property, and a lever to money.

TQ: What of television?

HB: The more seriously I've taken writing for television the less success I've had. And I've written well for it now, as the readings at the Royal Shakespeare Company (RSC) have shown. This is a very painful irony. My first was *Cows* in 1972, a domestic story, very much an exercise in the existing Play for Today convention,

I believed. I then wrote *The Chauffeur and the Lady*, and *Mutinies*, two half-hour studies in resentment. These were not much liked by the authorities there. Then *Prowling Offensive* was blue-pencilled. I submitted to this, in the wrong belief that it was better to say something than nothing, but even then they were out to ditch it. It was made and then abandoned, so the series it was meant to be a part of went out one short.

Mutinies was about an act of arson carried out by two poets in the employ of a Battle of Britain ace. *The Chauffeur* was about blind antagonism between a female rentier and a semi-literate communist. *Prowling Offensive* contained a lot of material later used in *Claw* – a pimp compromises a minister at a fancy-dress ball. I still wasn't done for, and got a commission for a play about negotiations between the IRA and a secret clique of civil servants. I employed every tactic to prevent it being rejected. I set it in a room like a studio so it would be cheap ('we can't afford this' is always an excuse for rejection) and named no names. But the subject was considered in itself grounds for refusal. Nothing else. No one said it wasn't good. On the Irish question there is no struggle for work, no argument. The entire establishment are in the business of resistance. I have done others – *I'm Bleeding*, *Heaven* and *The Loud Boy's Life*. Some of my best writing has gone there, poured down the drain. And now the commissions have dried up. I have become *persona non grata*. The terrible scandal of the drama department is not known to the public. There is good work there, in the bottom of steel cabinets.

TQ: Between the early satirical plays and *Stripwell* and *Claw* there's a gap of a couple of years. Does that also reflect a time when you weren't writing?

HB: No. There have never been gaps when I wasn't writing. Looking back, it might have been better if there had been. I have to keep on working through until I've exhausted a certain kind of play, before I'm in a position to develop in some other direction – unlike some writers, who may not write a play for a couple of years and then produce one which isn't obviously connected with their previous work. I knew when I'd written *Claw* – it was written before *Stripwell* – that I'd made a definite advance, largely because of the third act, which I regarded as a triumph. It was almost a new form for me: in prose, with very long speeches – even longer to begin with than they are in the final text. I was very surprised when Charles Marowitz said that Act Three just wasn't theatre, that it wasn't performable. I was confident that it was performable. And of course the play would be much slighter without that act.

TQ: In that third act you also seem to be offering an interpretation of the action in a way that you deny to audiences in your earlier plays.

HB: Yes. There is a withdrawal from the action on my part, too: it is less insistent. Nothing in the act relies on the shared assumptions that I have expected audiences to respond to in other acts. It was the beginning of a confidence to remove myself from a common ground. I dislike a play in which the dramatist overstates his intentions, making matters easy for his audience. It produces this rather unhealthy expectation that we should all know what it's about by the interval. To continually undermine the expected is the only way to really alter people's perceptions. Act Three of *Claw* does this superbly, but other plays also attempt to defy an audience, to force it to struggle a little. This tension is what costs me a lot of support – people must have it all in their hands, but the effects of my work are always underneath, always tending to dissolve associations. *Love of a Good Man* perpetually dislocates.

TQ: Are *Stripwell* and *Claw* companion pieces?

HB: I always think of them as mutually antagonistic. When Michael Codron first commissioned *Stripwell*, I deliberately chose to write a play for middle-class audiences. I wanted to get a play into the West End. I thought I could represent that familiar middle-class drawing-room milieu effectively enough to be successful in those terms. But the problems of the bourgeois individual were not problems I felt very strongly about. What I wrote was an attempt at a middle-class tragedy, and consequently it had all those values that sustain that kind of a play – a sweeping humanitarianism, elegant wit, a familiar situation. It involved tremendous self-discipline. Some of the moments, I thought, were effective. I produced what I thought were a lot of elegant lines which would go down well in the West End. They didn't. Essentially, I suppose, the play was too mean for that kind of audience to be nourished by. I can't do a Simon Gray. I'm quite glad to have found that I can't.

I suppose I believed that it was enough to represent to the audience their own habits. But I wasn't taking into account the need to stroke their backs. I thought I'd bent over backwards to soften my touch and only allowed my voice to come through clearly at salient points, like the ending. But then so much sympathy and concern was extended towards the central character, particularly because of the way that Michael Hordem was playing him, that the thought of him being wiped out came as a genuine shock, particularly since I'd created a situation where it seemed he had talked his way out of his fate.

In contrast, I was very concerned at one stage that *Claw* was too nakedly agitprop, that it might look crude in that respect – the way in which the father always holds the holy grail of political truth before him, and is proved right by the conclusion of the play. I was worried that that would look clumsy.

There's nothing worse for an audience than knowing you can more or less predict how the relationships in a play will operate. With *Claw,* I not only think that you can't deduce what the ending will be, I don't even think you can deduce the second act on the evidence of the first. In Act One, it looks as if the play will be a 7:84-ish tale of a working-class youth discovering the guts of society. The second act is very different, closer to *Stripwell* in its drawing-room elegance.

TQ: Do you feel there is an identifiable audience for which you are writing?

HB: At one time I would have said that there was – the young radical audience. When I wrote *Edward, the Final Days,* I believed there was a young, united, euphoric audience hostile to Heath and Toryism, optimistic about the prospect of a Labour government under Harold Wilson. I knew who I was talking to, and we spoke the same language – especially since satire is a very easy language to use and understand, because there is little ambiguity involved. But as my work has become more complex, the appropriate responses to political issues have also become more blurred. We've seen the collapse of Labour as a viable source of change in our society, and I've reflected that in my work. You can't rely on that shared optimism any longer. I find now that I don't get very much support from critics on the left.

   So I'm no longer sure where my audience comes from. I do have a following, I'm aware of that, but who they are I'm not sure. It comes down to how well you articulate the political sense of your time, because my work is not cohesively political, but I capture the bewilderment which is the common condition now. The fact that things are not tied down and easily explicable in my work is a virtue in that respect. The tension in the plays often comes from knowing what I don't like, what offends my sensibilities, but at the same time not being able to pose an alternative. I don't find that a weakness. I don't know that dramatists can pose alternatives.

   I like to think that my plays are very open and accessible. Fundamentally I'm a popular writer. It's always bothered me that I haven't achieved the breakthrough to bigger audiences that I think the work could command. But the popular dramatist, by definition, needs to reassure his audience that the manner of their lives is a correct one, whereas my work tends not to do that. Style alone can't make you popular.

TQ: *Wax,* your next play, seems to be in a much lighter vein […]

HB: Yes. *Wax* is out of chronology and incomplete. It is half of a two-act play my agent persuaded me to send out and I overruled myself. It is funny, but the funniness rests on nothing substantial, partly because the second act is missing. Act Two showed the hero dismissed from the army and setting up a strike-breaking force. I've always suffered from the left's obsession with the machinations of the eccentric right. It comes from reading too many newspapers.

TQ: What of *Heroes of Labour* and *Birth on a Hard Shoulder*?

HB: *Heroes of Labour* is a 30-minute TV play about a four-way relationship: it involves a property speculator; his mistress (also his secretary); a black Oxford graduate who is taken on as a rent collector and dressed up in menacing clothes to scare out ageing tenants; and one of those old men, a communist who served in Russia in the 1920s. I later reactivated that character in *Fair Slaughter*. They blow him up with one of his rusty old grenades, demolishing the whole block at the same time.

Birth on a Hard Shoulder came from a short paragraph in a newspaper item. When the Labour Party won the 1974 election, a doctor in Sussex was so disturbed that he shot his family and then shot himself. I turned the doctor into a stockbroker and set the play on the evening of the election. He shoots his family but then drives off into the night. He encounters two girls on a motorway, one of whom is about to give birth. He assists at the birth of the baby, which dies, and the three of them become drifters in London. He gets mixed up with a conspiracy of police officers and small-time crooks and property developers, who believe they can seize power in the country at a moment of crisis. One of the girls develops a political conscience; the other regards politics with scorn. The stockbroker is arrested and put in an asylum for the murder of his family. One girl dies in a fire and the other goes to Cornwall and sets up a pseudo-religious group, sending out pamphlets to sailors in bottles.

The central point is that a man who regards the election of a socialist government as fatal to his whole lifestyle has by the end of the play come to regard the prospect of his own side winning as equally alarming. It is about small discoveries, small advances in awareness.

TQ: There are character types which recur in your plays, even to the extent of some of them reappearing, like the two undertakers Hacker and Clout in *Credentials of a Sympathizer* and *The Love of a Good Man*.

HB: Yes. In that case it was because *Credentials of Sympathizer* was never produced, and an interesting relationship wasn't going to be used. The old Gocher figure in *Fair Slaughter* is a character from *Heroes of Labour*. I sometimes go back to characters if I feel that I haven't exhausted their possibilities. Sometimes a character with a very small role in one play will feature quite largely in another. And clearly there are other characters who are very similar to one another: you could link Jarrow in *Stripwell*, for example, with the sold-out Labour politician in *The Hang of the Gaol* – that kind of malleable Labour politician who is adept at exploiting opportunities, but in terror of change.

McPhee is a rootless individual with vast resources of untapped humanity. His survival is not the ground for optimism in the play. Survival is never enough for that. But he has achieved certain insights, and we know he will go on surviving, if only because he is never the victim of an idea. All the other characters are governed by thorough notions. All McPhee has is a passion for contact, and this overcomes persistent betrayal. I think that is good going as optimism goes.

The play is not so much about politics as about moral collapse – which I believe follows from bad politics: the loss of community, the fascist urge in sex and government. All the characters prey on decay. There are no positive gains from relationships, which are grabbed selfishly. Sensation is substituted for sensuality. I've already said something about Rhoda – that her contempt is actually fuelled by deracination – and I have no time for Orbison's limp liberalism. She has often been identified as the focus of sympathy. It's not true. Her humanism is defunct and essentially cruel. It is McPhee's limpet-like capacity for hope that makes the play vibrate. He won't be prised away from hope.

TQ: The chronological shifts from past to present that you have used in your more recent plays seem to go together with a search for some sense of historical development in the way that people have become disillusioned with society. Was *Fair Slaughter* the first time that you used that technique?

HB: Yes. I used it extensively, too, in the television play *All Bleeding*[4] and in the stage version of that. There are great problems in it, because such a long passage of time dissipates the degree of emotional commitment characters can expect. There's something in the unities. But history is a vastly important factor in my plays. It broods over most of my work, it lurks in the back of the characters' minds, and is a persistent justification for action. The right-wing characters invoke it continually (Flicker in *Loud Boy*, Nattress in *Birth on a Hard Shoulder*) and the left fret about its judgement (Stagg in *Hang*, Orbison in *That Good*). I'm very concerned about Europe, about its pain and its destiny. It's massively contradictory, full of agony, bent on suicide. In England the last 30 years have been years of defeat. Only recently have I come to believe in the possibility of overcoming.

TQ: What of *Heaven*?

HB: I'd been interested for some time in the subject of those 'traitors' who, if they'd remained in this country instead of defecting, would have become leading figures of the establishment. That spectacle of the massive move to the left by upper-class figures in the 1920s and 1930s is something I find very powerful. In some ways their treason was ambiguous, in that there's no doubt that all of them might have expected to come back to England as members of some socialist commonwealth – which didn't happen. At the same time, although they were communists, they subscribed to many ruling-class attitudes. In Philby's book *My Secret War*, when he's explaining why he became a spy, he says that he was offered the chance to join the most elite corps in the world – the KGB. How could he refuse? That is the voice of a ruling-class Englishman, locating where power lies and capturing it. Then there are also the people who remained here, like Tom Driberg, who maintained a classic communist position but didn't really find any way of using it in our society. *Heaven* was about those two options: either to remain here, in the Labour Party, and become a gossip columnist, or to become an outright traitor.

TQ: What of the character of the vicar in that play? I had the distinct feeling that he was likely to crop up again in your work.

HB: Moscrop is a nationalist, and so am I, though the word is contaminated with xenophobia and futile patriotism. I mean by it, defence of a certain culture against penetration from outside, in the form of commercial and cultural colonization. I am for an open culture but not a raped one. Moscrop is frantic with illusion, but also capable of great perception. I have very few characters with correct views. My latest play *Downchild* is about a man who believed, as Driberg did, that the gossip column was politically effective – a tragic misjudgement. He believed that if you were able to expose the manner of life of the ruling class – their squandering of wealth, their vulgarity – in a popular paper like the *Express,* you could produce a reaction of outrage and militant opposition. In fact, it merely induced envy and complacency. Some dramatists have made the same mistake. You have to use very impure human material to make good points in theatre.

TQ: Do you hope that the audience will sympathise with your characters?

HB: I want my characters to earn the love of an audience. That is why I don't like Stripwell; it's far too easy to like him. It's a bourgeois habit to insist on immediate identity, and left writers do it too. They place all their wit and sympathy with their hero, who becomes a strenuous voice of reason, knocking all the right targets. It's hard to like Noel Biledew, McPhee, Hacker, Erica, Downchild, but, because it's hard, they lodge the better.

TQ: With Fricker, though, in *The Loud Boy's Life*, I never felt that he would be successful in gaining national power. The chronological structure of that play shows him first at the city dinner where he receives the invitation to seize power, and then moves back in time, so there was something about him that made it clear he'd failed from the start.

HB: That play was originally written as a two-part television series in which the banquet was the continual thread and all the other scenes came back to it. When we did it at The Warehouse we had the banquet as a single scene and disposed of it in one go. Consequently, Act Two was the poorer for it, since the banquet is the best-written scene. I find Fricker – and Enoch Powell, on whom he is based, and all those people who overreach – very interesting. He's placed in a context where he's made to look horrendous because of his colleagues, because of the company he keeps – all those obnoxious social types who cast a large shadow over him. He despises them and at the same time controls them with a malicious elegance.

In all the plays of mine that deal with English society – *The Loud Boy's Life*, *The Hang of the Gaol*, *That Good Between Us*, the play I'm writing about Tom Driberg – I've always hoped to create a complex picture, to cover as wide a scope, as many classes of people, as possible. I have the feeling that this play about Driberg will be the last of those plays. I think I've done a good job of describing our society. I can't go on doing it much longer.

TQ: In the television play *All Bleeding* the character of the East European cartoonist presumably reflects that ambivalent feeling you described, which involves wanting to preserve the best of the British national identity?

HB: The character Bela misconceives what British freedom is all about. After a life in Europe, England in the 1930s was rightly regarded as a haven of liberty, and only a fool disregards these freedoms now. It is the institutional life of England which is so fundamentally rotten, and that's why parliamentary change has been so grotesquely irrelevant. But the really defensible – the traditional culture of liberty – is vital. What Bela does in the stage version of the play is to insist on blame – and the worst aspect of humanism is its rejection of blame, the idea we are all guilty. A wicked, paralysing posture.

TQ: It's quite striking that the female characters in your plays are very often given the most positive ideas.

HB: I agree women are frequently given good ideas, are positive about life in a way that men are often not. But they are also capable of illusion and error, so I'm not chivalric. I've already talked about Rhoda (*That Good*) and Angie (*Claw*). Even where they are right (Crystal in *Loud Boy*) they are capable of the same decay into opportunism as the men.

The older characters share a common turning away from sex, sensing it's a trick. The conversation in *Hang of the Gaol* between Jane and Matherson is almost archetypal, the coming together of women in an intimacy not known among men. But their political difference ruptures it, overcomes gender solidarity. Sexual love has not been celebrated in my plays yet, though in my latest play for the RSC I have tried to see sexual passion more positively as a need and an inalienable right, even an end it itself.

TQ: That play deals with a Middle Eastern country and the hangover of the colonial experience?

HB: Partly. It's about the perishing of dream when exposed to reality, and this struggle for affirmation occurs both sexually and politically. It has real-life figures in it, Lawrence of Arabia and Toplis, the English army mutineer. Toplis seeks out his old regiment, now on a colonial posting, disguised as a conjuror. He offers an apparently practical magic, the real magic of change, initiates a mutiny, but himself becomes the victim of the sexual magic of the colonial governor – a woman at the end of a career of promiscuity. It's about people refusing to settle for less than the whole. It's against compromise, and for the whole hog.

TQ: Have you felt – or do you feel now – any particular attachment to any of the theatres where you've worked?

HB: I've been on the move a lot – from the Royal Court to the Open Space and then on to The Warehouse. In many ways my work is probably more characteristic of the Warehouse style than anyone else's. The actors at the RSC mean a lot to me, and they know how to use my language very effectively. I can write on a scale that I like to write on. I hoped to graduate to the Aldwych – to have a second shot, after *Stripwell*, at filling a house. After *The Love of a Good Man* I was confident that I was popular enough as a writer to manage that.

TQ: Do you write with a certain actor–audience relationship in mind?

HB: Not often. I write with actors clearly in mind, and think about possible situations for presenting them. I have enjoyed working with Ian McDiarmid and conceived *Downchild* for him. Some actors I've had a long and stimulating history of working with. The great Roger Sloman, for example. I feel tremendous warmth for people who do my work well, go away and say I must do a part for him or her. Actually, I am enthusiastic for myself, because they have done my work so well, and am re-inspired by them. Jill Baker did this in *The Loud Boy*, so did Donald Sumpter. But I could list so many brilliant performances in my work. I am a performance writer. Look at McDiarmid in *That Good*, or Pat Stewart in the same play, Clive Merrison in *Loud Boy*, Fulton McKay in *Hang of the Gaol*.

TQ: What particular demands do your plays make on actors?

HB: A readiness to tackle quite difficult linguistic problems, and a vast amount of energy. The plays are in high gear all the time; there is little room to lean back. I probably don't get on with actors who work on psychology. Actors have to feel a 'type' quickly, and elaborate on that. Of course, comic ability, but not acting comic. It has always been good working with RSC actors, but it was interesting watching Max Wall in *Fair Slaughter*, too. Here was an actor with no formal training and little grasp of the play's ideology. But he grasped the dialogue naturally – it was completely truthful for him. He saidlines in a way no trained actor would have come across. And I'm no naturalistic dialogue writer.

TQ: An actor can play the part quite successfully without necessarily agreeing with what you're saying?

HB: There's a lot of lip service paid to the idea of an actor *completely* comprehending a
        text. Naturally I would prefer that. But I don't think it's necessary. I have worked
        mainly with young actors, most of whom share my convictions. Actors more than
        anyone else in the theatre tend to like my work.

TQ: What of the directors you've worked with? You've already mentioned Bill Gaskill.
        Who else is there you'd want to mention?

HB: Chris Parr was superb with *Claw*. My relationship with him ended with his tenancy
        at [the Traverse Theatre] Edinburgh. At the RSC I have worked with young men of
        my own tendency and convictions. That's very good. David Leland ran a superb
        company at Sheffield for *Love of a Good Man* and I had a flexible relationship with
        him. It was very democratic and the play revealed that. Bill Alexander works
        from his own vision, wants to allow that through, beyond all things. I would
        willingly work with Bill because he succeeds and he has enthusiasm. It's very rare
        that, compelling enthusiasm. I like intervening in rehearsal, though I know it may
        threaten some work already confirmed.

TQ: Have there been many foreign productions?

HB: I was once unperformed abroad. Things have picked up slowly. With *Claw* and
        Birth my reputation in Scandinavia is high. I have had superb productions there. I
        have had good performances and readings in America. I have not got to Germany
        yet, and don't know why. I am more concerned about the second production
        problem here. I'm not alone in this. Very few of my generation write plays which
        are done twice. *Stripwell* was done quite a lot, and *Claw* has crept in from the back,
        as I expect *Love of a Good Man* to. It says nothing of our plays that this is so difficult,
        only of the rank cowardice of managements. There ought to be a separate subsidy
        system for second productions, perhaps even a specialist theatre. There are so
        many good plays from the 1970s waiting for this.

TQ: Do you feel frustrated that you haven't broken through to big stage productions?

HB: It is rather frustrating after some ten years. I'd feel it more, though, if I weren't
        conscious of a very clear development in my work. The venues for large
        company plays are shrinking. The Warehouse, for example, doesn't appear to be
        that confident about its continuing existence as a venue for new plays. Perhaps
        dramatists will have to adjust to this situation – unless, that is, they're in favour
        at the National Theatre. The play I'm writing now only has nine characters.
            I am disconcerted about the critical hostility I sense towards my work. I do
        feel that people I might have relied on for support a few years ago no longer
        supply it with the same readiness. Critics like Michael Billington or Irving Wardle
        – that range of middlebrow critic – now seem to be actively hostile towards my

work. But I'm not hostile towards the critics: there is a good role for them. I had a lot of respect for Harold Hobson: he was an enthusiast who would celebrate something new and interesting even when he didn't fully understand it. Every new generation of writers, every new form of theatre, requires a new theatre critic to write about it. Outside the pages of *Theatre Quarterly* and *Time Out*, the mainstream critics seem not to know how to deal with what's happened in the past ten years. Consequently they live a truly parasitic existence, in that they're discouraging public interest rather than arousing it.

TQ: How would you describe your own position now, after ten years writing?

HB: *Downchild* is my final play on English society and politics. I hope I've made a significant contribution in describing a society and a time. I think, taken as a body, my 'English' plays amount to an indictment and a compulsive collection of writing.

   But, of course, I cannot and do not want to go on doing this. I want to say my final piece on the Wilson era, which I hated – to nail that. After this, I sense a change of direction. I do not feel safe, partly because of the welter of critical hostility. I certainly don't intend to aim for more 'maturity', 'fair-mindedness' or any other of the weary baggage of critical humanism. I've never been interested in fair-mindedness; it's death in drama. As I said before, nothing significantly new can expect to be carried by an existing regime of criticism. It has to find its own support system. This is slowly happening. Ten years is a long time, but I have changed, I have got better. Morally, I am moving nearer to a sense of overcoming. I have begun this in the RSC play, in the new Oxford play, in ideas for the future. But I develop slowly, over many plays. I feel, too, a move away from the 'populist' figures who have dominated my work, characters like Gocher in *Fair Slaughter*, Hacker in *That Good*, towards more intellectual heroes. I also feel the stirrings of some change in form, which cannot be thrust on a play, but comes out of failures. Every play is a failure on which you aim to build. If the form cannot contain your intention, you must break it. Finally, in retrospect, I am not happy with what I've done. I never am. I rejoice in the performance, but worry because I sense I have not written the play I thought.

TQ: Are you as prolific as you were?

HB: No, not at all. I've written two plays this year. That will be my year's work, since I'm doing a film script as well. There was a time when I'd perhaps do a couple of television plays and a couple of stage plays in a single year. So I've slowed down in a way. It's probably as a result of being more self-critical. I'm not a primitive any more. Perhaps I'm even damagingly self-critical – you can be too preoccupied with the power of a single word at times.

TQ: Have you been happy with the designs for productions of your plays?

HB: I've not always had the designs that I wanted. In some cases the flavour of the text has been interpreted much too literally. That has sometimes created an aura of melancholy and gloom which the actors have had to struggle to work against. One of the reasons why I despise setting scenes in rooms is because it always seems to produce a set of clichéd images onstage. I like props – I'm not that keen on sets.

TQ: What kind of changes have you made in converting *All Bleeding* into a stage play?

HB: It is about different things. You cannot return to a play after two years and simply reproduce it for the stage. It's still about two directions to insanity, but it's now more positive and hopeful – about a man being educated by life, making errors but in the last resort giving in to persuasion rather than pursuing the ego. It's subtitled *Scenes of Overcoming*. A lot of it is debate. And it now involves collaboration with two artists, in that the development of character is supported by manifestations of their work. It's still about madness, but it now says you must live with madness, not be destroyed by it.

TQ: Did reading history at university in any way provide you with tools for your writing?

HB: It made me refuse the obvious in the political play, made me cautious, even suspicious, especially of crude political solutions. It's also given me a profound sense of European suffering. Anyone who knows something of Russia in this century is bound to be both deeply moved by suffering and ferocious at the Cold War propaganda we are subjected to. History makes you angry.

TQ: What is it about the First World War that has fascinated you so much?

HB: The death wish of an advanced culture, obviously. And then there's the proximity of another world war now – it's never seemed more likely. In my more satirical vein I have poured scorn on our culture, but when it is threatened, I realize how much I care for it. It's a protective instinct: like social democracy in the 1930s – all the communists loathed it, but when it was threatened by Hitler, they flocked to defend it. I feel that about Europe. One only has to think of Hungary, say, or Poland – the suffering in those countries in this century compared with England or America. We are diminished by it.

TQ: In the past your work was often linked with that of Howard Brenton. Do you see any similarities?

HB: I found it interesting to talk to him recently about the question of the optimism of the will and the pessimism of the intellect. I think that Howard is much more inclined now to invoke the former. The fact that he is and I'm not is perhaps because he's a better socialist than I am. Those areas that we have in common can be traced back to our both having been satirists in the 1960s: the attack on establishment individuals, the anger at being in a society which is declining. In my appreciation of history, some societies have declined even though the forces did exist within them that could have regenerated them. In our society now the progressive forces exist, the analysis of the problems exists, but for historical reasons it is difficult to assemble the opposition. That's why I'm a pessimist in political terms. Brenton has the same fury.

TQ: Your characters are full of despair, or apathy, or ready to compromise at the drop of a hat.

HB: Not at all. That is a description of the political people, the office-holders, the Staggs, Clapcotts and so on. They are compromisers, but others are not: McPhee, Old Biledew, Gocher, even Fricker, cling desperately to their truth. Erica, Finney in *Birth on a Hard Shoulder,* are deeply principled. What I do rarely show is the bold, confident projection of left-wing ideology, flashed at an audience in the expectation of instant support. There are no guerrillas in my plays. There are the expedient and the resisters, and always a tremendous presence of pain, even in the eventual capitulation. Jardine in *Hang* cheats at the end, but is a great sufferer. What I celebrate is energy and the small discovery of dignity. I think that is socialist. From confronting the pessimism comes the will to change. I think if my work does anything it forces a changed perception, even reluctantly. And it does this by refusing the expectation at every turn.

This interview was conducted at Barker's home in Brighton on 26 August 1980 and first published in the journal Theatre Quarterly, *10:40 (Cambridge: Cambridge University Press, 1981). A shorter version appeared in the book* New Theatre Voices of the Seventies, *edited by Simon Trussler (London: Eyre Methuen, 1981).*

Victory. The Wrestling School, 1991. Photo credit Leslie Black

'Articulate explorers in an age of populism'

With Charles Lamb

Charles Lamb (CL)
Howard Barker (HB)

CL: Looking back over the last twenty years, which political events affected you most significantly as a writer. Obviously, some of your plays reflect attitudes towards particular Labour or Conservative governments.

HB: Well, I'm tempted to answer that by saying very few events as such – presumably, I take it, you're referring to key events, international events like the Vietnam War or the '68 Troubles. While I may have gone on the odd demonstration against Vietnam, I can't trace any signs of it affecting what I wrote. And it's certainly true that in '68 I knew very little of what was supposed to have been going on. So I'm obviously not like the rest of my generation in that those things, so far as I am aware, didn't make a lot of impact on my work. But it would be silly to say that events haven't in some way affected my work. Greenham was one of the starting points for *The Castle* – probably because my wife was involved in that. I found that a very symbolic event. It would be easy to point to, say, the third act of *Claw*, or *Credentials of a Sympathizer* and say I was moved to speak about the Northern Irish War. But in no play have I ever addressed a political event as such. My political sense derives from the past, and I view the present from the perspective of the past, at least as I have constructed it, in imagination. So that in *Victory* I am acutely conscious of the collapse of a political ethic in my own time, but my sense is always that we have been here before.

CL: I seem to remember you reacted very strongly to the Falklands War and that you saw *Victory* as somehow reflecting your feelings about that episode?

HB: I was very astonished at the whole jingoistic atmosphere surrounding that and *The Castle* reflects here and there the Falklands landscape – Krak talks about boys screaming on windy hills. But I never produced a Falklands play – in the reflexive sense. I watched the Falklands War with a sort of disbelief, the eruption of popular patriotism took me by surprise and I thought in any case, once the battle began we would lose it. I saw it militarily as another Gallipoli. But it turned out to be quite the opposite. The army won, the government did not fall, rather the Argentine military dictatorship fell. A curious residual imperialist episode became deeply significant […] The left still has not recovered from this, but the fact is, anything can be revived, and no sentiment is ever really defunct. A people contains in its psyche caverns of unplayed texts.

CL: What about *Downchild*?

HB: Yes, it's not specific to atrocities or war but my political plays are always critical plays of social significance concerned with the broad pattern of events, with an ethos. *Downchild* was the last of a series of plays about the betrayal of socialism – the corruption of socialism in the Labour Party. Actually it wasn't, because I went on to have a final hack in *A Passion in Six Days*. But the interesting thing about *Downchild* and its investigations is that it hangs from a pastiche – it is a conflation of two unrelated events of the 1960s, the Lucan murder and the peculiar resignation of Wilson, in the form of an English country house thriller. I could only approach the inertia of the Labour Party through the most extreme invention.

CL: To have had a sense of betrayal, you must have believed. Did you believe in the Wilson governments?

HB: Well, I suppose I must have done, otherwise I wouldn't have been affected so much. That seems naive now. *A Passion in Six Days*, which came after *Downchild*, is probably the play in which I articulate most clearly what I think is wrong with the Labour Party as a party. It must debate the forms of social progress. Now, in projecting itself as a pillar of family life and domesticity, the Labour Party has joined hands with the Tories. Glenys and Neil are now to become the archetypal domestic couple. If that's at the centre of the party there can be no possibilities of significant change. Perhaps the programme I wanted was in any case brutalist, crudely demolitionist. I expected a parliamentary party to embark upon a revolutionary programme, which shows a poor grasp of reality. I think I was groping towards not an economist criticism of English Labourism, but attempting to expose its intensely petit-bourgeois morality. This has peaked again in the person of Kinnock. But I won't be returning to the vomit.

CL: To return to *Cheek*, it has been stated that this was written as a reaction to Bond's *Saved*.

HB: *Saved* was one of the first plays I ever saw in the theatre – and I myself was not a writer then. So I suppose that seeing that the life of my own class and background could be represented on the stage made me want to write a play – and, perhaps, write it better. I do remember feeling that Bond's presentation of the South London working class was abominable and contemptuous. The inarticulacy, the grunting and the monosyllabics, being accepted as a portrayal of working-class people, did offend me and may have inspired me to write *Cheek*, which did lend articulacy to the characters. Laurie is quite adept verbally. So it could be seen as a reaction to the sterility of Bond's language.

CL: Even if it acted as a negative stimulus, presumably you did find it nevertheless a powerful experience?

HB: Yes, I must have done. But then, again, I remember being irritated by a number of things in that production. I remember that William Gaskill intercut the scenes by flashing up advertisements. That there had to be a relation between a commercially exploitative society and the depravity of those kids struck me as – not so. I couldn't connect with that connection. Though I was stimulated by seeing a theatre about people I was supposed to know, I wasn't moved to imitate it.

CL: Wasn't there anything you liked about it?

HB: Yes, the acting. Those actors [...] like Kenneth Cranham, infected me with the sound of their voices. I'd never heard those accents before – certainly never played in front of an audience. But obviously I was impressed because both my friend and I went back to see [Edward Bond's] *The Narrow Road to the Deep North,* so we must have been engaged by the play. I remember thinking that *The Narrow Road* was much better; I very much liked the scene where one of the priests gets a pot stuck on his head. I don't know why I remember that. I just thought it was [laughs] [...] good.

CL: That was one of the plays where Bond began to move away from the kind of naturalism you get in *Saved* into a more symbolic sort of representation.

HB: Yes, not knowing Brecht, I suppose I also found it rather exciting to see exotic places with Englishmen speaking colloquial English. Cockney monks provided a dislocation. I've never seen [Bond's] *Lear*, I've not even read it, but I've liked his work less and less. For example, I thought *The Fool* was a very depressing form of literary biography.

CL: You have said in interview that you admired Charles Wood's *Dingo*. What did you find interesting about the play?

HB: Well, it's completely unnaturalistic. It's set in the kind of location which has always interested me – which, I suppose are locations of catastrophe. In that particular case it's set in the western desert during the war. It features, in a very satirical way which then pleased me, various political figures like Rommel. And also the important thing for me about Charles Wood, whom I still think is a very underrated writer, is his joy in using English; speech and wit. That's the reason why I'd rate a play like *Veterans* which, though deficient in content, is brilliant in its language texture.

CL: When I read *Stripwell* and *Claw* after reading *Cheek*, I was quite surprised at what seemed to be a major move away from naturalism. In the interim you had written various unpublished satirical plays. Was this a conscious change of direction?

HB: Well, *Cheek* was a Royal Court apprentice play par excellence and *No One Was Saved* is not dissimilar – neither of them political plays. After that I then wrote a short play about Edward Heath called *Edward, the Final Days*, and when I did that I got back to a kind of satirical writing that I used to produce as a schoolboy. I suddenly got back that instinct to be satirical and plunged straight into that. So, after writing the Edward Heath play, I wrote *Alpha Alpha*, which is a satirical play about the East End, the Kray brothers. Then I wrote *Claw* and I was vaguely aware that I was getting on a helter-skelter of satire and I wasn't being at all engaged with my characters. It was only with *Claw* that I managed to drag myself back from what might have been a fatal precipice. The last act of *Claw*, which I still think is rather a fine piece of writing, surmounts and overcomes the satirical emphasis of the previous two acts. So, I was led off and recovered.

CL: Caricature was nevertheless important in the development of your own style. I feel that the influence of caricature is very apparent in all your later work. Though you have, in a way, moved beyond caricature.

HB: I think most of my work is in some way rhetorical. A character speaks his mind and very publicly. There's very little unspoken text, nearly everything that is thought is spoken. The sense of caricature has been increasingly marginal, has been located in minor characters. In the centre of the plays complexity and contradiction have replaced it. Partly this reflects moves away from class stereotypes. My protagonists are, and have been, by and large intellectuals, artists, teachers, military geniuses, wives of intellectuals, and even Skinner, who is a peasant, is a witch and therefore owns knowledge. There are few Hackers or Billy McPhees now. In an age of populism, I am drawn not towards the dumb victims but the articulate explorers. Schweik would be a most inappropriate vessel of hope in an age like this, where knowledge is under attack and desire soon to be criminal.

CL: As a dramatist, you show a considerable interest in character. In left drama criticism, character has long been regarded as somewhat suspect – linked to ideas of bourgeois individualism. The broad tendency has been to regard the individual as a product of social circumstance, thereby demystifying the concept. By using it as such a definite reference point in your writing, aren't you encouraging reactionary thinking?

HB: The idea of expressing collectivity on the stage seems to me not really desirable. I regard the conventional left position on character and the individual as defunct and sabotaged, a limp rag. The individual as the product of deterministic historical and economic forces leaves serious art with nothing but stereotype and ideology, all dead rhetoric. The individual remains the only source of imaginative recreation of society, and is the proper subject for art [...] I'm interested in the individual as the potential of many selves. We need to see self as a potential ground for renewal and not as something stale and socially made.

Characters create events through their own pain. *The Castle* is very much about an event –it's about the construction of a building but the building is a manifestation of the alienation of the characters. If Stucley, when he comes back from the Crusades, had not found sexual despair, then the castle wouldn't have been built. So, the actual event is, always in my work, the outcome of conflict within the selves. I think in *Saved* there is no form of resistance in those circumstances, whereas in my plays everyone always knows that intervention is possible and they call up forces within themselves which often fail but nevertheless respond creatively.

CL: In ignoring the socially determined view of the individual in your work, are you then rejecting the validity of this way of understanding character or is it the case that you don't feel the need to present stage character in this way?

HB: Both. My characters sense the warping, shaping and distorting effect of society upon themselves and then they struggle against it. They define themselves and create themselves in resistance to forces. Take Hacker in *The Love of a Good Man*: he is a part of bourgeois exploitation – he's a spiv; the war and capitalism provide him with an opportunity and he arrives at a certain point. But the play is not about the spectacle of Hacker dehumanized by capitalism; it is about Hacker discovering who he might be and therefore grappling with it – to some extent defining himself in opposition to those forces. At the end of the play he learns a great deal about himself and turns against those individuals who in a Bond play would stand for authority. Although people are initially created by situations, the trajectory of the play is about self-definition, about refusal.

CL: Isn't that rather close to a certain kind of bourgeois narrative in which the hero/heroine progresses from ignorance to self-knowledge?

HB: Is that a bourgeois narrative? It seems as much a Socialist Realist narrative. But the difference is in the definition of self-improvement. In the bourgeois play, the character is redeemed; he becomes socially viable. In the Socialist Realist play he becomes ardent. In my work he constructs a self whose integrity is sealed against socialized lying, which corrupts the other two models. Often they're destroyed by what they discover. They do find a sense of self, which they often don't possess at all. But the plays are not improving; they're not meant to reduce the audience to feeling, 'if I work hard or concentrate more I will improve myself'.

CL: Yet, in presenting characters who are extremely passionate and who are committed as forcibly and as impressively as they are – aren't they recommending passion and commitment to an audience?

HB: Yes, that does come across, but the implication is not that they will therefore be happier. Certainly the possibility of self-change is there, but not in the form that Brecht would propose it, that this can only be achieved satisfactorily through a form of collective uprising.

CL: Is it your intention to represent character 'as it really is' onstage or is stage character in your work something quite apart from real people (whomever they might be). Do they partake, for instance, of the nature of symbols?

HB: The main difference between them and observable people is, I suppose, that they are extremists. Under ordinary circumstances thecharacter remains unexplored, unexposed; the nerves are quite concealed. But in order to force that exposure on the characters, I always set them within catastrophic situations. The characters onstage are not simply in unlikely situations but usually disastrous ones; perhaps just in the aftermath of a disaster. I don't like the point of disaster itself, but what occurs after it.

        The Europeans is about the siege of Vienna – specifically after the siege when the Turks and Islamic conquerors have withdrawn and the Christian State has been saved. The play is about attempts to restore morality within that. But all my plays are like that: they're all about 'post havoc'. I'm attracted to those circumstances because at times like that people are disorderly. They cease to be the predictable product of social forces – not simply workers or bourgeois or rentiers; they are dislocated from those classic roles by the social struggle.

        The naturalistic and the Brechtian projects seem equally false to me. I neither believe in reproducing the voice and manner of the social person nor in identifying the sources of self in economics, ideology etc. I am interested in character as speculation; the stage character makes no pretence at existent life, or rather he bounds over it, leading the audience into areas of fantasy and imagination. The possible, rather than the probable, becomes the definition of action.

CL: Can we talk about narrative – perhaps the classical counterpoise to character? Here again, a lot of left criticism has stressed the importance of the story – the influence of Brecht and Bond to point out two significant examples – in that this lends itself to the presentation of the social dimension. It also facilitates parable or fable. You have indicated a discontent with narrative and I've had the impression from plays like *Hang of the Gaol* and *Victory* that conventional narrative formats (the investigation, the quest) have been used merely as vehicles. I don't think you've treated the forms respectfully – giving due weight to suspense etc. Why are you suspicious of narrative?

HB: (Laughs) I think now I know why. I've always been contemptuous of narrative in the way that one is dismissive about what one can do well. I can tell stories rather efficiently, but I was always slightly suspicious of that and I didn't know why. Living in this era now it is easier to understand why, because narrative has clearly become the property of the establishment. It's interesting that you should say that the left view narrative as a means of exposing society's evils. The Thatcher era is an era of complete contradiction; we now find that narrative belongs in *Eastenders* and *Dynasty* and the other soaps. So it's clearly been expropriated. If it ever did have the means of exposing social relations – as in Brecht – the situation has now been reversed. The epic novel that you can pick up on bookstalls, nine hundred pages long, by mimicking the attempt to expose in depth actually closes the mind of the reader. And therefore I suppose I now know one has an obligation to do without narrative in order to stimulate the audience.

CL: By 'narrative', I suppose we're talking about the action, the linkage of events dominated by the structure of beginning, middle and ending, especially the ending. Brecht had a lot of difficulty with endings.

HB: I think everyone does. Good endings tend to be reconciliations. One squirms at the idea of a good ending. Take *Victory*, which is a 'well-ended play'. The arrival of Ball and Bradshaw onstage together as two ends of a spectrum of defeat – one the republican and one the nationalist figure – both of whom have been betrayed by the system they felt affinity for, is actually an image of great reconciliation and reassurance – the notion that somehow, at the end of the day the lion will lie down with the lamb. There's an element of sentimentality in that which I felt I needed. Of course, it's one thing to say you're going to break narrative because you realize it's suspect and reactionary, but it's quite another thing to know how to do it [...] [Disrupting narrative] is getting to be a greater problem because audiences are less and less tolerant of interruptions because they're fed on narrative.

CL: One of the comments you made about *Claw* in an interview emphasized the importance of setting up certain audience expectations and then disappointing these. You said you wanted the audience to begin by regarding the play as a conventional piece of agitprop, but then suddenly it turns into something else. Also, in plays such as *Victory* and *Crimes in Hot Countries*, you employ stock farce situations, like mistaken identity, after which things suddenly get serious again. Do you find the transitions difficult?

HB: I don't find transitions difficult. They're native to me. I see life in terms of contradictions and transitions. I've employed a lot in *The Bite of the Night*. There's one scene where an army officer who's seized power and is running a populist State, is suddenly picked up by one of his fellow officers who has no particular ambition to authority himself – picked up in his arms totally spontaneously. This man says he can't put him down – otherwise they'd all be back in the same society. There's a long scene when he carries him around and the passenger says, "well, you've got no ideas, so you've got to put me down". It is actually a farcical situation. That – in a play which is actually bitterly cruel and sadistic about sexual things – reduces politics, at that moment, to a very basic dilemma. It's one thing to act and another thing to fulfil the act. I don't think it should be difficult for actors. But I don't think actors are trained to understand those transitions, those swoops, at all. And obviously they do produce confusion in audiences, but it's a good confusion for an audience to feel. I'm very interested in the laugh, in what constitutes the valid laugh. I'm interested in making new kinds of laughs. I always have done that. There's that one which is untrustworthy, a laugh which makes you ashamed of having laughed.

CL: Do you feel that actors should signal these transitions fairly abruptly because there is a tendency to strive for continuity and consistency?

HB: The moment at which the audience is lost between two conventions has to be the crucial moment in which you have power. It's a momentary chance in a lifetime of bad art to actually suffer a creative dislocation. I think, in a sense, an unhappy audience is the one I aspire to, an audience that has not found its feet within the work, rather than an audience that constantly knows where it is.

CL: In directing your plays, then, it would be advisable to look for these discontinuities and build the interpretation of the text around them?

HB: Yes. The actors obviously have to know when to let go of character consistency and to play reversals in their roles.

CL: Yet they tend naturally to do the opposite and positively strive for consistency of character, by 'ironing out' discrepancies.

HB: Yes, their whole training makes them do that. The question 'why do I do that at this point?' is a reflection of that kind of training. But it's quite difficult to answer that question sometimes, 'you *do* it because you've changed, or something's changed you'. I think that requires a sort of retraining.

CL: I'd like to talk about history. You disclaim that your history plays are history in the academic sense. Yet you have studied history. You employ deliberate anachronisms. Is this because you regard history – in the way that Brecht regarded the theatre of naturalistic illusion – as being a form of deceit, in that it attempts to conceal or suppress its most fundamental truth, that it is a form of literary fabrication?

HB: Yes, I suppose I do. I think history is an invention of both left and right. Both are equally false [...] When I go to East European countries I usually go to visit what they call a museum of the working class. And so I did in Prague – an enormous building in which no Czech ever sets foot, so I had it to myself. Having walked past enormous statues of Lenin which dominated a red-carpeted staircase, I then went into endless rooms of photographs – because the photograph is the icon of the artistic sections of the Communist authorities. In room after room there were photographs of people being shot, hanged, executed, being killed in battles, or cheering their cosmonauts. You realize that the party itself has commandeered the masses by this means. The photograph itself celebrates the individual face but, at the same time, by enclosing it in mass cabinets, the masses are entrapped by the party which claims to speak for them.

    I find that illuminating for the theatre in that history is always about the extension of the individual and one or other political grouping annexes the idea of the individual for some ideological function. The good history play tries to rescue the individual from that annexation which is what I'm talking about in subtitling *The Power of the Dog* as *Moments from History and Anti-history*. Anti-history is about people who try to resist that occupation.

CL: So you see history, then, as being a kind of narrative.

HB: Yes, it is a narrative. And I'm afraid I think the English liberal left's opposition to the two formal histories is itself a mirror image of those histories. What you get in our Labour Party culture here is the story of Daisy Noakes, a housemaid; and there you have 500 fairly illiterate pages of what it's like to be a housemaid. I see nothing to distinguish that from the biography of Lord Beaverbrook. It's counter – but its qualities are identical.

CL: You'd see history, then, as being inescapably concerned with the present?

HB: Yes. That's why we are in the process of writing plays about the Civil War. Because our common cultural diktat here was that the Civil War was about romantic cavaliers oppressed by authoritarian puritans [...] I wanted to approach that both from a vision of the defeat of the puritans and their own persecution at the hands of the other side, and in the form of a woman too. So, I'd reverse three things whilst, I hope, not producing a counter-cultural image of the English Civil War, which is what a conventional left playwright would do.

CL: You mean something like *The World Turned Upside Down*, which Keith Dewhurst adapted from Christopher Hill's book?

HB: Yes, it's what they would call the hidden side of history. In fact, it's not hidden at all; it's just not exposed by this regime. It's there, and that play simply reproduced the story of the Diggers. What Bradshaw does is both to be the reverse of the historical model and to subvert it as she goes along. She liberates herself from her own husband's influence.

CL: History, then, is a particular form of oppression which exploits the individual?

HB: The leading woman character in *The Europeans* has been raped, maimed and made pregnant by the Turks during the war. And, at the beginning of the play, she tells the story of her maiming to the Christian bishops' enquiry into atrocities. So, she narrates what has happened to her, and quite unashamedly, so the State has a record. But the expectation on the part of the government is that she will leave it at that. She refuses to do so and says, 'I am about to give birth, but I will do this in public, in front of an audience'. The more she refuses to allow her own suffering to be subsumed within history, the more unpleasant she becomes to the regime. Even though they are Christians who might have milked her for anti-Islamic propaganda, they also want her to lie down and, in a way, that goes back to the museum: 'you've paid a terrible price for being part of history but now your suffering is not narrative'. If you refuse that, as she does consistently, you therefore disrupt that programme.

I believe the experience of history is an experience of pain; the words are interchangeable. Just as the individual, in the years following trauma, likes to recall the trauma, so does society insist on reproducing its dislocations, but always in a laundered way, which invokes necessity – 'struggle' is a word much beloved of the left. It has lost its meaning, become stripped of its pain, and cloaked in anodyne romanticism – and anaesthetizes memory. The individual is robbed of his experience of agony by being forced into a participation he could not at the time recognize; in other words, he is re-individualized.

This returns me to the emphasis I place on the individual as the centre of all resistance. Solzhenitsyn tells us that the most successful resisters in Stalin's camps were the religious, when they must have been persistently battered by a conventional wisdom that told them religion was a comic characteristic of pre-civilization.

CL: This is consistent with your focus on the individual. Perhaps, extending out of that, there seems to me to be in your work a curious, but persistent, loyalty to the dead. To give some examples, in *Fair Slaughter* Gocher's loyalty to communism is inseparably linked to his loyalty to the dead Tovarish, whose hand he carries round in a bottle. In *That Good Between Us*, you endow a murdered, tortured corpse with speech to communicate with the torturer's daughter. *The Love of a Good Man* is, of course, permeated with concern for the dead; the battlefield *séance* springs to mind. In *Victory*, Bradshaw's quest is motivated through loyalty to a dead man. In *The Power of the Dog*, there is the issue of Ilona's dead sister, and at the end of *Downchild*, the hero's last words express his love for a dead defector. Can you comment?

HB: I don't know if I can. All that you say is true.

CL: Do you think it's important?

HB: I think it's terribly important. The dead are the mute victims of this plundered agony. They receive nothing but the title of 'the sacrificed', to whom an entirely spurious respect is shown on specified occasions, the falseness of which is well articulated by Bride in *The Love of a Good Man*. They are, of course, wrongly perceived as innocent, or as victims, but whatever their reality, they are the most expropriated by the successor regimes, and much hatred and mischief are invoked on their behalf. In fact, an ugly struggle goes on over the dead. They beckon to the living, because their 'sacrifice' (which never is sacrifice) is employed to justify further 'sacrifice'. They are forever calling more people 'over'.

CL: Linking this with what we've said about history, is it a question of giving the ultimate victims of history the voice which has been denied them?

HB: The most significant revival of the dead occurs in my narrative poem *Don't Exaggerate*. In that case it's the voice for someone who has suffered not only in his own life but also, in being revived and given an intense level of articulacy, actually plays with the living. And so he plays the ahistoricity of his own existence to the audience.

CL: Bond, after writing what he called a series of "question plays", accepted the responsibility to provide "answer plays". You view Marxism as yet another form of oppressive historical myth, what do you replace it with?

HB: I'm against messages. As far as answers go, perhaps it's necessary to resist the questions. After I finished *The Bite of the Night*, I wrote a series of ten short plays called *The Possibilities*. Given that all persuasion lies in one direction at any particular time, there is still within the individual the power to resist that direction. In each of these plays, very compelling reasons why, for example, you should not do something, are shown to be resistible; [we see] the possibility of not being persuaded by a compelling argument, since argument, logic, has now become a lever.

CL: Isn't logic, however, intrinsic to language, [isn't it] the technology of writing, if you like?

HB: Yes, logic may be intrinsic to language, but is not intrinsic to poetry, which is the method of my writing. I suppose these plays celebrate emotional resistance, spontaneity, whatever the consequences. I can't think of a theatre of answers at all. I'm not sure I believe in dramatists' responsibility.

CL: What about *No End of Blame*, where the cartoonist hero accepts the verdict of the Soviet Writers and Artists Union that his anti-NEP cartoon was irresponsible? Would you go along with that attitude?

HB: No. That play is the only play I've written which has a tangible and conventional hero. And, though it's subtitled *Scenes of Overcoming*, one of the things he overcomes is his own sense of self. For example, in that scene he thinks something passionately but he represses it in the interests of the overriding definition of the people's interests as defined by that committee. I think that's wrong and I don't regard that as a good form of overcoming. Your individual consciousness as a writer cannot be compromised with a commitment to something which you can't actually see.

CL: Have you felt the lack of large-scale financial commitment to your work?

HB: Yes. I think the best production of my work I've ever seen was not done in England but in Finland; a large theatre committed six months of its rehearsal time to doing *The Love of a Good Man* on a massive scale. The huge, non-naturalistic set was the first to allow the entrances to work. [By contrast] I saw *The Power of the Dog* – in which the entrances are crucial, because you can't have Stalin appear casually – being done in a studio space; the casualness, the banality of Stalin's personality is a point made theatrically by its counterpointing with his office, his costume, his ostensible power; in other words, his entrance.

CL: Studio spaces have problems in presenting the emotional impact of that kind of power, which demands huge dimensions.

HB: What you get by putting big plays in a small space is a frisson of imagination. 'This is a space which is meant to signify the Battle of Agincourt if you're prepared to make that effort'. But I think it demands too much of an audience who have the right to experience a play without having to keep imagining space and scale. I'm certainly unhappy that so many of my plays have been refused the scale of production they require. That's a vicious circle too because if they're not put on the big stage, they fail, at a certain level, and therefore they don't get the level of audiences they would have got if they'd been put on in the right space in the first place.

CL: In this country, I suppose, the largest productions of your work would have been at the Royal Court?

HB: Yes, leaving aside Sheffield Crucible's production of *A Passion in Six Days*, which was on the main stage and, therefore, big. The conference scenes did work well, because Roger Glossop designed those conventional elements of the party conference – such as the speaker's stand and the podium on which the party members sit – on a scale which was greater than life. That gave the scenes a properly epic element.

CL: Being deprived of main auditorium space is a common complaint amongst contemporary dramatists.

HB: Yes. Mind you, not many contemporary dramatists really write epic plays. When Howard Brenton talks about wanting to play on the Steinway, he's not actually filling the space. When I saw *Weapons of Happiness*, two characters were talking and a tank appears, and you go, 'Oh, a real tank!' But that's not what epic theatre is, it's not getting all the junk on that he could have if it was real. I saw David Edgar's *Maydays* at the Barbican; there's a street scene during the battle of Budapest, when people rush across with flags, and there's a bit of smoke drifting about which is not really necessary. You only have the scale when the thing commands the scale. You don't fill it with dross in order to create pseudo-cinema. But I think my claim to the bigger space is based not just on the fact that most of my scenes happen outdoors and in big spaces, but that the language itself is rhetorical and epic. And because people speak speeches they need space. I don't get that, so one's continually telling actors to pipe down.

CL: With regard to the rhetoric, isn't it necessary for actors to counteract the text to an extent?

HB: Yes, that's absolutely right.

CL: You have said that you feel there are subtexts in your work and, surely, a complete surrender to surface rhetoric isn't going to bring these out?

HB: What happens often in a speech of mine is that a character plays one line of thought, which is then subverted by another line of thought; then he drops that and returns to the first line. So that within one speech, someone is labouring with, possibly, two completely conflicting ideas, such as pity and violence. A line might go, 'If I could get my hands around your throat, I would certainly kill you!' And then, 'Oh God! I'm so miserable!'

CL: Couldn't you have the actor say, 'If I could get my hands around your throat', etc., and *act*, 'Oh God! I'm so miserable!'?

HB: Yes, you could. That's a lot to ask, and it's not my style to do that. That would be a subtext. I think with that rhetorical thing […] maybe it's not rhetorical; perhaps we should find another word for it, the way it develops is that the characters often feel that they themselves are performing. They don't just say what's true; they say something which they know will create an effect on some of the other characters onstage. The character performs to himself and then to others. It's complicated.

CL: I find that interesting. Do you know F. Scott Fitzgerald's definition of personality at the beginning of *The Great Gatsby*, where he says personality can be defined as, "an unbroken series of successful gestures"? That definition has always seemed to me to be what many of your characters are aiming at. I wondered whether you saw your characters as striving for that kind of completeness?

HB: People trying to create themselves? Yes, I do feel that the character gives a performance that he then proceeds to subvert, so that they pre-empt other characters' right to judge them. The character says, 'I know myself, my qualities. So, don't think you can accuse me, because I already know that'. That's the way a lot of the political figures negotiate.

CL: Do you think that impenetrability is sustained indefinitely? In David Hare's *Knuckle*, the hero talks about his merchant banker father as having a personality like a pebble, smooth, no cracks, no way in, no point of vulnerability.

HB: No, because they can't really do it. It would be a fault if they really were impermeable. But they attempt it, because they can't resist the power of their own emotions or their own pain.

CL: So we should see these 'performances' founder?

HB: You see the performance attempt and the failure. And the reason the performances are put up is because people need carapaces in order to endure what history has imposed on them within the play. This girl in *The Europeans*, who's been raped, plays complete absorption and a complete understanding of her situation. She continually plays self-knowledge, but, as the play progresses, this is continually demolished.

CL: This suggests, with its interiority and exteriority, that an actor could approach certain parts, at least, from a naturalistic point of view? The Stanislavsky approach to character.

HB: Yes. I suppose that's so.

CL: Concerning layers of 'performance', I particularly enjoyed directing those scenes in *Fair Slaughter*, after the escape from prison, where Old Gocher has to keep up a continual ambiguity about the journey back to the USSR, pretending, or perhaps, believing that they're in The Steppes, when they're only a few miles south of London.

HB: [He does so] for the benefit of his friend, who needs to think that he can make it. That's a double bluff, isn't it?

CL: Gocher thinks Leary needs to think that he can make it, the mirroring goes on to infinity. And it also plays with the ambiguities of the staging; the scenery is only visible through the dialogue. It's very funny and, at the same time, very moving.

This previously unpublished interview, conducted in 1987, is an appendix to Charles Lamb's doctoral thesis on 'Irrational Theatre' (Warwick University: 1993).

The Last Supper. Nick Le Prevost (Ivory). The Wrestling School, 1987. Photo credit John Haynes

'The idea of hidden life'

With David Ian Rabey

David Ian Rabey (DIR)
Howard Barker (HB)

DIR: Lvov's assertion in *The Last Supper*, "Only catastrophe can keep us clean", echoes Bianca's line, "Catastrophe is also birth", in *Women Beware Women*, and Starhemberg's forcible tuition of Concilia in *The Europeans*. One definition of catastrophe is the experience of living beyond the point where death is preferable to continued existence, and I wonder how close this is to your own sense of catastrophe as potential explosion of spurious notions of life's worth or purpose, opening up tormenting roads to liberation. Your characters discover capacities to perform realignments in their selves through catastrophe which are incredible even to them, the phenomenon described by Helen in *The Bite of the Night* as the human ability to lose one's mind and yet find others, to lose one's sight yet see through other channels; and these characters are purposefully disturbing in begging the question as to how self-conscious or self-aware they are in their compulsions to excavate, explicate and perform their selves.

HB: Catastrophe in my theatre is willed, as opposed to simply endured. Bradshaw's horror at her husband's quartering is only the beginning of a journey she undertakes. Her pain is a door to catastrophic experience, which she wills upon herself, almost as if she wished to expose herself to the whole range of possible disaster, and like a piece of wood or linen, to accept the warping which hostility inflicts on her. But the fullest manifestation of catastrophe occurs in the choice Savage makes in Act I Scene I of *The Bite of the Night*, the discarding of family, the passage of sacred barriers which inhibit knowledge. This is a rupture which is made in isolation from the external. His wife, on the other hand, seizes a catastrophic opportunity with the fall of Troy to deliberately lose herself. And others also interpret bad fortune as a concealed escape, for example, Bianca's reluctant acknowledgement of meanings attaching to her own ordeal, and a forced examination of her own sexual nature. And in *Brutopia* Cecilia exposes herself to the risks of insanity or violent death in her ruthless relationship with Henry VIII.

What lies behind the idea of catastrophe is the sense of other varieties of the self repressed or obscured by politics, social convention, or simple fear. Bradshaw's journey is ostensibly one of piety – the collecting of her husband's parts – but it leads to acts of outrageous impiety. Savage commits impious acts as the condition of his tour. The will to be whole, and perhaps more than whole, is discovered in opposition to collective sentiment. Dramatically, the technique for summoning the will for this act of persistent rupture consists in constant self-description, the exhortation which found its first expression in a rudimentary form in Billy McPhee's last words in *That Good Between Us*.

DIR: The most compulsive characters in your recent plays – *Women Beware Women, The Bite of the Night, The Europeans,* and *The Last Supper* – are self-appointed liberators who consciously inflict pain to stimulate. Is the willing of catastrophe on self and others the same as the impulse to tragedy?

HB: The tragic resides in the refusal of the individual to leave the personality unexcavated, the eruption of will into areas of social piety. Savage's painful expression of secret thought, and the act contingent upon it, brings both him and Helen into the tragic arena. On the other hand, conventional tragedy demands punishment for transgression – mental disorder or death. It is the revenge of the collective upon the savage ego. Savage is not punished, at least not by the collective, and Starhemberg defies the collective to the end, drawing Katrin with him. So these plays are not tragic but catastrophist. The tragic denouement, the restoration of discipline over self by society or deity, seems to be in Shakespeare a neutered thing, a watery agency without vigour, unfelt and unbelieved. The punishment Savage receives is terrible loneliness, the effect of knowing too much. Starhemberg and Katrin discover new life through a love that can only be discovered in the extreme of resistance. As with Livia and Leantio, their claim on each other is conditional on rejection of reconciliation with the State. Lvov dies, but then he wishes to.

DIR: A recurrent theme in your work is the body, its mutilation and forcible mutation by self and others; Helen wonders, "What joint or knuckle, what pared-down shredded section would be the point at which your love would say stop, *essential Helen?*" The drive to discover how much can be done to the human body before it ceases to be desirable, talismanic or powerful emerges as unsettlingly vital. The transgression of ostensible physical limitations and ideals breaks, by association, conventional socially restrictive notions of beauty, desirability, and endurance. For example, in *The Europeans* Starhemberg's ruthless adoration of Katrin leads him into rebellion against the aesthetic ideal of beauty which sends shockwaves into the State's ideal of order.

HB: The body as conventional ground for controlled desire is one of the undeclared cornerstones of the State. It is inevitably associated with youth, especially with fertility, and effectively locates sexual charisma at the shallowest point. The freedom that some of my characters discover in locating sexual power in the frame of experience, e.g. pain, relates desire to the interior life rather than in the skin-deep fascination of the icon. Helen of Troy is described by Homer and all who follow him as youthful, beautiful, impossible-to-see-without-desire, etc., and Helen herself as reluctant, the victim of her appearance and so on. But we know beauty has nothing to do with desire, and that a beautiful woman cannot launch a thousand ships, whereas we suspect a desirable woman might. This distinction is at the crux of *The Bite of the Night*.

The State depends for its continuation on the cult of family and fertility, and fetishizes it by its collusions with the propagation of the beautiful, as thing to be possessed, as body owned and sold. I emphasized this in *Women Beware Women*, but also showed Sordido's ravishing of Bianca as the reverse of the coin. In *The Europeans*, Katrin's atrocious condition is a spur to desire in Starhemberg, her eroticism lying precisely in her impossible-to-assimilate history. She has none of the functions of fertility, being unable to feed an infant. By loving Katrin, Starhemberg publicly breaks the silent contract of socialized love.

But the body as locus of abuse and fetishization goes back earlier than these plays, certainly to *The Love of a Good Man*. The State has always played fictional games with the flesh of the dead. The Unknown Warrior is a response to the phenomenon of incomprehensible slaughter in the twentieth century, and designed to be an anonymous representation of sacrifice. In other words, the annexation of the innocent for the purposes of the State. I examined this proposition from a number of angles in the play. The symbolic and the actual coincide in the games played around the identity of a single corpse in the midst of monumental mourning.

On the other hand, the State's ferocious dismembering of its enemies is, of course, the motor to *Victory*. The personal ache to recover the murdered, euphemistically called 'The fallen' in the Great Wars, but the 'criminal' after great revolutions, reaches its apotheosis in Bradshaw's theft of her husband's head from the sleeping monarch, who transports it about with him, a more powerful talisman than the works hatched inside it. This hypnosis induced by the presence of the body defies rationalism, as we can see in the supreme obscenity of Lenin's tomb. While you are a useful pretext for social policy your body is mummified. As soon as you are discredited, your remains are attacked. Stalin was turfed out of his mausoleum. His flesh had to be abused as well as his ideas; and this in the super-rational society.

DIR: *Women Beware Women* and *The Europeans* depict speculative, disruptive actions which defy the sentimentalities of false democracies; these actions attack the ideal of 'kindness' by which populism discourages completeness of the self and the individual's will to know the true nature of his or her desires.

HB: I have tried to open the idea of kindness to examination because it is so frequently employed as a ban on action, a means of stifling will and self-expression. There is a form of kindness which is nothing to do with [being] 'kind' at all, but is a relentless charity which distorts the nature of the doer. Thus, to be kind to one's relatives might be to stunt oneself, to be kind to the weak might stunt the ability of the weak to develop their own strategy and so on. Kindness becomes a form of oppression, enabling us to refuse courses of action on the grounds they might injure others. Against this regime of delicacy, Livia's ruthless setting of Sordido on Bianca in *Women Beware Women,* and Starhemberg's despatch of Concilia in *The Europeans,* are acts of calculated violence which are creative to both the perpetrator and the ostensible victim. I have tried in *Brutopia* to look for a creative form of kindness in the person of Cecilia. She looks for a truthful form of it, declaring she cannot find kindness in the company of the kind, knowing as she does her father's kindness to be the fake virtue of a Renaissance egotist. More was, in his political relations, a most unkind man, vituperative and merciless, whose Utopia is socialized oppression based on sexual abstinence.

DIR: In *The Last Supper,* Lvov is an incarnate offence to populism in his completeness of self, when populism promises the provision of so-called 'essential' complementary elements and contexts which prove to be debilitating, intoxicating and addictive. I'm reminded of Nietzsche's identification of the herd instinct and its enshrined apotheosis in religion. You also seem fascinated by the promises and images of religious faith.

HB: Lvov creates a religion out of denial, insisting always on returning responsibility to the individual seeker. He is never placatory and rarely congratulatory, making independence of self the first condition of freedom. He plays two versions of kindness against each other, knowing that only by repression are we able to perform acts of social kindness, whereas only by acts of self-affirmation do we achieve the other sorts of kindness, truth to character. The persistent acts of rupture he performs with public morality entail an isolation from alternative sources of power. It is paramount for Lvov that he will not play the messiah to those seeking simple moral consolations; the officer asks for a pacifist lecture and goes away empty-handed, as does the farmer, a sinner whose sin we never learn. At the end of the play, the returning officer, hardened and revolutionary, declares that those will be punished who did not make their messages clear – the first priority of power being the unambiguous repetition of moral postures.

I am less interested in writing exposures of religion than in describing the constant swing between submission and independence that religion generates. Sloman, after attacking Lvov for his refusal of democracy, cannot resist the man's sheer self-assertiveness, which he finds immaculate, and, after a collective act of cannibalism, it is he who asserts the unity of all who have participated. It is Sloman who is the potential high priest of the cult. Thus, his [call to] "Hold hands!" is both a cry of solidarity but also of mutual enslavement. The accommodation which the individual is prepared to make to sustain faith is inordinate, a kind of longing for servitude of mind, and this can be observed in the great rationalist religions also. When Gisela is brutally exposed to bad sex by Lvov, an attempt to break her loyalty, she manages to turn her very proper anger into a controlling pity for him, and it is a source of bitter frustration to him that he cannot break their will to servitude. But the best religious figures are those who are essentially corrupt, and know their corruption. As Stucley declares in *The Castle*, what help can the perfect be to the imperfect? Only the imperfect can help the imperfect.

DIR: Whereas populism seeks to impose restrictive definitions of the self, the polar opposite force might be desire, which challenges even the *self-defined* limits of the self in a surge of derationalizing intuitive legitimacy, a liberation available to all yet defying generalization.

HB: Passion destabilizes the character, and by extension, the social cohesiveness of the polity. It is literally incapacitating, which was why it has been regarded as an infliction or a sickness. But desire, reciprocated, directs energy and makes transformation, both internal and external. Thus Ann and Skinner together can move mountains [in *The Castle*] but Skinner alone becomes a monument to defiance, strenuously powered and a subject of desire in herself, who has no access to desire any more. The cult of Skinner and her wound, her terrible absence, lends her the prospect of real political power, but it is a sterile thing compared to her original state. On the other hand, there is something condemned about Ann's hunger for Krak, and his own dissolution in it. It is unequal and ill fitting, and its cruelties are not creative in the way that, say, Starhemberg's are in *The Europeans*. In all the relationships of desire in my work, up until *The Bite of the Night*, there is a stronger and a weaker element, whether it's Ann's weakness vis-à-vis Skinner or Leantio's vis-à-vis Livia. But between Helen and Savage there is a relentless and ferocious drive that finds a mutual inspiration, an inevitable passage of destruction.

DIR: It strikes me that impulses to severance are crucial to your work – demanding the courage to act on one's love or hatred, or, most disturbingly, one's inextricably mingled love *and* hatred.

HB: "Impulses to severance" is a good phrase, raising once again the spectre of self-inflicted pain as a means to new knowledge, and yes, the hurt done to a loved one – and by extension, to oneself – is the supremely catastrophic example. This is difficult to articulate. It is near to the subject that occupies much of my attention as a writer, the nature of the bad spirit, the meaning of wickedness. The rupturing of conventional pieties is a common theme in my work – Savage's murder of his father in *The Bite* (it is technically a suicide, but Savage demands it), Orphuls's killing of his mother in *The Europeans*, Cecilia's ecstasy in her father's death in *Brutopia*, all of them gateways to self-development, but also appalling and traumatic.

There is an earlier form of this in Bradshaw's conscious dehumanization of her son in *Victory*. What the characters do in rupturing these bonds is to create morality for themselves, as if from scratch. They insist on a carte blanche, however impossible. It is as if they were seeing their own lives as theatre, and demanding the right to invent themselves.

DIR: The simultaneous co-existence of love and cruelty, or desire and pain, in your work is a more complex theme than can be encapsulated in the simplistic terms of deviancy, 'sadism' and 'masochism', in which social notions of deviance have their own effects of oppressive cultural (non-)legitimization. Lvov describes love as "doing the undoable". How might we distinguish love from desire?

HB: To take the first part, you are correct to expose terms such as 'sadism' and 'masochism' as attempts to bolster a spurious normality in sexual relations. Not all acts of cruelty between lovers can be interpreted as sadism unless a real hatred of the other, as opposed to the profound resentment that lies at the root of desire, is the source of it. By 'resentment' I intend this – the anger, and even shame, felt by the partner in the presence of the inextinguishable power of the other's sex, the spectacle of endless servitude (and ecstasy is a servitude) that sexual power (i.e. sexual difference) lays before us. This is a landscape of hunger which (like cunt in Krak's futile drawings) has neither edge nor width, and forever entails the abolition of dignity and even self-knowledge in the birth and rebirth of wanting. This resentment at servitude lies at the heart of wanting itself, and produces the ambiguous sense of despair and fascination which might lead to violence, a violence shared by both parties. Now, this is nothing at all to do with De Sade's monotonous savagery, where the orgasm is the single end of all imagination, and the attainment of orgasm an ever-diminishing prospect, available only by further refinements of cruelty. De Sade's violence is never mutual – it is not shared pain, but infliction.

The word love is not uncommon in my work, but I only edged towards a meaning for it in *The Europeans*, which is subtitled *Struggles to love*. And here it is in many ways not mediated through the body as desire is. What Starhemberg does for – and also against – Katrin is to insist on her right to self-description, resistant to the categories invented for her by the State and refusing the false reconciliations of history on the one hand, or parenthood on the other. His love for her is a love for her completion, her pursuit, which he perceives and perhaps judges more finely than she does herself. This certainly involves "doing the undoable".

DIR: *The Power of the Dog's* subtitle, *Moments in History and anti-History*, seems your first step towards identifying a mythic power in individual pasts as opposed to national pasts. This power is increasingly identified with sexuality in your work, particularly in *Women Beware Women* and *The Breath of the Crowd*, which highlight exposure and realization of the unlived life, the uniqueness of each personal testimony and the sense of cumulative power involved in sexual encounters.

HB: There is little or no aperture in *The Power of the Dog* for celebration or the catalogue of restorative things that are commonly associated with the humanist theatre. But what it does assert is the capacity of individuals for alternative experience and private history, which both dives under and is swamped by collective politics. In a world of 'Historical Method', blunderingly performed by Stalin with materialist rhetoric, an alternative fetishism is created by the dislocated, a viable private madness in collective madness.

The image of Ilona, fashion model and atrocity addict, is not easily prised open by psychological or political interpretation. She is a self-invention of the historical moment, absurd and yet powerfully evocative of wrong-rightness. In this, the play prefigures *The Possibilities*, which are all approaches to the idea of wrong-rightness. They are amoral plays, but powerful assertions of human imagination at the moment when reconciliation is a greater disaster than extinction itself. The willed creation of private history (Ilona's collection of photographs), its resistance to world-historical forces (an appalling category if there ever was one), and its insistence on private perception at all costs (she will continue with her narcissism no matter what the objective conditions) come yet more defiantly in *The Europeans* where atrocity itself, as personified in Katrin, refuses to submit to absorption into historical material (the dead, the executed, the unknown warrior, the fallen, etc.). Katrin is the 'Screaming Exhibit', a phenomenon that rocks the 'Museum of Reconciliation'. In all these plays, and, as you indicate, in *The Breath of the Crowd*, sexual history is made between characters with an authenticity that cannot distinguish their political actions. The dignity that is discovered in this struggle even lends a quality of beauty to the otherwise wholly disreputable. I'm thinking of Scadding in *Downchild*, for example.

DIR: Your characters insist on absolute truthfulness, in self and others, in sexual relations, however harrowing the consequences. For example, Skinner in *The Castle* tells Ann to leave nothing out of her description of her relations with Krak: "If I know all I can struggle with it, I can wrestle it to death [...]" Thus Skinner seeks relief from the self-torturing fascination of "the imagined thing", which gnaws her to madness.

HB: The demand for absolute truth in the sexual relationship is simultaneously the key to Skinner's evaluation to semi-divine status and a kind of emotional death. The truth is the devastation of hope. In a state of hopelessness she acquires the will to catastrophic experience, passing from passionate love life to adamantine stoicism. As long as Ann remained untruthful, the possibility of reconciliation existed, though as a sort of half-life, the wanting in pursuit of the unwanting. But by submerging herself in scalding pain (the very last detail of infidelity), Skinner sheds a defunct self, a dead skin, and even seems to regard sexual madness as nearly comic, when Krak exposes his loss of self to her, his bewilderment in the state of passion.

DIR: *Don't Exaggerate*, a direct address to the audience, seems a crucial development in locating obligation in the theatre audience on the specific occasion of performance. The prologues of *The Bite of the Night* and *The Last Supper* similarly emphasize the importance of what the witnesses choose to bring to, and give to, the theatrical experience.

HB: The importance of *Don't Exaggerate* in my theory of theatre lay in its employment of contradiction and digression as means of returning the onus of moral decision to the audience. I now believe in the dethronement of the audience, the abolition of its judgemental character, and the assertion of the stage over the auditorium. By this I mean the restitution of power to the actor, not as demonstrator of a given thesis, but as the figure who encourages the audience to abandon its moral and intellectual baggage and permit itself the greater freedom of an imaginative tour, essentially a destabilizing experience.

The proposition of a moral posture, and its immediate demolition ("You exaggerate! You do exaggerate! You know you do"), has the effect of loosening ideology, implying the absence of objective truths, and forcing the audience to make its own decisions about the actions shown or described. What the audience is given, its reward for this dangerous exposure, is beauty (truth having been annexed by political or psychological theory). *The Last Supper* is beautiful in language and form (I am thinking particularly of the parable entitled, 'The obscure origins of domesticity'), whilst being wholly un-ideological. The play is no longer a proposition about politics at all, though it is certainly about freedom. Rather, it is a journey without maps and without clear instructions to the audience, which is sometimes pained by the absence of hidden orders ('detest this character', 'see the manipulation here', etc.), especially when the character himself lacks stability (Ella in this play is both without words, then highly articulate, and Marya's contradictions are only superficially madness – they are, in fact, perfectly commensurate with frustrated dominance). In all my work after

Don't Exaggerate the audience is unable to withdraw into the security of known moral postures. This alone serves to eliminate 'entertainment' from its experience, since entertainment is impossible without very firmly drawn demarcations.

DIR: *Scenes from an Execution* dramatizes how, "artists have no power and great imagination. The State has no imagination and great power". Do you think this relationship is essentially antagonistic, one describing the limitations of the other's reach and reference?

HB: It seems to me impossible that the State and the artist should enjoy anything but a fleeting similarity of interest, usually in the aftermath of a revolution when the artist mistakenly believes his imagination will be licensed as part of the cultural rebirth of a new order. The rapid restitution of economic and social priorities and the assertion of the collective, or its mediators, over the individual interpretation of society, make this inevitably short-lived. States are mechanisms of discipline, and perpetually involved in rewriting and reordering experience, annexing it and abolishing it in the interests of proclaimed moral certitudes. The artist, as long as he is in profound union with his imagination, inevitably finds himself opposing ideological imperatives and exposed to censorship. This censorship will always take the form of 'protection' of sensibilities (the weak, women, virtue, the family, our past, etc.) no matter what the ostensible pretensions of the regime – a left regime has to protect 'class' and 'reason' as well as all the rest, and is likely to be more restrictive than certain inert reactionary ones. Women have to be protected against abuse, and the family against its perpetual, but never total, dismemberment. The State is a mass of fictions held together by superior power. I believe this has been the case as long as the State has existed. The problem is to judge which fictions are necessary ones.

DIR: How might the compulsion of audiences to witness transgression, as depicted in Jacobean drama, and your own, be distinguished from voyeurism? Can the stage release, as well as depict, the unlived life?

HB: All descriptions and propositions of and about life in drama entail the possibility of imitation. But my plays do not operate as models of behaviour, recommendations or exhortations. They are not pathways out of collective life or manuals of mayhem. They do not attempt to demonstrate wrong life or detail paths to self-knowledge. Every play is provisional, just as every statement must be provisional. I have nothing to teach anyone. In any case, the pain and despair experienced by my characters hardly invite imitation, though conversely, there is no tragic denouement which reinforces the existing moral consensus. Rather, the plays remove, plank by plank, the floor of existing moral opinion in order to plead other, unarticulated causes. The audience (if there is such a thing, and since I do not seek a solidarity here, I ought to talk of individuals) feels itself bereft (and frequently exhilarated as a consequence) of its usual critical or empathetic equipment, and even insecure in its laughter, which is the last refuge of uncertainty.

But this disarray is not sterile. Since there is a distinct absence of moral convention, the transgressor is not punished, the audience is obliged to arrive at its own judgement, not of situations it knows, but of ones it does not. What occurs in my plays is only partly life as it is known, after all. Mostly, it is unknown life. The audience is stirred at a subconscious level by the sheer volume of imagined life which the actors present. This is not voyeuristic, since it is not a fetishism around an observed action which leaves the witness transfixed but still hermetically sealed in his own moral posture. The possibility that is unlocked in the relations between characters drags the idea of hidden life into the forefront of consciousness. It is an acutely painful, and a half-reluctant, experience, to which individuals frequently return.

DIR: When surrounded by normative systems of predictions, connecting with further normative systems of predictions, rather than with lived experience, one is in danger of being enmeshed in a climate of accrued debilitation – to quote *Don't Exaggerate*, "the liars operate in the imagination, too". But the subversive power of the imagination, and its address to an unwontedly full sense of human integrity, might reside in its unpredictability. In discovering integrity in action, the individual invents freedom for himself or herself in a non-ideological way, and becomes answerable to nothing and no one for validation. How close is this to the spirit of enquiry at work in *The Possibilities* and to your sense of theatrical surprise in general? Do the subversive powers of both comedy and tragedy lie in their demonstrations of essential incongruity? Is the vital essence of theatre a power of dislocation?

HB: The hidden purpose of much modern drama has been the exposure of wrong life. The play states more or less overtly, 'beware not to live like this', or, in an age of ideology, 'you must put an end to this'. Both comedy and the sorts of tragedies we variously encounter conspire in this missionary intention. And it would be absurd to pretend audiences do not hunger for this instruction as vehemently as writers long to provide it. It is theatre's old obeisance to certain governing conventions. When the play fails to provide instruction in wrong life, unease is created and, frequently, a piqued resistance. In *The Possibilities* I persistently refuse the answer an audience anticipates from the predicated situation. There is an element of frustration in it, but what prevents the witnesses of the plays from becoming vociferous in their unwilling subjection to the wholly unpredictable nature of the pieces is the peculiar, simultaneous ecstasy of recognizing the appalling strain of being human. They are not led or instructed by the story. The onus of dealing with the pain is theirs.

There is no right course, or wrong action in *Kiss My Hands* or *The Philosophical Lieutenant*. Nor is there a generalized protest at the way we are, or at our unkindness to each other. The audience suffers this, but the pain is somehow positive. It can only be that out of the deepest exploration of pain, unmediated by ideology or morality, a certain strength is lent by performance. The power of these pieces in production reveals the meaninglessness of the notion of 'pessimism' in art. It is not pessimism at all; it is the excoriation of experience.

DIR: I know you resist sentimental or intoxicating celebratory invocations of 'community' such as some would identify as the characteristic cohesive effect of the theatrical experience – the descent (or imposition?) of communality which Hilton and others worship in mystical terms. Rather, you've emphasized the individual reflection of the single audience member, concentrating and witnessing in the darkened stalls. But what, then, is his relationship to his fellow spectators, and to what extent is this salient to the theatrical experience?

HB: Yes, I am against the solidarity of the audience. It is easily manipulated and frequently, albeit unconsciously, authoritarian. The best moments in theatre for me are those in which solitary movements can be discerned, in which a sense of contest can be registered between the stage and the disjointed audience. These solitary contests are, of course, determined by the fact of the existence of others; they would be harder to achieve in isolation. The tension created by an assumed collectivity of response, which then disintegrates, leaving individuals exposed to the effects of actions on the stage, is to me a valid condition of experiencing art.

The audience has to sense its moments of division as well as its moments of unity, which I would not deny, though I wouldn't locate this unity in the usual places, perhaps. The unity should surprise as much as the disunity. Often this sense of isolation is affirmed by the light of the foyer, where the normal buzz of the consensus is replaced by a wariness to articulate what is still undigested. But I do not intend the individual to be without a guide. I come back to the actor, who by sheer bravery becomes the focus of hope and the source of security that cannot, in my work, be found in the usual forms of the message or the verisimilitude. In the actor's courage, the audience individual finds his own.

This interview was originally published in 1989, in the first edition of the book of Barker's theory Arguments for a Theatre *(Manchester: Manchester University Press, 1989 [1993] [1997]).*

Hated Nightfall. Ian McDiarmid (Dancer) and Keith Osborn (Arrant). The Wrestling School & the Royal Court, 1994. Photo credit Stephen Vaughan

'A laboratory of human possibility'

With Charles Lamb

Charles Lamb (CL)
Howard Barker (HB)

CL: You're writing increasingly on theoretical matters, about theatre in general and the social function of theatre. Have you felt it necessary to do this? Because it could be seen, perhaps, as a rather dangerous direction for a creative writer to take.

HB: Anyone who has worked consistently at an art form for a number of years has a theory of creation and production. It is only a matter of articulating it that separates 'theoretical' artists from others. In my own case I undertook it as a work of self-defence. Unlike most ostensibly 'controversial' writers, I had no critical support that was visible. Where it existed, chiefly among younger academics, and abroad, it couldn't express itself in the public domain.
         With the 'Fortynine asides' [published in the theory collection *Arguments for a Theatre*] I recognized that the aphoristic was the most suitable for me, given the poetic nature of my writing style. But the theory changes, as the plays do, in temperament and form. I have never thought it likely the style of my work could be dominated by a theoretical posture I had adopted, but rather the other way round. I am seeking to justify, in a post hoc way, what I arrived at imaginatively – that seems the only way an imaginative artist proceeds, blindly, wilfully, and chaotically, in the first instance, conceptually on reflection. But I was inevitably drawn towards questions of function and the social context of theatre. There was no theory of production which did not see theatre as essentially a critical medium. I was bound to collide with that.

CL: Two things occur to me: one is that there has been a tremendous dominance of theory in this country in post-war theatre, in theatre as studied in universities –

I'm thinking particularly of Brechtian theory and the influence of Stanislavsky. This seems to centre on theatre being a form of communication which disseminates messages or truths to its audience. But the problem with your kind of theatre is that it doesn't do that. Derrida has said that the literary work should be "insupportable", meaning not only that it should somehow challenge our tolerance but that it should resist analysis in terms of current theoretical positions – that it should not depend on or refer to theoretical positions for validation, rather it should question theory. And in a sense it seems to me that what you're trying to do with your work involves a reversal of the normal assumptions. Critics go to performances expecting to come away with something – theory, message or whatever; they do not expect to have their own assumptions challenged.

HB: This challenge to existing critics and existing audiences is not a politics on my part, not a mischief, but springs – at the point of creation – from exhaustion with forms and assumptions, the obsession with clarity, for example, that I regarded rather early on as being a lethal ingredient in practice. After all, I never write from clarity, I have none, nor do I ever know the structure or narrative form, let alone the content, of any play I am writing. How could a theory of production that depended on clarity of 'meaning' and 'intention' have any relevance to me? Those who clamoured for meanings and messages were requiring the theatre to reiterate social propaganda within the framework of a governing social humanism, a compact of mutual celebration which had degenerated into massage.

    My first assumption became – a statement from bitter experience – that the audience and the stage are not united – rather, that the theatre is a place of discomfort, and that its prevailing mood is one of anxiety. It occurred to me, almost as soon as I had emerged from an ostensible 'socialist' form of 'critical' writing (not that it had earned me any friends among 'socialist' critics) that – given the plethora of media information, social propaganda, collective affirmation, humanistic accord, that falls here like a drenching rain – theatre's only function now could be speculation. [Theatre needed to go] beyond the existing humanistic compact, in other words [...] the theatre [had] to become an illegal space. Instead of taking theatre into the street, as if it could speak automatically to all people, it should assert its privileged nature, its secret character, claiming privacy for the very reason that privacy in a populist culture is anathema and the subject of perpetual violation. In a sense, it should be hard to get at. Obviously, this is the opposite pole from the national obsession with 'access'. But access is only control in another form of control.

CL: Brecht and Stanislavsky, and the notion of the play as having a 'ruling idea' seem very prevalent in the kind of director's theatre we have here. The theatre theory of the twentieth century pivots round the figure of the director – not the figure of the writer. And that shift is especially concerned with the exercising of a kind of control, the control of the performance.

HB: That is true, but writers have conspired in this; since Brecht in particular, but it extends far back into the Enlightenment [...] They have conceived of themselves as civilizers. If you think your function is to civilize other human beings, you can't permit yourself the dangerous luxury of seeing the performance 'degenerating' into ambiguity, the actors playing contradiction and so on. It is primarily a matter of disciplining the audience and the performers into a condition where they are able to 'receive' the dispensed wisdom of the text. In essence, I believe the actor to be a symbol of mayhem, an unreliable reservoir of emotion, a licensed player of the illicit. Modern directorial practice has been to pin him to a rack of ideology – in the supreme interest of the collective, of course. He is diminished by this, and so is the theatre.

CL: I wanted to talk about the actor, because the best response to your work has been largely from actors, and I would have thought their response would come on a more immediate, experiential and instinctive level, whereas the position at the moment is that your work is not acceptable to the major theatrical establishments, which are essentially directorial establishments.

HB: Yes. I don't think it is possible to exaggerate the absolute seizure of the theatre environment at the moment. This seizure is the outcome of a peculiar collusion between liberal theatre directors and populist culture as a whole. The values of entertainment and the degeneracy of a critical theatre into a new sort of sentimentality have produced a theatre which is indistinguishable from other dramatic forms, but almost certainly inferior to them. It is my view that theatre has been good only when it disassociated itself from the governing ideology, that it made its business the experience of outlawed life – and I don't mean the fashion for criminality. The natural outlaws of society are artists, of course, and not criminals, who merely mirror the values of ruling systems. I'm referring to tragedy, which is trespass. Directorial theatre distrusts tragedy. It gets out of hand, is irrational. Most directors are uneasy with irrational qualities onstage; they give them a sense of redundancy.

CL: Regarding the business of performance, then, do you feel that there is a need for a new approach? One of the things that interested me in studying your work, considering it from the point of view of performance, was that it did seem to question the established functions of director and actor and the way in which these might approach the work of rehearsal and, finally, the performance itself. One of the things that struck me was the actors' insistence on the openness they found in your texts, so that when they went out to perform there was a sense that they did not know what was going to happen next.[...] That sounds like nonsense, because, of course, the text is there, but perhaps they did not know what the motivations behind the words were going to be, what the implications would be, in which particular direction the ambiguities were going to tend, or how another actor was going to play a line which they would then have to respond to. That openness interested me. One actress in particular, I seem to recall, did a lot of work on her part, examining all the different possibilities of the different situations but she would approach a performance with a sense that those possibilities were all still open.

HB: This sense of fluidity – some actors might regard it as insecurity – reflects the manner of the production of the text itself, which, as I said before, was written in that state of chaos;which I regard as normal with regard to my own work, and life in general. Do we possess 'intentions', with regard to one another, which are not in permanent overthrow? Do we not depend on a high degree of resourcefulness in our dealings with one another, seizing, abandoning projects, opportunistic at one moment, craven the next? The ambiguities that lie within speeches in my plays, the fact that characters proffer themselves, withdraw, exercise a desire, and even pretend to a desire, in order to witness its effects, mean that both actions and speeches are ambiguous even to the character himself. An argument might be ridden like a horse by a character until a better presents itself – if only because argument in my work is frequently spurious, and only emotion is trusted, emotion conjures the argument out of need.

Thus an actor will find it hard to lay down a line on a character from any rational point of view, all he can approach at any given moment is the emotional demand generated by his character encountering another. This must change night by night, and no actor can ever play this work blindly, or soporifically, as they frequently do with texts which are cemented; it is also why members of the audience frequently return to watch again and again – partly to witness different aspects of the overwhelming density of it, but also to see performances in flux. This means the director's role is a different one. He cannot be the fountain of 'meaning', his autonomy is distinctly limited, and authority is widely distributed. His crucial function is to orchestrate. It is an aesthetic judgement that is called for here, a fineness of sensibility to the overall experience.

CL: One of the things that interested me in this connection is the business of bluff. It seems to me that quite a number of your characters, in quite a number of plays, are bluffers – they fake. And I feel that this is an important characteristic of a lot of performance. The ambiguity of a situation connects with this in the sense that you can have a character who plays a reaction which is – for want of a better word – 'genuine' or 'unpremeditated'. [This might be] for example […] pain […] [A]t a certain stage [this can] turn into [a] performance […] [in which] the character realizes the effect this is having on others and begins to exploit it. This is the kind of area where the actor actually has choices […] at what point does the bluff begin and the spontaneity end? It struck me this was an opportunity for the actor to live the situation differently every time.

HB: It is the reason why the work is violently unnaturalistic, for naturalism takes fixed character for granted. This acute self-awareness in characters is the absolute in tenderness, in thin skin. The word 'bluff' implies a conscious manipulation, but this is not strictly true. The character is always governed by powerful desires, ones which are more or less permanently out of control, and therefore in crisis; he grasps, expediently, desperately, at whatever lies to hand, sometimes with yet further appalling consequences. Stucley, in *The Castle*, Charles in *Victory*, my Vanya in *(Uncle) Vanya*, nearly everyone in *Ego in Arcadia*, to an extent perform their own emotions and exploit the opportunities lent by their fascination. Stucley's long speech to his wife on his return is a tortuous series of attempts to undermine her resistance to him, but they are not calculated so much as driven by need, a sort of brilliance born of panic. In this panic, a number of narratives are going on at the same time.

CL: Yes, that's a good example. You can actually have the opposite thing. Stucley performs his weakness – and he is performing – but he can also be seduced, presumably, by his own performance? And, actually, although he sets out to control this whole thing from a strategic point of view, the performance can take him over and he can end up being taken back by it, becoming the victim of his own performance.

HB: When the character expresses an intense emotion – released by the breakdown of stratagems or appeals – it flings open doors, opens vistas to new grounds of invention. The attack on the Bible and the Christian message by Stucley, for example, is primarily an expression of pain and loneliness, but hearing his own articulation of it provides him with a new resource. He attacks the Bible, he rejects it; then he retrieves it, annexes it, for his own purposes, by inventing the theology of Christ the Lover. The spontaneity of these emotional swoops forces him into new postures, so he does become both the victim of his emotions and also the shrewd exploiter of them. Characters therefore swing between control and loss of control. Naturalistic theatre is always bound by the possible, in effect, the already known. In Catastrophic Theatre, the impossible is drawn into proximity.

CL: Presumably this is where language is very important, because the language carries the momentum of the drama and the characters, through using language, can be seduced by their own articulation. So there is a sense in which, perhaps, the words speak the character rather than *vice versa*. I think this is another area in which there is a problem with contemporary performance theory, which teaches actions – the Brechtian idea of 'gestus', where one considers the action as a whole, and the words are merely part of it. In considering the text, one looks at the line and decides what the action is, the motivation, and then speaks the words following up that particular action.

HB: In such a theory, the words become of diminishing importance, they might even be incomprehensible, whereas I have argued that the power of language is crucial to the authority of theatre, but [also] that it has to be continually reinvented; the dramatist must also be a poet, just as the actors must equip themselves to speak. The speech is specific to theatre, one of its highest principles and what most distinguishes it from film or television. In the speech the actor breaks the bonds of the real, disrupts the familiar, scattered syntax of naturalism, with its domestic associations, and draws the audience into a state of intoxication. It is the antithesis of critical realism, with its "on the one hand [...] on the other" formulations, its commitment to objectification. And the speech does speak the character. Articulation in such torrents subverts reason, unbalances the complacent notion of stable character. In floods of temper or despair we say, "I did not know myself [...]"

CL: Moving from the theory to the work that you are writing, it's changed very considerably over the course of your career – especially these last few years. But if I actually look right back through your drama, there do seem to be certain central issues and concerns which are remarkably consistent. In fact, I was very surprised at the way certain situations which loom large in plays of the 1980s are there in embryo in plays of the early 1970s. How do you feel that the direction of your work has changed recently?

HB: There are new themes, but also, as you suggest, themes which are entirely re-viewed. The idea of sacrifice, for example, which could only be approached satirically in early plays, has taken on enormous significance in recent work. Smith is the first of these self-sacrificing figures, the first example of pure devotion that I have managed. Indeed, the whole of *Rome* is about the conflict between definitions of self and the abolition of selfhood. Then there are the servant figures who predominate in my more recent work, beginning with the servant in *Ten Dilemmas*, a man morally and intellectually superior to his master, but moved to terrible acts of service by pity, and the former tutor Dancer in my latest play *Hated Nightfall*, who converts a passion for revenge into a supreme self-immolation. Some of these investigations can be traced back to *The Possibilities*, particularly, perhaps, to the Groom in *Reasons for the Fall of Emperors*, whose infuriating self-abnegation is only slightly ridiculous.

Another theme which colours recent work, but which, it now seems clear, had earlier, cruder manifestations, is the idea of the insufficiency of the world, of the impossibility of discovering a place in it for those whose souls are, in a sense, too large for their environment, whose curiosity is too intense for the mundane necessities of social order, but too desiring for solitude. This is very much the texture of *The Europeans* and of *Rome,* but you are right to say it appears embryonically in earlier plays [...] [such as] *The Castle*, where the emotional ambition of Skinner cannot discover an equivalent, or *Crimes in Hot Countries,* where Erica is condemned to spiritual loneliness for daring to dream of her equal. This ill-fit with the world was solved in *The Europeans* only by a series of semi-barbaric acts of existential will, induced by Starhemberg, [and] suffered by Katrin. The search for a reason not to commit suicide lies at the heart of my work, and what is distilled from that is a sense of melancholy. The most melancholic of my plays is perhaps *Golgo*, though *Ego in Arcadia* is also profoundly melancholic. I don't mean depressing. Only a populist, entertainment-obsessed, comedy-obsessed culture confuses melancholy with depression.

CL: I remember you saying once that one of your major interests was character. You also said that you were interested in the point where the personal intersected with power and the political element, this latter coming to be seen especially in the shape of ideology. With this emphasis on the individual – and a lot of your characters are concerned to discover or follow their individuality – isn't this, perhaps, another kind of ideology […] [in which] will becomes a thing solely in and for itself? I'm thinking, in particular, of the attitude expressed by, for instance, Stagg, the Home Secretary in *The Hang of the Gaol*, when he asserts the importance of 'clinging' – with all the negative connotations that word implies. Your political figures are often 'clingers' in the sense that they sacrifice everything to their will to power; and in this sense your political figures are, in their grotesque-ness, perhaps your most conventionally 'realistic' characters. I suppose what I'm suggesting is that there is desire, but when this desire meets with resistance it can be sustained by will and that, at a certain point, the initial desire evaporates and there remains only will.

HB: The political figures might be divided into the active seekers for power, and those on whom power is pressed. If Stagg is the ultimate cynic of a discredited democratic system, with its honours and compromised loyalties, perhaps Skinner is at the opposite pole, one for whom political power is the ironic gift of resistance to authority. The former exists in absolute circularity. The latter is burdened with the moral dilemma of inventing a new system out of the ruins of the old, and the horror of it causes her to repudiate power itself. It is only when she perceives – in a spasm of pure feeling – her chance to indulge her appetite for revenge that she picks up the keys again. These are different varieties of will, one sterile, one passionate. You could include Toplis, Park, Lear, Livia, Ridler among the willed, driven figures who are both made and, ultimately, broken by their collision with power. There is nothing remotely ideological about these, if ideology means, as it must do, system, structure, law and inhibition. They are transgressive, morally innovative, insisting on a personal identity which the collective seeks to eliminate. This reaches an apotheosis in *Ten Dilemmas*, where impotence is reclaimed as a form of opposition, and punished. This is not a case of will outlasting desire – pure negativity. The self denies social manipulation, even if self is partially – and I would insist only partially – socially produced.

CL: This obviously links with another aspect of your thinking which is concerned with the feeling of being menaced by increasing social authoritarianism. I recall you once saying that desire would possibly be made illegal. How real would you say this danger is?

HB: The political and social project of the twentieth century has been the elimination of pain, the elimination of conflict, the prolongation of life. The corollary of this is the promotion of happiness. Apart from regimentation, which has been tried, the best means to achieve these ends is to create a barrage of propaganda about harmony, and this requires definitions. Profound moments of desire are disruptive, because, by nature, they do not relate to given norms, they defy the definitions arrived at by opinion-makers, whether it be intellectuals or Welfare State managers, media bosses, or vocal minorities. The increasing level of social propaganda, disguising itself as news and information services, entertainment and the various sham manifestations of 'participation', eventually must locate its enemies; it cannot define harmony if its opposite isn't visible. We have experienced some of this in the identification and paranoia over 'abuses', which has clear undertones of the medieval, the witch hunt. The resource one possesses to oppose legalized happiness is imagination, of course, but we observe that in the theatre – to take one example – it is distinctly subordinated to social realism, now an oppressive form, as I have said elsewhere.

CL: One of the things that strikes me is the quantity of common ground you share with the classical Greek tragedians where one finds the opposition of collectivity and individualism formalized in the division between tragic protagonists and the choruses; the former demonstrating hubris by overstepping the bounds, the latter tending to present conventional social wisdom. You have attempted to assert the value of tragedy in a culture which is resolutely bent on endorsing comedy as being both 'healthy' and moral. Though what comedy does more than anything else – as Bergson points out – is reinforce collective values and attitudes.

HB: I identified, some time ago, the pernicious effect of the comedy industry on moral autonomy here – it is one of the oppressive social characteristics that appears like a plague in *The Last Supper*, and, as you know, I have regarded political and social satire as the essence of redundancy.

CL: Another aspect of this is that you seem to share the Greek suspicion of the idea of happiness. This mistrust is a constant theme in the classical tragedies – "Call no one happy until he is dead". I think most people today would find this obsessive or morbid. Perhaps the Greeks felt that there was something more valuable than happiness – beyond happiness, which they saw as illusory.

HB: It is the social endorsement of happiness – its politicization – that renders it more oppressive as a principle of existence even than when it was first institutionalized by the utilitarians. It has become a 'right', along with numberless other 'rights' that a populist State vomits from its cornucopia. Because the Greeks understood the pleasures hidden in the spectacle of pain, as well as its place in life, its supreme irrationality, even its comedy, they did not resist it in the way we do, even though it horrified them. They saw the malice in things. We have never really come to terms with the Christian god, because he has repudiated malice, it is not part of his will, despite the terrible fate of Job. Inevitably, the liberal humanist State dare not contemplate it either, actions of ill-will can only be the product of social malformation, psychological disturbance and so on. Malice was a characteristic of the Greek gods, so that ill fortune was not greeted with the nauseating incomprehension that afflicts us, the rage at the "unfairness of things". Also, they knew as well as we do that the acquisition of an object, or a person, delivers rather little satisfaction. The heroic consists in reaching beyond gratification, in rendering gratification irrelevant. Thus the idea of being happy does not concern Draper in *Ten Dilemmas* – it is not part of his consciousness any more. That he is bound to a woman with whom he cannot experience conventional 'fulfilment' is a source of fascination, and fascination is the highest state a character can experience in my work – an abolition of ends, absolute desire.

CL: You have characters who transgress and who break conventions and taboos in ways such as we've been discussing, but there are always consequences to these actions. One of these seems to be that the character comes to an increasing solitude; they are progressively isolated.

HB: Not inevitably, though solitude is a state I cannot say I find appalling or contemptible. It would be a most unimaginative culture that could not see the virtues of solitude, or the reasons why one might opt to exclude oneself from society. Men and women have chosen it for centuries. It is true that the relentless pursuit of knowledge can lead to nothing else – it's the fate of Savage in *The Bite of the Night*, and of Park in *Rome* – Park is physically deprived of the means of communication anyway.

[Solitude] arrives to some as a consequence of their supreme powers of resistance – they become idols: who in *The Castle* can discover the means of communicating with Skinner, for example? And in *Victory* it is an irony that Bradshaw spends the remainder of her life with an enemy who has also lost the power of speech [...] though there is a physical intimacy there. This isolation is a testament to their heroic status. Some are able to suspend it – Galactia, in *Scenes from an Execution,* is prepared to submerge it in a dubious form of celebrity, Lear in *Seven hears* is prepared to play chess with a cheat for his whole life in order to engage at some level with another human being, but it is primarily the erotic that provides the sole recourse [...] It is the erotic that enables Starhemberg and Katrin to overcome the blandishments of the liberal State in *The Europeans,* and the erotic subverts Ridler's missionary zeal in *A Hard Heart.* At a certain point, however, there is a transition, a triumph, where solitude is resolved into a moment of universality. I am thinking of the sacrifice that Dancer makes in *Hated Nightfall,* when he expresses desire in a form which precludes the erotic. He draws catastrophe upon himself, and upon the family he has been ordered to execute, as a gesture of spiritual independence: more than a gesture, it is a rebuke to a world in which both the reactionary *and* the revolutionary are decadent [and] intolerable.

CL: Is this what happens with Draper in *Ten Dilemmas?* Because he ends up in a position where he's more or less forcing the others to kill him, but he himself pre-empts that by taking his own life. In that situation there were other choices available to him – he could have bluffed, or pleaded. So that would be an example of someone going beyond isolation into sacrifice [...]?

HB: *Ten Dilemmas* is a play about rebellion, in its most extreme form, ultimate rebellion. It is a rebellion against nature, against sex and against procreation. Death is inevitable, and the collective – in this case the family of Draper – are prepared to murder him in order to break the fascination that exists between the fecund woman (Becker) and the impotent man (Draper). Draper's self-sacrifice might be seen, therefore, as peculiarly 'responsible [...]': Becker can do nothing but resort to another man, which she does in the last scene. But Draper's suicide is simultaneously the sacrifice required by the collective in full cry against a dissenter, and the act of a disdainful aristocrat who never for a moment doubts his power even if he suffers shattering despair. I cannot pretend to fully understand *Ten Dilemmas* yet [...] perhaps I never shall. In many ways *Hated Nightfall* is clearer to me [...] Dancer's lucidity, the defiance with which he sacrifices himself for a family who are not worthy of his sacrifice, is a perfect contradiction.

CL: We've talked about how you frequently present characters who assert their own individuality and are prepared to take this to excess, but you also show characters who do the opposite, who attempt to resign their individuality in servitude. Presumably, you would not value this tactic of resignation of the will as highly as its assertion. Is it not as valid?

HB: The idea of 'excessive' individuality is interesting. It suggests there is so much possible play in a personality that is submerged in the interests of order, discipline, political and social convenience, and if this is the case, then the theatre – as ever – poses the opposite, the unfettered, demonstrative ego. There are few victims in my plays – even the most resolutely punished of them all, Helen of Troy in *The Bite of the Night,* who is made the scapegoat for every failed system, turns her ordeal into a resource; her maimed body becomes an increasingly powerful talisman the less there is that remains of it. Armless and legless she remains an erotic fetish for succeeding generations. Katrin repudiates the idea of the 'victim' in *The Europeans* by thrusting her condition into the public gaze, an unrepentant hater. The victims of State power in *Victory*, Ball and Scrope, reverse roles: Ball becomes a silent, innocuous pet on a rope, while Scrope screams slogans at his tormentors. In a few cases, power becomes itself becomes a tedium, and 'personality' a thing which, painstakingly made, loses its glitter. I am thinking of Toplis in *Crimes in Hot Countries*, Lear in *Seven Lear* – [who is] exhausted by enquiry – and the most potent example, Lvov in *The Last Supper*, a charisma at the end of its tether. Lvov has a household of 'servants', all of whom have renounced or try to renounce their egos in the interests of service to another. It is not until *Ten Dilemmas* that I dared to imagine the individual who yielded up his independence entirely to others, as opposed to the many characters who swing between submission and rebellion, as Lvov's disciples do. The servant in *Ten Dilemmas* is recognized by all around him as a man morally superior, intellectually superior, to those he has chosen to serve, who are themselves conventionally immoral. He does this from a profound sense of pity – not the lifeless pity we approve of socially, but a passionate love for two people engaged in a struggle *à outrance* [to excess] with a mundane world.

CL: With your play (*Uncle*) *Vanya* it seems that you wanted to confront an aspect of English theatre which is reflected particularly in the popularity of Chekhov's plays. This is a kind of aestheticizing and celebration of hopelessness and apathy.

HB: Works of art undergo changes of meanings from age to age, decade to decade. What I confronted in rewriting *Uncle Vanya* was the contemporary condition of the work. Chekhov may have thought his plays were comedies, but inevitably they have been annexed for other purposes, principally the endorsement of moral and sexual failure. The materialist argument that Chekhov was describing the decline of a particular class in the climate of gathering revolution may lend this moral weakness a certain documentary authority, but from the point of view of a living theatre, the effect has been to provide English audiences with an alibi for denying the speculative or the tragic. Chekhov, who seems to have hated the episode with the gun in *Uncle Vanya*, was so embarrassed by human action on the stage, as opposed to endless inaction, that he regarded this moment as melodramatic [and] shameful. I took this as my starting point for an unfolding series of incidents that obliged Vanya to reach for characteristics in himself that he could not normally expose, in other words, to lend him will. This castrated man is restored to his sexual powers and seduces Helena. Astrov, a fashionable ecologist, but still someone who cannot complete a desire, is murdered. The characters revolt against inertia.

CL: It's interesting that the shipwrecked Chekhov takes refuge in the room. In the sphere of theatre practice Chekhov is a very important figure – with regard to the development of Stanislavskian acting techniques. The 'system' could have been written to complement Chekhov's artistic vision – one of the striking characteristics of which is that there is no significant interaction. The plays dramatize the impossibility or worthlessness of this – as you say, it's a condition of negativity. So you have characters who are ceaselessly yearning towards each other but the play shows this to be hopeless and the only 'answer' is 'work'. The 'system' condones this vision by its emphasis on the primacy of the 'character' [and of] 'emotion' arising from the character's interior, which serves to create an impression of the *role* as a precious but sealed balloon of subjectivity. Stanislavsky's 'system', like Chekhov, ignores the possibility of significant emotion being generated in and by the interaction of self with the other.

HB: Yes, you have identified the crucial difference between my theatre and Chekhov's and between the Stanislavskian mode – with its domination of contemporary theatre practice – and what is required for my own practice. There is no carbonized stability of character in my theatre, no one is immune from the effects of others – on the contrary, the need to influence, subvert, annexe, seduce others is the very definition of existence. The consequence of this perpetual emotional imperialism or craving – it is a matter of judgement – is that action is the permanent state of affairs, that change is relentless, that the obligations of choice or denial cannot be evaded, and that selves are in constant play, every character has the potential for its own opposite. I have said often that the audience is – on an individual basis – given authority and autonomy by this sort of theatre, it is not trapped within the existent, not reminded, confirmed in its powerlessness. This dark, enclosed space, detached from the world, is a laboratory of human possibility. It has religious connotations, but whereas religion affirms disciplines, restrictions, theatre explodes them.

CL: A number of your plays – particularly recent ones – have contained clerics. And in *Rome* the central focus of the play is strongly ecclesiastical, involving not only individual characters but also the question of cultural identity as to exactly what 'Rome' is.

HB: I think one has to examine the possibility that faith is one kind of freedom. We discussed the idea of servitude. What Smith performs in *Rome* is the absolute in priestly self-abnegation. She endures as literally as possible the ordeal of the man who has, stage by stage, become a god, just as God in this play manifests a terrible longing to be a man. Park, the immaculate Pope, is better at being God than God himself is, which is why he is condemned to suffer so inordinately. The reason Park has such authority is that he represents something superior to God – culture, 'Rome', the accretion of human artistic and social practice, which is, in the end, located in a fragment of a teacup. Smith's adoration of Park is inspired principally by his sexual pathos, but transferred to a set of values associated with 'Rome', few of which are ever identified: but that isn't important. What matters is her invention of an identity when social identity (the culture) is overwhelmed.

CL: The play is subtitled *On being divine*. I'm interested in what your conception of the divine might be. Initially Benz is divine, but clearly feels the need to engage with the human. He becomes engaged in a seductive deal with Beatrice, which seems to propel him towards the human, while she, on the contrary, overcomes what might be called her humanity; I'm thinking of her response to Benz's killing of their child. She says, "There is the fact and the emotion. They come apart and in the gap's divinity".

HB: What is divine cannot be human, and what is human cannot be divine, therefore divinity is inhuman. We mean this even when we talk casually of 'divine beauty', meaning such exquisite beauty it is barely comprehensible; but there is a corollary to this, which is its moral detachment from human values. We know the Greek gods were without conscience, that the Old Testament God was jealous and vindictive. We even know that Jesus ran out of patience with the sick and tried to avoid them. We are frustrated by our own consciences and put limits to them all the time. [There is, in *Rome*, a] perpetual pull between the moment of authentic pity (which is rare), the trough of socialized pity (which is gesture, insincerity, public obeisance), and the violent repudiation of one's relations with others (which is a divine moment of moral autonomy); [the latter would be], of course, obscene if it were to become systematized [...] [This tension] is the substance of the theology of *Rome*.

This interview was originally published in 1993, in the second edition of the book of Barker's theory Arguments for a Theatre *(Manchester: Manchester University Press, 1989 [1993] [1997]).*

'On puppetry and *All He Fears*'

With Penny Francis

Penny Francis (PF)
Howard Barker (HB)

PF: You are a well-known playwright, always attracting critical attention and often controversy. How, briefly, did you come to theatre? Do you know what drives you to write for this medium?

HB: No other art form satisfies my particular assortment of powers. I am a poet and an artist; I require language as the primary resource of my existence. On the other hand, I have an interest in the context in which this speech is delivered. I could not be satisfied with only writing radio, for example, though I do so frequently. The visual image is critical, as a counterpoint and enhancement of the verbal content of a scene. It is true that I could make film, but it would be more difficult to accommodate a spoken poetry, as opposed to a visual poetry, in film. Theatre allows a profusion of resources; it is excessive, overabundant; it suits the chaotic nature of my imagination. I like to inundate an audience with experiences which attack all the senses, or most of them at any rate.

PF: The offer of a commission to write a play for puppets – animated figures – must have surprised you? Why did you consider it and finally accomplish it? What contact with puppetry did you have before this?

HB: I was not entirely surprised. I have written for theatre, radio, film and opera. I consider that a poet who has a voice, and has refined that voice over a number of years, can employ it across all media. On the other hand, I was aware that puppetry conventionally discards density of language. I thought of it primarily as a poem, but I wished to ignore any problems that would arise in the staging of this poem. I ignore all problems of staging a play also. The achievement frequently comes out of overcoming these problems. I had seen no puppetry.

    When I began writing for theatre I had seen virtually no theatre either.

PF: Was the idea for the play in your head before the commission? If so, had you imagined it as needing a form somehow different from conventionally played drama?

HB: Not at all. The idea of a philosophical journey nevertheless seemed eminently suitable. Perhaps if this commission had not appeared, *All He Fears* would have had no existence in any form, but been diffused in other works. The idea of a character who colludes in his own dread would have occupied a place in some drama, but not on its own. It would have been an element in a stage play, perhaps.

PF: Did you take some part in the process of staging it? Puppetry is thought to be as much about fine art, design and movement as about verbal communication. Was the process a new way of producing a text? Were you aware of more or less constraints, for example?

HB: Unfortunately not. I understand the importance of fine art elements in puppetry, but this does not seem more critical than in living stage. But as for movement, yes, I knew at once here was a clear distinction from stage practice, as well as in the extent to which the director/operator possesses absolute control of the creation of mood. Those constraints of speech – the puppet cannot articulate – did not seem a reason to *reduce* speech, however. The speech and the demonstration of movement in the body of the puppet gave precisely that detail and excess I aspire to. To speak melancholy and to express melancholy simultaneously in the body – how many actors can do that? Very few.

PF: How did you – do you – view the result? Were your original ideas and artistic intentions reinforced or distorted by the aesthetic and the puppetry of this production? Would you like to see it interpreted another way if it were produced again with puppets?

HB: There was much to applaud in the production. But the Movingstage Company was learning as I was, dealing with new things, dealing with excess. The brilliance of some of their solutions amazed me – such as the massive leg that extended into the grave – hugely disproportionate to the little figure in the dark [...] and the climbing of the endless rope, [which would be] impossible in live theatre. It was, perhaps, slower in tempo than I would have liked. But companies have their styles, and I don't criticize the dreamy, spacious feeling of some of the scenes. My dramatic instincts told me to move more swiftly, I was for hastening the narrative. But this is perhaps less crucial in puppetry, where other aesthetics prevail. To be quite truthful, I preferred the stark black and white scenes, the moonlight effects, to the carefully coloured outdoors. I look forward to further interpretations of this text, as I do with all texts. Perhaps a crueller, less humanistic manner would yield other pleasures.

PF: How differently would you expect an audience to react to it if it were played by actors? Perhaps you have seen it played thus.

HB: No, I have not seen the text played by actors, although a ballet is in prospect. It was, of course, recorded by actors – Ian McDiarmid and Harriet Walter were the principals. I sense to stage it with live actors would be to steal some of its ambiguities, and the last scene, in a heavenly place, peopled by cannibal horses and such like, with the passage of the crucified louts – [the] stage could never achieve the surreal qualities required. On film, it would be possible.

PF: Would you consider another commission to write for animated figures, or consider the inclusion of puppetry within a play for actors? Practitioners believe that an awareness of puppetry will widen the choice of expressive options for a theatre writer or director.

HB: Of course I would write again for puppets. I have a constant reservoir of half-formed notions for texts that have no particular locus. I would agree that on the whole, the freedom of the puppet stage would or should stimulate better stage writing. But I have never lacked those elements in my stage work. Again, I think the freedom of imagination – its promiscuity – should be a tool for any stage writer. It is only the fatuous domination of naturalism that has separated out these media, and I have never written naturalistically.

    In my latest stage play, for example, an anatomist carries out a post-mortem on himself. A rush of blood inundates the entire stage. Now, there is a problem for theatre! But it is also a problem for the puppet stage. I see no essential difference. What puppetry lent me in this instance was a purity of expression that came from the very non-humanity of the 'performer'. When a puppet *contemplates* for example, the element of mimicry of human contemplation lends a huge emotional injection [...] one is faintly *charmed* [...] and yet this charm, born of intense mimesis, is also *frightening* [...] this is what I mean by the ambiguity of it, in so far as I am able to express it.

PF: Has the experience of *All He Fears* changed your perceptions of communication through theatre in any way?

HB: From what I have said above, you will see that essentially the answer is no [...] and yet [...] every experience that imitates behaviour is suggestive of further possibility. I would say that *All He Fears* in production showed me a prospect of different acting styles. What they might be I can't articulate yet.

This interview was first published in Puck *(the review of the International Institute of Puppetry) in Charleville-Mezieres, France in May 1995. It was republished in the British journal* Contemporary Theatre Review 9:4 *(London: Routledge, 1999).*

'A demand for the problematic'

With Dan Hefko

Dan Hefko (DH)
Howard Barker (HB)

DH: You write in *Arguments for a Theatre*, "Plays are much too short [...] One day a play will be written for which men and women will miss a day's work. It's likely this play itself will be experienced as work". Your 24-hour play *The Ecstatic Bible* is scheduled to be performed in the year 2000. Do you envision it as the sort of play you describe above?

NB: What I was articulating in this part of *Arguments* was my sense that a society of absolute leisure can only induce mass insanity. Naturally it won't be recognized as such. But one of the symptoms will be the sort of spiritual exhaustion we can already discern among intellectuals, the majority of whom have forsaken any kind of discriminatory or discerning attitude towards – to take a single topic – art or literature. In this general miasma of entertainment, if the human spirit exists at all in odd pockets of resistance, it will identify itself in a demand for the problematic as opposed to the celebratory, the enigmatic as opposed to the accessible, the secret as opposed to the transparent. Naturally this demand entails moral and intellectual labour. Authentic works of art will be seen as hard work, as they have frequently been in the past. But in this soporific climate, hard work will be seen as a privilege. Not only this, but these works must – can only – infringe the laws of the soporific order. They will perhaps be illegal. Who knows?

DH: In 'A Conversation with Charles Lamb' you say that "the theory changes, as the plays do in temperament and form". How has your art brought about changes in your theory in the time since the second edition of *Arguments for a Theatre* appeared in 1993?

HB: I suppose the answer to this lies in a close reading of the third edition (1997). I have moved further toward the idea of art as secrecy, as operating in the zones of the unforgivable, not simply the irrational. Whilst all entertainment exists in the mechanical sphere, so do most so-called serious works of art, so-called good films and so on. They are soddenwith the conventional wisdom of their time, they exude a decayed and trivialized humanism, and in the sexual and erotic field they are almost entirely sentimental. An aspect of this is the failure to create powerful visual poetry and the continuing decay of language. What do you do to oppose all this? Well, you simply oppose it. Not everything can be a strategy. You work to your convictions and you listen to see if this response reverberates. If it does, good, but you cannot *intend* the reverberation, or you become habituated to the same marketing practices as the industrialized art you would like to annihilate.

DH: You've rewritten (is that the right word?) plays by Middleton, Shakespeare, Chekhov and Lessing, to name a few. How is *The Ecstatic Bible* different from or similar to those plays as a work of imaginative revisionism?

HB: *The Ecstatic Bible* as it stands is one testament, and it ends with the birth of the Son. Of course, I have written of this Son already, in my finest play, *The Last Supper*. Perhaps I will do that again, I don't know. But *The Ecstatic Bible* owes nothing to the Old Testament. It does, after all, contain a taut narrative which, whilst occasionally obscured by new narratives, always reasserts itself, and this is the passion of the Priest for Gollancz. I almost called this a hopeless passion, but of course it is not; on the contrary it is utterly hopeful; it is the essence of hope by virtue of its never knowing a consummation. The Old Testament is, however, an appalling record of cruelty and revenge, usually inflicted by a God whose relentless self-affirmation is no more nor less devastating than the godless climate of my play. "Europe is Death's Estate", I once wrote in *Don't Exaggerate*. It will always be so. Such a culture, so dazzling in its extremes, so absolute in beauty and horror, can't simply convert to the Garden of Eden overnight. Look at the painting of Bosch and the prose of Celine. Four hundred years separates them, but their Europe is the same. So is mine. It's not a revision of the Bible, therefore, as say *Minna* is an overturning of Lessing. One might say, in its torrent of agony and defiance, it imitates the Old Testament in its mood. Of course, it's also humorous, which the Bible never is.

DH: I've heard you say that you don't consider your art to have been influenced by any particular writer or school of thought. What contemporary playwrights/poets do you most respect?

HB: What influences any artist? Not necessarily those he might respect, for one can respect others for technical reasons whilst despising their ontology. I can more easily identify painters, film-makers, philosophers than I can writers who have exerted profound influence on me. [In visual art]: Bosch; Cranach; Altdorfer; Goya; Watteau; Gericault; Hammershoi; Spencer; Bacon; Rothko; Beauys (perhaps the list is predictable). In film: Bresson; Buñuel; Pasolini; Tarkovsky. In poetry: Apolinnaire; Rilke; Attila Jozsef; George Oppen. In theatre I have always sensed my solitude, certainly from the time I became myself, from the time I no longer desired to be a part of anything, or to serve anything.

DH: You have said, "The dramatist must be a poet". In the poem 'On Plethora' you write: "The play of plethora/ being a poem/ cannot be reduced". I'm curious what, if any, distinctions you make between poetry and plays. It seems that some of your poems, 'On Plethora' for example, are more theoretical, argumentative, didactic and/or explicative than your plays. Do you make different arguments for poems than you make for plays? In your essay 'Art of Darkness' you suggest, "When one reads a poem, the poet's identity is immediate, so intimate that the reader feels he is a collaborator in a struggle of articulation". And yet many of your own poems like 'Don't Exaggerate' and those collected in *The Tortmann Diaries* are dramatic monologues of sorts, aren't they? How much of your own identity is there in Tortmann, "a solitary and diabolical figure, an ecstatic roamer of cities and later self-imposed exile, who from his rock of misanthropy subjects himself and the world to an unflinching critique"?

HB: Increasingly I make no distinction between the plays and the poems, or indeed, the paintings I paint or the films I write (none of which will ever be produced, I think it is safe to say). In certain early poems I was simpler, more direct in vaguely socio-critical terms. So I was in the early plays, however insecure those politics were. But now I regard a poem like 'Tortmann in the Wilderness' as precisely like a recent play, say *He Stumbled*. In both cases, nothing can be deduced in terms of a morality; they share a common language, and they are intensely imagistic, in a way which is nothing to do with recognition. I avoid all recognition. I regard the visionary artist as one who does not concern himself with reproduction, only invention. The frisson of pleasure an audience might discover in finding its own experiences reproduced can never be experienced in any artistic product that emerges from my imagination. Of course these works are human, but the ecstasies come from unexpected collisions, unlikely juxtapositions, and the peculiar power of prejudices which allow passions to perpetuate themselves. Choosing to continue to live under any circumstances is, after all, a prejudice. It's perfectly true, as you suggest, that in works of this kind one is brought very near to the author, perhaps uncomfortably so, because these sentiments are hardly anonymous. But to return to an earlier distinction, you always know a Goya painting. Unlike a work by any number of social realists from the 1930s (USA or USSR) the identity is tangible. But not, it is worth remarking, in an autobiographical sense. I don't tell my own life. You might deduce things about my life, but it's not the substance of any play that I have written.

DH: The use of rhyme seems more prevalent in *The Tortmann Diaries* (1996) than in your previous collections. Is there a reason for that?

HB: Yes, but I think there is plenty of rhyme in *The Ascent of Monte Grappa*. I like rhyme, it is a distinctive quality of the poem, one of its engines, and rhyme is apparent in the plays also. Rhyme in a play establishes a certain condition for the audience, it affirms that we are out of the naturalistic obligation.

DH: Again and again in your creative work you seem to me to exemplify the quality which Keats ascribed to Shakespeare's greatness: negative capability. Keats described it variously as, the ability to be "in uncertainties, Mysteries, doubts, without any irritable reaching after fact & reason […]" and the poetic quality of "enjoy[ing] light and shade; it lives in gusto, be it foul or fair, high or low, rich or poor, mean or elevated – It has as much delight in conceiving an Iago as an Imogen. What shocks the virtuous Philosopher, delights the camelion Poet. It does no harm from its relish of the dark side of things any more than from its taste for the bright one; because they both end in speculation". How do you respond to such a comparison?

HB: I have always sensed that what I have in common with Shakespeare above all other things is a certain freedom from moral earnestness. That may seem a strange thing to say of him, because the Shakespearian tragedy until *Hamlet* is affirmative of certain moral platitudes, but always I sense in him as with all the Jacobeans, this is an act of will or political expediency, their hearts are not in it, they do not really believe the world punishes and rewards in any relation to just desserts at all. On the contrary, meaningless pain is the thing that drives Shakespeare into his highest ecstasies – as a *writer*. And this painful ecstasy cannot be seized on as a plea for civility, as an eloquence in favour of any social order; it simply *is* […] so it is with me […] and I have affirmed over and over again that we, the audience, need to know this; we need to know the limits of social and political action and to witness unrelieved pain in others as a thing of beauty. Without beauty it's sheer prurience. Here again, therefore, the issue of language is paramount. It is how we speak the pain.

DH: In *Arguments for a Theatre* you write, "[…] the play is not a debate, it is literally 'play', and like children's play it is 'world-inventing', requiring no legitimation from the exterior". Would you say that your plays put adult audiences in the position of children (or perhaps even infants), of not knowing and not understanding? Certainly the childish and infantile can also have negative connotations. You've written that, "The infantile notion of the reward, which still dominates the serious theatre, is based on critical clichés […] Infantile critics are forever in search of 'important' plays".

HB: I do not attempt to infantilize an audience. On the contrary, I pay them the respect due not only to adults but to curious adults. I honour them by taking it for granted they do not want to be told what they already know; indeed, I take it for granted they do not want to be 'told' at all. I don't posture with 'truth', which it is my 'duty' to impart. I do not assume a higher status than the audience; I only present the meditations that obsess or stimulate me. They may find things here to arouse their own curiosity. They may discover, in this world of extremes, something of a need they did not feel they possessed. Who knows? I try not to study the audience except from this point of view – that I do not consider an audience a single object which I wish to manipulate, but rather a diffuse, disunited body, and secondly, I do not let any consideration of the audience affect my ways as a writer. No serious works of art are driven by the audience, even if arguably, they once were (from the point of view of patronage […]).

DH: You've written at length about the connections between poetry and theatre. Do you think of your visual art, which appears on the covers of a number of your collections of poems and plays, as being connected to your dramatic art?

HB: I produce rapid pen and ink sketches, watercolour wash drawings, even full-scale paintings, of scenes from the plays even while they are being written. They stand for a particular moment of visualization of the text. Very rarely do these images transfer to the productions that I direct; they are stages on the way to the performance, and therefore, being first instincts, are the first to go.

DH: In your play *The Castle*, a character named Stucley says, "Everything I fear, it comes to pass. Everything I imagine is vindicated. Awful talent I possess […]" This idea plays itself out to an even greater extent in your later play for marionettes *All He Fears*. After having brought upon himself "everything he dreads", Botius says, "All I feared […]/Has come to pass […]" Is the "awful talent" which Stucley and Botius possess a common trait of characters in your plays or are they its primary recipients? Did one character grow out of the other?

HB: Stucley's boast that he is prescient is not founded upon much; rather it is an element of his growing hysteria, a sort of documentation of his paranoia, and as with many individuals driven to despair, he welcomes any scrap of evidence that not only he, but the entire world, is doomed. But Stucley is simultaneously a heroic figure, which Botius is not. Botius wills his ordeals one after another, disguising his pleasure in submitting to self-abnegation by identifying the agents of his distress as if they arrived by accident rather than invitation. Stucley sets a great engine in motion that crushes him, and he screams with a passionate delirium as it does so. Botius fears life itself and squirms to avoid it. But it's true they are to varying extents complicit with circumstances. There are some others: the model and war atrocity addict Ilona in *The Power of the Dog*, who makes passivity into a system, and the youthful Lear in *Seven Lears* begs the mountain to fall on him. Perhaps there is something in such apparent senselessness that attracts and appals me also. I have never much presented the 'progressives' and 'life-enhancers' in my work, even if I have always felt the tragic narrative is itself life-enhancing as an aesthetic, vastly more so than so-called plays of 'celebration […]'

DH: I read somewhere that you write three or four hours a day with no rewrites and that typically you publish two plays and one other project per year. Is that accurate? What becomes of the other writing?

HB: I produce two or three dramatic projects in a year, generally speaking, and this reflects two circumstances of my life. Primarily, this productivity is enabled by the fact that few of my texts are 'successes' in the conventional sense. I am therefore not much drawn from my creative work into following the typical trajectory of a 'success […]', i.e. transfers to New York, films of the play and so on. Secondly, I have not so far in my life been frustrated by a lack of material that I wish to explore. And the fact I also write poetry and paint creates an ebb and flow between the forms that stimulates me. This year I have not directed a play, so I have written a full-length stage play (*Ursula: Fear of the Estuary*) which I expect to direct next year, a radio play (*Albertina: the 20 Duologues*) commissioned from the BBC, and purely for my own pleasure, screenplays which I have no expectation whatsoever will be produced, one full-length, one short. That is not untypical. Obviously, a massive piece like *The Ecstatic Bible* absorbed nearly two years. It stands to reason that, given my status as *persona non grata* with the national theatre institutions, I now write more than can be produced. My own company, The Wrestling School, will do *Ursula* in Spring 1998. Others will be given premieres abroad, in foreign languages, here by students, or not at all.

DH: You speak with great reverence for actors, and they in turn have been some of your most articulate supporters. Actor Gary Oldman once said, "Good male acting comes from the soul and from the cock – which is what Barker's writing gives opportunities for". That sounds like it could be one of your own aphorisms. Would you add to that? What is the relationship between "the soul and […] the cock" for you as a writer? Does good female acting come from analogous places?

HB: Oldman was a dazzling stage actor. It's a pity he's lost to the theatre, and my work always throws up parts he might have dazzled audiences in; I could name half a dozen roles where a kind of self-seduction, a challenge to the self, would have matched his powers. Too bad. But what he says is really a description of what I attempt in all the major roles, male or female. That is an affirmation of the possibility that life contains just some elements of ecstasy that can be *created out* of so much base metal […] not by narcotic use […] not by reacting to another's system, be it industrialized music or pulp film […] but by will and primarily, by the seduction of another, the struggle to love, to quote the sub-title of *The Europeans*. Is that what Oldman calls 'cock'? Possibly. It's desire, anyway, it is mutuality, it is oscillation on the edge of destruction, and it occurs between men and women because the male–female union is so *difficult*, so doomed, so fatal. It also occurs on the margins, in the extremes, and on the outside, of the social compact, never inside it. And certainly – obviously – actors are driven to play to their highest qualities when they are themselves stimulated by what they are saying, and sex is said a great deal in my work, though not in any naturalistic way – rather the opposite, it's bold but it's linguistically creative. Sexual expression needs recreating all the time to hold its charge, and that can be done by successive waves of argot (the American film) or by very poetic metaphor, sexual *situation* (a good example might be the Vanya/ Helena seduction in my *(Uncle) Vanya*). And yes, I do revere actors. They can be transformed by what they say, the words reach into their unconscious and lift all manner of energy to the surface, much of it erotic. They are licensed to utter and in doing so they enable others to utter. It is a pity that film culture is generally so poor that this utterance only impoverishes its public.

DH: Harrison Ford says in a recent interview, "People require stories to help them define their relationships to other people in the world [...] I am part of that storytelling department. I find myself being tedious in repeating it, but there are very few places in our culture where we have an opportunity to confirm our common humanity more than when we go into a dark room and sit alone with a bunch of strangers and all feel the same thing. I think that makes us feel closer and more responsible to others". Anyone familiar with your writing would expect that those sorts of comments might make you nauseated. Can you explain why that is?

HB: Bad democracies perpetually stress harmony as the first fruit of their ideology. What they are really talking about is unanimity. The more sham the democracy becomes, the more it talks of 'celebration' and 'the people', the more it borrows defunct slogans from the old Communist system. Ford's political aesthetic here denies the authentic truth of the dark room, be it stage or screen, which is that darkness is a license to transgress, permission to think what illumination – exposing you to the gaze of others – submerges in a false collectivity. By employing the word 'storytelling' he hopes to endow the industry with a false innocence, as if we were children at the knee of a kind old man. But he also accidentally reveals the politics of the narrative, which, when it remains at the stage of storytelling (middle, beginning and end) obviously deals in the market of morals, cheap ethics based on justice and reward. That is what the industry requires of its 'artists'. The Theatre of Catastrophe (which theoretically would apply to a filmed Theatre of Catastrophe also) doesn't seek to gratify the collective moral appetite at all. On the contrary, it requires such a moral baggage to be left at the door. The onus is shifted onto the audience as individuals to make an ethical choice from what it sees. It divides the audience.

DH: A specimen exam question for an Honours Theatre Studies course at the University of Glasgow directly quotes you: "'Tragedy is not really concerned with enlightening social behaviour; it is primarily concerned with pain; in attending it we leave our morals at the door'. To what extent would you wish to qualify such views in the light of your reading of Greek tragedy?" With your aversion to 'academic work' in mind, I'm curious how you would respond to that question.

HB: Greek tragedy isn't a monolith. It develops, presumably according to the stresses and strains in Athenian society, and we don't have to take the word of a single critic (Aristotle) as to its efficacy, the intentions of its makers, or the results of watching it. And we can never escape the fundamental paradox of all literary theory – does the author ever know his intentions, and worse, can he relate his intentions to the semi-anarchic nature of creative impulses? This applies to me as it has applied to the Greeks, Shakespeare or Brecht. So let us say that according to tradition, Greek tragedy is – in the purest form – political, since it purges the audience of its unsocial instincts and reaffirms the collective wisdom of the polis. Who knows? The fact is that in the pre-Socratic Greeks justice has rather little to do with anything. The individual is simply *crushed* by circumstances to which he has no recourse, for which he has no actual responsibility. What does the audience see here but the savage nature of existence, pain for its own sake? It cannot compel you to *live your life differently* (the absolute purpose of the Brechtian theatre), nor does it comfort you in the knowledge of the *sadness of things* (Chekhov […]). Rather, this witnessing is a desperate need, and in this moment of witnessing, a triumph of the human soul emerges – the conversion of this horror into *beauty*, the spectacle of your own potential agony in a world of absolute indifference finds a compensation in the poetry of pain. That is what I believe early Greek tragedy achieves. I believe it is also at the heart of Shakespearian grief. Pain is, ironically, a sort of commodity. People are always trying to steal it from others who endure it. They put it to use. One man's suffering is the pretext to inflict suffering on another. A tragic theatre doesn't really permit that incorporation – perhaps that's why Brecht hated Greek tragedy. The Greeks didn't say the misery of x was a reason to attack the house of y.

DH: In an interview published recently in *Paris Review*, American theatre critic John Simon says, "There's theatre that has something necessary to say – it may not even be good, but it has an insight it must express – and there's theatre which may be very slick and accomplished but has nothing to say". In an imagined dialogue between a critic and a dramatist you write that, "Art is strictly useless, which is its rebellion". Elsewhere you write, "Slowly, the audience will discover the new theatre to be a necessity for its moral and emotional survival". Is the quality of its necessity located in its uselessness, in the fact that the play "has something necessary to say", but that something isn't, by necessity, insightful or enlightening? Or does the play contain nothing which is "necessary to say"?

HB: My aesthetics try to take account of the social panic of the day, which is why I have affirmed the strictly useless nature of art in a social moment of extreme utilitarianism ('who does your play help [...]?'). It is – as the quotation says – pure rebellion to state the uselessness of some activity in the contemporary climate. But I affirm it. 'Why are we in the theatre tonight?' is a question that wouldn't be swiftly answered if a text of mine was playing. I can answer the question of why I came to write it, but the audience would find it hard to say what drew them there because they know – given my reputation – that it can't solve anything for them; it is not going to be a lesson in good behaviour, social solidarity, harmony and so on; it won't offer a demonstration of a good life. What's more it doesn't entertain, it fails to provide the usual elements of the contract which lie hidden in most performance (pleasure/enlightenment [...] the ticket price). But it's precisely the absence of the enlightenment project that will ensure the work's survival, because the populist/democratic project of absolute leisure can only result in nausea among those able to resist its blandishments. They will repudiate education, they will vomit at the prospect of any more information, and most extraordinary of all, they will deny themselves *access* (the word of our time) knowing that it is precisely access to nothing. They will ache for the secret. And my texts are secrets. They are secrets to me.

This critic presumably has his own idea of what is 'necessary' and 'unnecessary'. What I am trying to articulate in those apparent contradictions is that great art has no truck with the market, nor does it serve as a clinic for social improvement. It cannot be reduced to a function, therefore, and, strictly speaking, is useless. It is precisely this uselessness that renders it powerful and ensures it can't be subverted. At some moment in the triumph of leisure and information, this uselessness will become highly valued by those for whom 'use' has revealed itself as another aspect of the control system. For them, its innocence will be a powerful reassurance. They will sense the work has no designs on them, in the way that apparently benign 'liberation' or 'critical' texts always do (Dario Fo, for example). The openness of the text, not insisting upon its 'necessity' at all, but being driven solely by the demands of the imagination, will create the possibility for individuals to redesign a morality out of it, to take it as a refuge from the relentless music of the happiness system. Obviously, these texts are not immune to the manipulation of the director. They can be harnessed. Anything can.

DH: In the title poem of your collection *The Ascent of Monte Grappa*, you write, "Mountain/My own silence might darken even yours// I shall be granite to all theorists/ And their regiments". Is this Howard Barker speaking? Going back to your poem 'On Plethora', you write that the "play of plethora [...] cannot be abbreviated/acknowledged/or/approved". Is this to say also that it is impervious to criticism? What, if any, should be the criteria of the critic?

HB: I think I am not very silent. I have felt compelled to speak theoretically by the sheer weight of hostile reviewing, much of it *ad hominem*, hysterical and profoundly destructive. I have tried to set out some of the positions from which this work must be viewed, and these are not the same positions from which most drama is viewed ('Shouldn't I feel sympathy for the character?'; 'Do I recognize this as typical?'; 'Why is the language so strange?'). The play of Plethora, of which *Rome* and *The Ecstatic Bible* are good examples (not all of my texts fit this category), certainly requires the audience (and the critic) to arrive with a different attitude, just as one wouldn't apply the same criteria to the painting of a neo-classicist and an abstract expressionist, for example. But there is so much dogma in theatre criticism, it seems eccentric to even suggest this. The critics police the culture, obviously. The fact that the current generation of police are liberal, humanistic, so-called progressive and so on doesn't mean they are not forever the police, permanently fencing out the work that may infect the placid garden of wit and civility.

DH: Reviewing The Wrestling School's 1996 production of your version of *Uncle Vanya* in the London *Times*, Benedict Nightingale wrote, "Howard Barker is not a chap to stand cap in hand before anything, least of all someone else's masterpiece". It seems he would have had to qualify that statement had he read 'Notes on the Necessity for a Version of Chekhov's *Uncle Vanya*', in which you write, "When we approach a great writer, we come naked, with a certain innocence and fear. We fear what subtle damage might be done to a carefully constructed life. In Chekhov, this painful exposure is not satisfied by what might be experienced as an act of love. Rather he sends us away more than ever bound in our own clothes". Is there any truth in Nightingale's conclusion that you don't respect the craftsmanship of Chekhov's *Uncle Vanya*?

HB: No, I am not disputing the quality of Chekhov's text, and it was typical of the critical class to make that wholly wrong assessment of my intentions. What are you to do when confronted with that quality of reviewing? I wasn't examining Chekhov but the function of Chekhov, the *use* of Chekhov, how Chekhov's status is employed for certain disguised socio-political ends. This was a genuine interrogation of the way theatre is used socially, a proper project for a modern writer to undertake. I took this inquiry to the point of asking how, when a writer disingenuously claims he is only 'showing the world as it is' (the naturalistic fallacy), he drills the audience into sharing his ideology. Chekhov removes hope from the theatrical landscape; in my view, he makes us collaborate in our own defeat at the hands of circumstance. This does not mean he is not a great writer. That wasn't my contention. I only wished to demonstrate that a different narrative could restore energy to the audience. Sterility and impotence can become seductive and glamorous in Chekhov. Perhaps at certain social moments a culture longs to be sterile and impotent. Is that why so much Chekhov has been played recently? These were the matters I addressed.

This interview was first published in the United States, in the journal Sycamore Review *10:2 (Purdue University, 1998).*

(Uncle) Vanya. William Armstrong (Vanya). The Wrestling School, 1996. Photo credit Stephen Vaughan

'It has always been possible to improve on God'

With Charles Lamb

Charles Lamb (CL)
Howard Barker (HB)

CL: One of the most frequently encountered adjectives applied to your early work – apart from 'political' – was 'angry'. Critics and audiences experienced a sense of indignation; some described it as hatred. This was interpreted as outrage at injustice – particularly as regards the behaviour of political figures. I'm thinking not simply about your very early satirical work, but plays like *No End of Blame*, where you have Bela, the politically committed cartoonist, opposed to Grigor, who believes in a more traditional notion of high art. Bela says, "When the cartoon lies it shows at once. When the painting lies it can deceive for centuries. The cartoon is celebrated in a million homes. The painting is worshipped in a gallery. The cartoon changes the world. The painting changes the artist. I long to change the world. I hate the world [...]" Would you say that anger has disappeared now – like Skinner says in *The Castle*, she waits and the anger goes?

HB: I'm not sure the plays are characterized by anger. There is anger in them, but I believe they are more significantly marked by a rudimentary tragic consciousness, which must eliminate anger as an ethical redundancy. Although these plays appear to possess a socialist outlook, they never went down well with the socialist critics here. They never earned me friends on the left, or the right for that matter. I suspect these critics detected a missing element in them, something which committed art must have, if it is not to become simply testament, and that is optimism, because it is not possible to make effective propaganda – which is what the political play is – without optimism. If you are recommending to an audience a certain course, a certain attitude, there has to be a clear implication that it will possess utilitarian value, i.e. it will increase their happiness. No play of mine has ever aimed for, or achieved, that. If my life at that time made me political, it didn't make me want to enlighten anyone. The quotation you gave from Bela never did speak for me. Perhaps people have assumed it did.

CL: The character was based on the cartoonist, Vicky?

HB: No, it was a greater cartoonist in my estimation, Illingworth, whose work was characterized by a Goya-esque darkness, it was less functional than Vicky. But to revert to your question, my work was certainly fuelled by class anger, but not dominated by it. I could not impose a political doctrine on it, for all that I felt myself to be political.

CL: Do you still feel angry about things?

HB: Not in my artistic life. Which is not to say I do not have opinions. I have many opinions, but I no longer think them worth anything in the wider world – certainly not in my own theatre. I trust my imagination, I don't value my opinions.

CL: So you feel that the anger would be a useless emotion?

HB: Not useless, but I never derogate instincts. It is the same with violence.

CL: You said to me a few years back, "I'm afraid I'm going to have to write increasingly about sex [...]" Well, you've done that. I was interested in the way that you put it – the note of regret – as if writing about sex were problematic. However, we seem to live in an age which is saturated with sex; it's ubiquitous and normal. On the other hand, the regulation of sexual activity still provokes anxiety and hysteria. Why did you feel that your work had to take that particular direction?

HB: It was always in my work, and slowly it acquired its own profound metaphorical value; it became a way of life and not a marginal expression of needs, a theatricality as such. Because of its complexity, and its threat, it is not simple to address it without some apprehension. I think that is what I might have meant by my suggestion that it caused me anxiety. But, after all, I value anxiety in theatre above all else, so it was inevitable I would expose myself, as well as the public, to it for my work. For me, the sexual is the ungovernable. In tragedy I esteem it for that. In society, it is perhaps very governable; it can become a social soporific, a commodity. Certainly the social obsession with sex has not enhanced its mutinous potential. But the potential is there.

CL: Do you think, perhaps, that the concept of sexuality is not a very useful one – because in your plays, sex is intermeshed with desire?

HB: Yes, it is more useful to talk of desire than sex as far as my theatre is concerned. Sex is essentially the biological, crucial but unreflective. All the sexual transactions in my plays are self-conscious, and therefore characterized by desire, a desire which is accumulative, a willed extremity which separates the participants from the cultural milieu in which they live. In all my work I reassert the catastrophic potential of the sexual encounter.

CL: I was thinking – in this connection – of Dreux-Breze, in *Rome* [...]

HB: Oh yes, the last scene [...]

CL: Where he feels that love has been tainted by the Enlightenment project [...]

HB: Yes, he does say that and whereas he appears to hold these bourgeois women in contempt, he enjoys his possession of something which, however unenlightened (perhaps especially because it is unenlightened), makes him irresistible to them [...] There's a necromancy about him in the end. He's walled up in a tower, ignored by the authorities, presumably for his mild eccentricity, but a source of fascination to the 'knowing' new class. He is in possession of the secret, of course, which revolution reviles.

CL: But what about the end of the scene where, after dismissing them, he collapses quite spectacularly?

HB: He cries out for love, which he senses the new system has abolished, as each generation senses the loss of love in each new political order.

CL: He does say to the women that their touches are bargains.

HB: Yes, it is the pursuit, isn't it? There is a pursuit in these plays of something immaculate, which is not beyond reach – it is just that it oscillates at such a high frequency that it doesn't endure. I suppose that the endurance of sexual desires is one of the most fascinating aspects of them; is it, for example, possible to create a permanent sexual desire between individuals?

CL: It would be socially useful, I dare say.

HB: In ensuring the triumph of the domestic arrangement, you mean? But it militates against that. However, that said, desire degenerates unless it is perpetually invented. Marriage is an institution which announces itself in the erotic and then proceeds to suffocate the erotic, to substitute property and children for that eroticism. Desire, on the contrary, lives only by the secret – unlike marriage it abhors the public place (except to desecrate it [...]). It values nothing above the sexual encounter with the loved one, but it is simultaneously permeated with a despair – that the encounter cannot be repeated [...] These are the secrets that I make my subjects now.

CL: So, in a sense, you are enlightening? You are pursuing an enlightenment project?

HB: No, because they are never explained, they intensify their own mystery. There is no therapy in my theatre, no exposure. The more closely one looks into the ecstasy of the sexual moment in desire, the more threatening it becomes.

CL: I wanted to ask you about that word 'ecstasy', because you make considerable use of it in your plays. People not only talk about it, but they devote their lives to the pursuit of it – to the detriment of everything else. But there is a range of different ideas of ecstasy: in *Crimes in Hot Countries* for instance, there's Erica, who rejects happiness and commits to her lover with an heroic crime; then there's Porcelain, whose idea of ecstasy is taking tea with his mother.

HB: Every individual would want to define it for himself. I was thinking of it in the sense offered by Erica, as a contradiction to happiness, long ago seized by utilitarianism for its anaemic collectivist programme of contentment. I'd go on to say that ecstasy is also beyond pleasure – the obsession of contemporary society, which, when it isn't talking about pleasure, is usually talking about medicine, [which is] only another aspect of the perceived pleasure in living forever. Those who pursue the difficult category of ecstasy – with all its risks – are effectively denying society.

CL: It's more individual.

HB: Yes, and this mutually created individualism is antagonistic to the collective.

CL: And it has a shattering effect. The notion of pursuing ecstasy seems to contain, of necessity, the idea of things being destroyed.

HB: Yes, it is fatal. But that is also its intimate bond with the tragic, which invites death to participate in its transactions.

CL: This vertiginous dual relation dedicated to the pursuit of ecstasy – to what extent would you say that its structure is essentially narcissistic? I was thinking of Placida's analysis of marriage when she says that the matrimonial condition is sustained only by vanity – the mirroring of self in self – "and that forlorn hope that in another's flesh might be discovered that refuge from solitude which in reality pertains only to God".

HB: I think it's not narcissistic at all, but an attempt to break out of the solitude of the self – not into marriage, which institutionalizes and destroys the erotic, and creates a different solitude of a particularly toxic kind, but through the dislocation of desire. Placida's judgement is, of course, conditional on her not yet having encountered the erotic herself.

CL: As auteur, are you aware of scripting non-verbal text more than you used to? I have an impression that your more recent work contains more stage directions and more prompts for physically expressive performance. (For example, the page of stage directions at the beginning of *He Stumbled* and the detailed stage directions for *Found in the Ground*).

HB: It's possible. An earlier work like *Victory* has barely any stage direction; I wanted to give ground to the director, thinking the dialogue my principal concern, and the stage picture his. I admit I have, since directing, taken the disposition of actors in the space more to myself. In my own productions the staging has acquired huge importance from the entire anti-realist inclination of them. I permit very little deviation from a structured arrangement.

CL: When you talk about an anti-realist inclination, that suggests the evolution of a particular production style with formal conventions. Do you feel that you have arrived at where you want to be with this, or is it a continuous process of development and experimentation?

HB: There is a very strong aesthetic system at work in my own productions. I don't demand that these values be applied in other circumstances, they are the outcome of my own relation with my texts. But, of course, they haven't appeared arbitrarily, but through long practice, a sense of what is possible given that neither entertainment nor commercial success, nor political effect, is part of my programme. In eradicating these aspects of common theatre practice, I feel liberated to think of methods peculiar to the needs of the work; strictly imaginative resources come into play that defy the expectations of realist theatre. But the style here – and what is style but the moral authority of an aesthetic – must change to accommodate more ambitious texts.

CL: In your work with The Wrestling School, have you found economic restrictions a problem?

HB: Certainly, but it isn't a simple equation of resources/achievement. The Wrestling School is a very poor theatre, but you would not guess that from watching the productions, for two reasons: the first is the powerful acting talent we have attracted and retained (and it is virtually an ensemble), and the second is a strong sense of design throughout, at every level, from costume to sound, all governed by a single imagination – one couldn't call it collaboration […] But we are driven into smaller theatres by management economies; our audience remains stable and, therefore, we rarely gain access to those big stages where the scale of these plays can breathe, as we did for example with *Ursula* in Birmingham. The illusions, the choreography of scene change, all go to nothing in studios.

CL: You have said that you're writing a non-dramatic work on the subject of theatre and death. Could you say a little about what this entails?

HB: It may seem obvious to some, but as someone dedicated to the writing of modern tragedy I am persuaded that tragedy is essentially – even simply – about death, [and] the means by which a character arrives at death, admits it to himself. By this I also imply that all disciplines in tragedy – such as social value, ascribed to it by Aristotle – are irrelevant to its purpose, and I do not say function; I think it has no function. I have always sensed [that] the supremely spiritual quality in tragedy marked it out from all dramatic forms, and this arises from its abolition of all values in favour of this profoundly healthy engagement with death.

CL: When people talk about death they tend to think in terms of a finality, a nothingness. But in *Rome*, there's Pius, who continues in an ambiguous state of suspended life.

HB: It is perfectly permissible to think of death as nothingness, and that is as valueless as thinking of it as something-ness. The compelling attraction of death lies in its domination of life; it is not only the 'Other' – it has a secret domination of most, if not all, lived action. Of course the political play can't and dare not admit this. We concede to death – I think even when death is said to be 'instantaneous', we have to admit it. That's evident in my play *Gertrude*, where Claudius is helped willingly into death by Gertrude's terrible narrative, a vastly more moving exegesis than Hamlet's own gesture in drinking publicly what he knows is poison. (Hamlet in my play, of course […]).

CL: And you still see death as a finality because Pius talks about death as endless – a series of antechambers.

HB: How can we know if it is a finality? The fact is we know nothing whatsoever about it, except surely, the single fact that it can't be yet more life.

CL: Pius' position interested me because – whereas Heidegger sees the subject as defined by its being towards death, conceived as a nothingness – Levinas sees the subject as confronted by a being that cannot be refused. That the ultimate horror is that it goes on and on.

HB: Yes, there may be no finality. And worse, what is the quality of that non-finality?

CL: He uses the expression *'es gibt'* – meaning 'it gives' – emphasizing the 'it' quality of utter impersonality which is in many ways more appalling than, say, a cruel God.

HB: I talk about the gesture of suicide and what a gamble it is. The suicide wants to leave the world but he doesn't know what he's going into. It might be even noisier, or cruder; there might be as many different versions of death as there were of life. And that's why I think the River Styx remains a powerful image. We keep talking about the other side; we have to talk about the other side because we don't have another metaphor for it. Those on the other side are those who might want to impart something to you but can't; it's very beautifully described in Homer, where Odysseus seeks his mother on the other side and she has something to tell him. He goes to grasp her and of course he can't – she's not there. That infinite negotiation with the nothingness seems to me to fill life, to inform it profoundly.

CL: One of the things that struck me about *He Stumbled* was that Doja appeared to be a central consciousness and that the audience perceive the world of the play through him. This is particularly evident in the reversal that occurs at the end where he realizes that they've duped him.

HB: It's essentially a thriller, the last case of a brilliant specialist. But he becomes the case himself. His status – based on evidence, proof, logic and so on – is eroded by the desperate power of the erotic; a relation he also thinks himself expert in, but which is supremely exercised by the 'deceased' king and his wife. The protagonist only redeems himself – and his own claim on eros, it must be said – by the supreme gesture of dissecting himself beneath the gaze of his mistress, and, as in *Gertrude*, she applauds him.

CL: Presumably he cuts very skilfully around everything [...]

HB: He excises his own heart, which may be possible for all I know.

CL: I assumed he would leave cutting the vital vein or artery until the very end.

HB: Who knows? It is perfectly possible to stage it without so much detail.

CL: It seems to me that his professional armour for protecting himself from the horror – the ritual, the instruments, the Latin – and his natural revulsion of corruption, all of this serves to support his ego. Finally, after all his catastrophes, he falls back on and asserts himself through an ideal of his work.

HB: The work ethic as a final dignity? That is a possible interpretation; certainly it is a flourish of recovered pride. But, as I suggested, the challenge is again to sexual status. He recovers this by the sheer scale of the gesture. She has not ceased to love him, even if he was, in the last analysis, an instrument of her own sexual passion for another.

CL: She states that.

HB: Yes, and her way is to permit him to die – almost, but not quite, to accompany him.

CL: That gesture – of allowing someone to die – figures in *Rome*. Smith, who carries sway with the Devots, allows her mother to commit suicide by defying them. She says, "Everybody understands that in the severest test of love […] to love is to allow".

HB: Which, again, emphasizes the superior importance of death over sheer survival. How you die – how you make your entrance into death – is so important in tragedy, I think – not the idea that life is everlasting, and should be everlasting, and that I will save you and I must save you. Those gestures are weaker.

CL: In *Rome*, one of the main themes – and indeed the subtitle – is *On Being Divine*. Benz, obviously, is the character who is supposed to be God.

HB: But he is the least divine of them, if we think of divine as an expression of perfection. *On Being Divine* means to overcome the meanness of man. Again, so much social propaganda asserts the common ordinariness of human beings, the solidarity of the frail, as if we were destined to love one another. Park's assumption of divinity is in his overcoming of common humanity – in the scene about the war hospital, for example. His divinity is repudiation.

CL: Well, he encounters God, doesn't he? God is angry with him because he's […]

HB: Proud.

CL: Because he's proud, yes […] and what these characters seem to *require* to be divine is people to worship them. Smith worships Park. I think there is a point where she is kissing his feet and he says, "I should not let you do that […]", but he doesn't stop her. This relationship between the worshippers and the worshipped seemed quite an important aspect of the process we're discussing.

HB: Yes, but it has always been possible to improve on God; the more he reveals, the more this becomes obvious. Park's assumption makes him vastly more moral than Benz, whose tempers are those of an Old Testament Yahweh.

CL: Benz says to Park, "I am not moral [...] I am devoid of all morality [...] I am will. Will only".

HB: Yes. Well that's what makes him a god.

CL: As Heraclitus says, "For the gods all things are just; for men, some things are just, some unjust [...]"

HB: Yes, and that returns us to tragedy. I once wrote in 'Fortynine asides' that tragedy makes justice its purpose, but I now think it is categorically the opposite; it has no truck with justice; such things as equity seem beneath its gaze; there are no unjust acts in tragedy – to put it another way, you would be wasting your time protesting the immorality of actions in a tragedy – the characters are only what they are, or indeed, precisely what they are. [They are] immune from ethical protest. The play is on another ground.

CL: It seems to me, however, there's no escape from the ethical which is there in the relationships between the human beings.

HB: The ethical is there to be disposed of.

CL: Yes, I think the characters often overrule it or violate its demands. They are acutely conscious of it, however. Doja, for instance, at the beginning of *He Stumbled*, when he finds he has to disappoint the fourth woman sexually, he immediately complains about remaining susceptible to a sense of 'obligation'. He says, "My infamy, whilst making me an object of desire, must not create in me some nagging and reciprocal responsibility to those who suffer that desire surely [...]" Now surely by saying all this, he's trying to divest himself of the unspoken ethical requirement?

HB: Yes, Doja has to struggle to disembarrass himself of his (or society's) ethical education. If that tension did not exist there could be no tragedy, only a torrent of atrocities.

CL: With the character of Park in *Rome*, there is a stage where the torturer says to him that he has to think of his torture as the finishing of one life and the starting of another.

HB: Yes, the torturer is conceived as rather social.

CL: You mean the happy family man with the child and the lunch box, etc.? Isn't that again an example of somebody, like Doja, fortifying himself with professionalism against the chaos and madness – abjection, perhaps – of what he actually has to engage with?

HB: That would be a humanist reading of it, as if in some part of his consciousness the torturer was appalled at what he did. But I see no sign of that in very cruel people. What he succeeds in doing is normalizing chaos.

CL: Yes. He does say, however, that he's been upset on occasions when he admits his victims have "broken" him.

HB: Yes, but that is his professionalism outraged, isn't it?

CL: And he also says he was disconcerted by Park's running commentary on his own decline.

HB: Indeed, the amoral can always be thrown off course, I dare say.

CL: And when he is indignant about the status accorded to thieves being denied to his profession, doesn't this suggest a vestigial ethical sense in him which has been outraged? Or is he merely cynically appealing to a morality in his auditors which he himself does not possess?

HB: I resist the idea that these statements are ethical, if only because, within the society we inhabit – [which is] that of the play also [...] – the ethical can so often be discerned as borrowed, hired and significantly *performed*, part of the individual's claim on the attention of others.

CL: To return to Park, he does actually seem to experience a rebirth, which is emphasized with the suckling.

HB: I'm not sure. He's infantilized by torture (by Benz, by God, through the torturer, to be precise) and makes a recovery of some kind.

CL: He goes back to a kind of abjection, doesn't he? His world – his ego – is destroyed in that process. The decision as to him going on the pillar, is that more Smith's? Beatrice says that he's going on a pillar but then she says, "[H]e is wanted. So it hardly matters what he wants".

HB: Yes, all such celebrity eventually loses control of its own identity, this is a very material example of that. He is his own relic. Relics have uses, they are fetishized.

CL: She 'interprets' him, doesn't she?

HB: Yes, she interprets him to the Devots, so she's critical in all this. He is merely symbolic, though he sings a song at one point – at a vital moment.

CL: Yes, the song at the end, but that is where he has experienced this change – a bit like Old Gocher at the end of *Fair Slaughter*, he discovers a humanity.

HB: What do we mean by humanity here? It's a longing for love […] He knows he is human, I suppose, and perhaps he had doubted that.

CL: He says Rome is "wanting". And presumably he consents in his death at the end, where Benz comes and wheels him out into the sea. Smith orders thatshe tells the Devots to abandon him to the incoming tide.

HB: And she is left by herself. A totem of true significance and not a negativity. This solitude – in her case a blind solitude (I think she's still rather immaculately dressed) – doesn't seem to me to be loss but a triumph, the ability to exist alone. That these people suffer to the extent they do gives an audience a sense of human potential beyond the norm. And I do think that's why tragedy is a necessary art form. It doesn't make you feel [that] life is good – or anything like that, or we can do it better, or wouldn't it be good if collectively we sorted something out […] It is purely the fact that its extremity, however painful, lends the audience power.

CL: Individually.

HB: I think of the audience as individual.

CL: A point I've had made to me quite frequently, mainly by admirers of your work, concerns the sheer quantity of incident that you incorporate in your plays. I've heard people say that – with a show like *Gertrude* – they would have preferred to watch the first half on one night – presumably gone away and thought about it – then returned to see the second half the following night. They find the work immensely stimulating but can only digest so much at a time.

HB: I aim to be profuse. It is profusive. It is excessive, and the excess is part of the experience. I don't apologize for that at all. The fact that people find it an overload could be merely a reflection of their ability to concentrate at this given moment in culture. I suspect they can't take *Hamlet* either, frankly. So it's probably that I haven't geared myself to the diminishing concentration levels – but that would be a purely technical fact. What I'm most interested in is loading the emotions. I've no belief at all that most people can follow all of it or even hear all of it, and that's why I think the directorial aspects are pretty critical in being able to provide a sort of magnetism between the performer and the audience which overcomes the alienation created by loss, because the audience is forever getting lost, I know it is. It listens to a long speech and I know it gets lost. But somehow there has to be an adhesion.

CL: It happens in Shakespeare all the time. You listen to a speech; something is said that causes you to reflect [...]

HB: Yes, and consequently you miss the next five lines. Is that necessarily a bad thing? The principle that shapes productions around the audience's mastery of the stage is a wrong one and limited to *meanings*, which interest me less than the compulsion of the experience. The compulsion must come from different angles.

CL: And this is principally the task of directors, performers and designers?

HB: No, in the first instance it is the responsibility of the dramatist – the quality of the ideas, or if not ideas, the imaginative world described – *that* dictates the outcome. The director has to present physical form for this, not to clean it up to make it 'accessible', or to civilize it, but to increase its anxiety by stimulating the ear and eye of the public, to maintain the tension that exists in the text. As I said earlier, it is a profusion of body and image that overwhelms tolerance, eliminating any pretence that we are being 'entertained'.

CL: You have for some years been interpreting your own work as director. Economic restrictions aside, should we regard these productions as definitive? Or are you happy with the potential of your work to be interpreted by others in radically different ways?

HB: It is never possible to talk of the definitive in play production; the idea of the definitive must be provisional. All I have sought to do, in developing a clear aesthetic for these texts, is to satisfy myself that, on this occasion at least, I the author got the kind of presentation I am most nearly satisfied by. I have seen these plays performed in wildly different ways, sometimes [altered] beyond recognition [from my own vision of them]. That's all right, because the text is public property in the last analysis. I have even seen some of these texts played better than I myself did them, but interestingly, on these occasions the directors shared my analysis of the theatre – they were not reduced, simplified to single messages or ironized.

This interview was conducted on 24 August 2003 and published in Charles Lamb's book The Theatre of Howard Barker *(London: Routledge, 2005).*

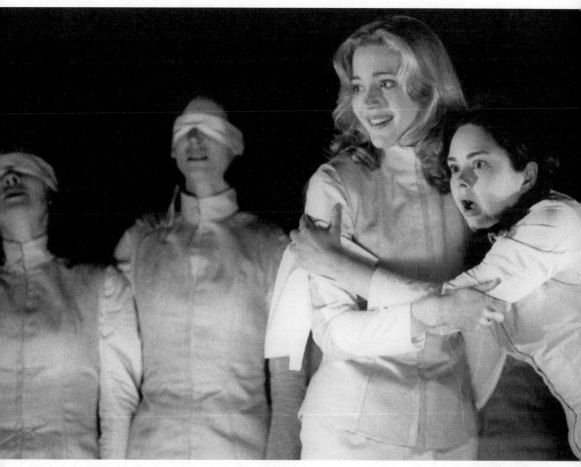

Ursula. Claire Price (Ursula) & Jules Melvin (Leonara). The Wrestling School, 1998. Photo credit Stephen Vaughan.

'Death as a theatrical experience'

With Aleks Sierz

Aleks Sierz (AS)
Howard Barker (HB)

AS: Would you say a few words about the origins of your latest play, *Dead Hands*?

HB: It's always difficult for me to talk about this because they're always embedded in one's personal past. I've always been interested in death – I've just got a new book out about death as a theatrical experience. It's always seemed to me to contain a contradiction at the heart of it, which is its effect on the living, which is, of course, to destabilize them, as all bereavement does. But it also engenders a mild hysteria, which is to do with the spectacle of the cadaver, its lifelessness, its stillness; that generates an artificial, but hectic, energy in those who view it. I know we think of funerals as very sedate occasions, but actually they are, internally at least, riotous, and this is all contained within the formality of the funeral.

As far as the sexual goes – which is, of course, the key instinct of life – that seems to me to be something that is generated by death. This play is, to some extent at least, about that sudden eruption of sexual energy created by the death of a father and the spectacle of that death. That's one aspect of it.

The second aspect, which is equally important, is the way in which the protagonist of this play, who is called F – symbolically, I suppose – finds himself brought nearer in his instincts to the life of his own father, who exists in front of him as a body. He suffers that rather appalling sense that we all get at times in our lives that we are not so very different from our parents, even though we may not have had much time for them.

AS: The play is about a dead man, and shows what happens to his two sons, and to his mistress, while he is lying there onstage in his coffin. It feels as if all three characters have become liberated by the old man's death, and that they allow their sexual fantasies to take flight. Is that right?

HB: No, I don't think so. I think what happens is that what appears to be a liberation develops into another form of bondage. One could extend that to politics if one wanted to, but, in this instance, what seem to be acts of free will suddenly appear to be terribly conditioned. That, for me, is the alarming – I wouldn't call it tragic – possibly despairing aspect of the piece.

AS: In common with your other plays, you do create this other world. It's not a recognizably naturalistic place, but, obviously, the emotions, the desires, the dark thoughts are recognizably human. How do you relate this invented space to the everyday world?

HB: Theoretically, I don't think the theatre concerns itself with what you call the "everyday world". Whilst much theatre has been about reducing the barrier between the audience and the stage, I've always wanted to enhance it. For me, every technique on the stage, including my technique as a writer personally, negates common experience, in the normal sense of social realism, which I find a sordid habit, frankly.

On the other hand, whilst all these situations are deeply speculative, they're not fantastical; it's very important to make that distinction. They're not escapist – as theatre might have thought of itself being at various times. In fact, it's an intensification of experience that you're seeing on the stage, even though I expect no one in the audience to say 'I recognize that', because for me that statement is futile and of no value to me as a writer at all. So, these are real, instinctive feelings, but the context is strange, and that's the distortion I always aim for, both as a writer and as a director.

AS: Clearly your exploration here of the erotic means that you are pushing out the boundaries of theatre. Could you talk a bit about how you do that with this particular piece?

HB: Firstly, one has to talk about language: after writing for 30 years now, I've refined a form of discourse for the stage which is very much my own, but is also quite natural to me, so it doesn't require a great deal of investment of struggle to produce that kind of language. It is now my discourse, as every writer who is experienced has his own discourse. The characteristics are that it is non-naturalistic, it's also poetic, it permits metaphor, and what's more – and this makes it interesting for actors, who like that kind of work – it's almost got its own rhythm. So, there's a musicality in the language. That's the first thing, I think, that separates it from normal theatre.

The other thing is that, when I direct, there's a very clear use of specific sound. The whole design concept is very particular. So, as you suggest, it removes it from the real world, but, at the same time, it's thoroughly of the world. It's speculative, it's not empirical.

AS: Do you see it also as moral speculation?

HB: Let me say at once, I'm not a moralist. This is what separates me from nearly every other writer operating in the English theatre. I'm not interested in the theatre as a moral space. On the one hand, by giving rein to the instinctive and the imaginative, one can't avoid infringing various moral rules, the governing moral principles of society; and the governing principles of theatre, it's got to be said, which is a very moral place at the moment, and has been for some while. So, you take a chance, if you write this kind of work, of running into an awful lot of critical flak for doing so. If there's a moral debate there [in the play], it's one that's not set up by me. It's more of a consequence of allowing a character to follow a thought to its conclusion.

AS: You mention critics. Do you think that they've misunderstood your work?

HB: No, I think they've probably understood it too well. I've been **doing this for** 30 years, and I've run into flak from the beginning. I've always been disliked by the establishment critics, because the plays are not moral. They recognized that very early on. One has to talk about the whole spectrum of the English theatre to sort this out, it's very interesting. My case is the most interesting phenomenon. Leaving aside my feelings, my career prospects and all the rest of it, the actual, pretty well wholesale, rejection of my work by the critical establishment is a meaningful and rather fascinating phenomenon.

You've got to put it in the whole context of what England, as a place, is. Primarily, it's a non-speculative culture. It's an empiricist, moralist, utilitarian culture in which everything has a use value. Michael Billington is that kind of critic *par excellence*, who always asks, 'what is the value of this text socially?' In other words, 'does it have a function?' Which seems to me to wipe out the whole use of tragedy as a genre, because tragedy has no function, so [Billington's position] eliminates that.

Then there's the National Theatre and what that stands for, its meaning as an institution; we can't ignore any of this.

AS: I know that you see much of the current British new writing scene as a bit banal, especially as regards its naturalism, and I think you've already mentioned its social realism. Could you say something about that and how your own project differs from it?

HB: Yes, that's a big question, an extensive question. When I began writing in the early 1970s, I produced a couple of plays that were of the sort required by the Royal Court, inasmuch as that was the key theatre at the time. They required that kind of play, and I could produce it. So, I wrote about my own life, as a south London youth. My nausea at that kind of writing, and my suspicion of what goes on at the Royal Court, as a producing house, and an ethical centre, developed quite early. I was, therefore, drawn to a sort of theatre that did not rely on narrated experience, or personal experience, as being the functional engine of it. I wanted to write plays that were imaginative, and took their whole authority from the imaginative.

In many ways, the whole roll-call of the so-called 'revolution' of the 1950s and 1960s has now become profoundly reactionary. It merely reiterates the idea of the street as the source of wisdom, the street as the source of authority and so on, which diminishes imagination, corrupts language and, worst of all, turns the actor into a member of his own audience. You see these kind of plays, and the audience knows it can do what they're doing. In other words, the fracture between stage and public is diminished. Naturalistic speech is something anyone can do. Drama schools don't teach voice anymore; you hear this all over the place. The status of the actor is reduced. And so, the whole experience becomes banal.

AS: One of your recurrent themes, and you've already alluded to this, is reinventing dramatic tragedy. Could you say a bit about what tragedy was in the past, and how your idea of it differs from that?

HB: *Dead Hands* is not a tragedy. It's very hard to write a tragedy. I'm interested in it. I've done it a couple of times, perhaps. I hope to do it again. It's a very difficult form to achieve.

Essentially, tragedy is about death. It's about our relationship with death. It brings death into the theatre immediately, either through murder or criminality. And the audience must be ready to receive death, and let it into their lives, at least for that amount of time, which doesn't happen with any other art form, I don't think – certainly not the thriller or the murder story. It is essentially about how one comes to death, and one therefore watches the protagonist in their struggle both to arrive at the moment of death and to diminish the importance of death.

I think tragedy's social and psychological value is huge. [Because of its profound relationship with death] tragedy cannot rehearse social values all the time. Aristotle – who is, after all, only a critic, let's get him into perspective – turns tragedy into a socially organized art form which makes everything better for society. This seems to me a complete misreading, certainly of Sophocles to begin with. When one writes tragedy, one is drawing an audience into something in which their normal value systems are not applicable, or at least they become eroded very quickly. This is what is exciting about the theatre. Hard as it is, and corrupt as it is, it is still the best place for moral speculation that is open to us.

Tragedy, let us be quite clear, is not a sad thing. Let's not use these words that Michael Billington uses, like 'pessimism' and 'optimism'. 'Pessimisim' and 'optimism' are useless categories in the theatre, likewise 'utility'; these are all useless. Tragedy is not sad. Chekhov writes sad plays, but he doesn't write tragedies. Tragedy is to do with someone overreaching. There's not a tragedy in somebody like Uncle Vanya, who doesn't do anything. Tragedy's about doing things, and, essentially, overreaching yourself. *Macbeth* is a wonderful example of that. Of course, at that moment, it's also replete with sex. *Macbeth* is unthinkable without Lady Macbeth.

I repudiate the whole idea of social value in tragedy. I'm interested in how the individual reconstructs him or herself from an experience of catastrophe. Those tragedies I have written involve that individual, phase-by-phase reconstruction in which characters cling both to instinct and to sexual passion, as a means of defining themselves in a world which is catastrophically damaged, as they appear to be.

AS: I know you didn't go to the theatre much as a child. How did you discover the theatre in the first place?

HB: It's a very good question. I grew up in a working-class, artisan family; we didn't go to the theatre, except at Christmas for pantomimes, and I don't remember having any strong feelings about it then. As a university student I wrote poetry, and I still do that.

It probably goes back to radio, which is a wonderful dramatic medium. It's completely undervalued, hardly heard, but superb; and I still write radio plays for the reason. When I was a very young, inexperienced writer, I wrote plays for radio specifically, and the BBC was then thoughtful enough to provide advice to young writers, which I doubt it does now. They actually said, "why don't you write a stage play?" So, it really came from there.

Because of that advice, I went to the Royal Court and I saw a few plays there; I didn't really like them very much. It is by not liking things that you're inclined to want to write. I always think that artistic development is a result of nausea. You see a play, it nauseates you, you think, "that's wrong, I can do something better"; however arrogant, as a process, that sounds, it is how progress is made in art, I think.

AS: I know you won't like this question, but what have you tried to say in your plays, partly as a confrontation with these traditions of naturalism and social realism that you found in the theatre?

HB: You're right, I don't like the question, because the idea of 'saying' is totally alien to me. We're now obliged by the Arts Council to meet audiences after shows; we're supposed to 'talk back' afterwards. So, you can produce an intense moment of poetry and visual ecstasy, and then you're asked to come onstage, and the actors have a glass of beer in their hands, and they're supposed to talk to the audience about precisely what they've just experienced. So, you destabilize the very thing you've just spent two and a half hours achieving. Behind this lies the idea that everything can be taken apart and understood. For me, a poem cannot be understood, it's just a poem, and that must apply to stage plays too.

So, to the idea of *saying* – one is always asked, 'what are you *saying* in this play?' I don't say anything. I'm completely resistant to the idea that I'm actually saying anything. If you say something, you must have a moral intention, and then you produce a work of art to fit the intention. That's not the way I work. I work from the imaginative idea, and I put it into the form of a drama. What is said may or may not be interpreted by other people. It's certainly not interpreted by me. So, I don't recognize that I'm saying anything.

AS: What, then, would be the driving force? What compels you to write? I think you write a play a year.

HB: Maybe sometimes two. I don't want to analyse myself, because I don't think it's very useful to do that. But, clearly there is a psychological need for me to express myself in this particular form. When I was very much younger, and a communist, I probably thought it had a function as well; in that the class war seemed to be something that needed to be shown, but, of course, everybody was doing the same thing at the same time anyway, so I don't know, in retrospect, what value that would have had. Now I don't think in those terms at all. I think of the theatre as a deeply philosophical, emotional and psychological experience, which can't be reduced to anything else.

AS: I remember once you said that you didn't want to cast light into the theatrical darkness. What's that all about?

HB: The stage is a lit area in a dark room. My antipathy to Brecht is partly to do with lightness. Brecht talks about light. Why do Brecht and his heirs want light in the auditorium? I think it's a fascistic instinct, that people should judge each other, and the audience can see itself; they can act as censors and policeman on each other. Whereas the dark auditorium, which I like and aspire to – complete darkness; I don't even like to see exit signs – allows the individual to fracture himself from the collectivity of the audience, and to respond personally to what's going on on the stage. This is a vastly more dangerous experience than the light is.

Let's take this word 'light' into its context – 'Enlightenment'. This is a western concept which is about me elucidating you. I don't believe writers have sounder judgements about politics than any other individual. All they have is imagination. That we trust. If you trust a writer's politics, you're a fool to do so.

AS: So, would it be wrong to see your work, especially in the past ten years, as political?

HB: It would be, in one sense, but I'm not so foolish as not to realize that all things contain a politics. It may not be my politics, but you drop a stone in a pool, it makes ripples. My work perhaps, inadvertently, has a political consequence, but it doesn't have a political intention.

AS: You've described your work as the Theatre of Catastrophe. Could you explain a little bit more about that?

HB: I was trying to do that when I was talking about tragedy. I was trying to separate my form of tragedy from, let's say, for the sake of brevity, Shakespearean tragedy. The end of the Shakespeare play is usually weak; I think most people recognize that; all great texts have got *longueurs* and weaknesses in them, obviously. What weakens a Shakespearean ending, for me, is its attempt to tie up a moral message, and it is a message. There's a message in it, for whatever reason; maybe it's the power of the Church in his day, who knows? There is an attempt to produce a reconciliation. It's as if, having put the audience through something like *King Lear*, it was necessary to say that, actually, he learned his lesson in the end. The worst example of that is the death of Edmund [in *King Lear*], which is pitiful and silly, really.

I don't do that. For me, the catastrophic play doesn't resolve, because there is, to me, no reconciliation, no resolution. In a frank way, I think very great personal experience only leads to one place, and that is solitude. The catastrophic play always leaves the protagonist in solitude. Whether solitude is of negative value is a matter of choice; it's an informed solitude. That's where my tragic plays lead to.

AS: Your plays have been much more successful in Europe than in Britain. Why do you think that is?

HB: I think it's quite easy to explain that. Something really awful that happened to England in the sixteenth century was the Reformation. We're constantly told how wonderful it was – maybe it had its advantages – but one of the things it eliminated, gradually, was the speculative habit of thinking, and also the idea of the dark, the Catholic, the confessional, all the sorts of things that make European, non-Protestant culture, at least, quite different from ours. The French – despite the French Revolution, despite the rationalism of the French and so on – are actually vastly more open to what you might call a philosophical text than the English are. They're not frightened of a writer who dares to think the unthinkable. That fits into the framework of their culture. The English are continually asking, 'what is the value of this text?' It's quite sordid, really. I think that explains my ability to work better in Europe, and America, it must be said.

AS: I read somewhere that your main influences – apart from Shakespeare, of course – have been poets rather than playwrights.

HB: Yes. As I said earlier, I started writing poetry long before I started writing plays, and I still do that. I don't have any dramatic heroes, apart from Shakespeare – his influence is unavoidable for anybody. These poets tend to be European, with the exception of George Oppen, who's a very fine American poet, in my opinion. They are poets like Rilke; Apollinaire is an absolute master: and also Paul Célan. What Célan represents, for me, is the attempt to identify the catastrophic – albeit in hermetic terms. Adorno said there could be "no poetry after Auschwitz", and I'm a huge admirer of Adorno – a Marxist who was also a bourgeois, and they're the most interesting ones. But Célan knows that, when he's trying to talk about the untalkable, the only language is a hermetic one; it belongs to him; it's a hermetic one. If you come into the Célan poem, you have to fight your way through it, and will you find the centre? You don't know if you will or not. I find that very inspiring, as a dramatist, that you cannot unlock every door in a play or a poem.

AS: You describe yourself as a "European". What do you mean by that?

HB: I've felt it since I was a child, and I can never quite identify why. As a child in a working-class, London family, a family of soldiers, policeman, tram drivers – an ordinary, working-class London family – it was very odd that, at the age of seven or eight, I began to think of myself as a Viennese or something. There are no European connections in my family at all; I just felt that. I can't say why I felt it, but, as time went by, I began to articulate it intellectually. My favourite authors tend to be central Europeans – Joseph Roth is a fantastic writer; Thomas Mann is another.

        The idea of being a European seems to me, crucially, to be able to span both the rational and irrational in one mind. I don't know many other cultures that can do that, or aspire to it. For me, the finest novelist of the twentieth century is Louis-Ferdinand Céline, a fascist, but a great writer. On the other hand, you have Thomas Mann, a democrat of immensely rational powers.

        It's the same in painting. Take Rembrandt and Bosch; there aren't two painters more opposite. To contain all that within your own fevered mind is what it is to be a European. It's a wonderful inheritance for us.

AS: Since 1988 The Wrestling School has been producing your work. How did this unique company come about?

HB: My best friends in the theatre, my allies, have been actors. After some experience of years in the RSC, some of those actors felt the work had not been properly directed; it was not understood. I don't know if that's true or not, but that was the feeling. Kenny Ireland in particular, who became a director, said, "why don't we do a new [Barker] text and direct ourselves, independently of the big companies?" We formed the company just to do *The Last Supper*. After that, we thought we'd try another one. So, in a sense, ad hoc-wise, the company has progressed year after year, and we're never funded except on a yearly basis. So, it's a very shoestring affair.

When Kenny went to take over the Lyceum in Edinburgh, I decided to direct the plays, and I've directed them ever since, in a very different way from Kenny; there's a complete bifurcation in the history of the company, between his method and mine.

AS: You're famous for saying that you send all your plays to the National Theatre for rejection. Can you tell me why you said that?

HB: Why I said it, or why I did it? I don't do it any more. I did used to do it, because I wanted to put a play on there, because the resources are enormous and theatres are enormous. It's just right for me, I write big plays – that's the theatre for me – the Olivier, for example.

I then became intrigued by the fact that under five different artistic directors I'd never been let in the door. People get very angry on my behalf about this; they say it's a scandal. It is a scandal, of course, but I'm not interested in pursuing that line. I'm much more interested in the question of why this happens, what it means.

People in Scotland want their own national theatre. I keep saying to them, "don't have one! They're no use to you, they're a terrible waste of resources, and you could run ten independent companies for that money, and you should do".

What is a national theatre? It's no longer a patriotic theatre– we don't have royalist patriots running things any more here – but it's still the *national* institution, and therefore it must reflect the national ideology. The national ideology is, more or less, *The Guardian* and *The Independent* rolled together. That's what that place now manifests in itself.

The reason my work is not performed there is not because I don't write well. Clearly, they're breaking they're contract, which is to produce the best writing in the country. If I'm not there and everyone else is, there must be a reason for that. The only reason I can see is that, in some way, my work continually infringes the liberal humanist tradition. Whatever they say in terms of, 'we have no animus against this writer', their refusal to stage my work must represent a resistance to it.

AS: Is it painful to be, as you once said you are, an 'internal exile' in this culture?

HB: Yes, of course. It's very nice to go abroad and be welcomed into national theatres in almost any country in Europe, and painful never to be welcomed into my own. That's not related only to them [the National Theatre]; it applies also to the Royal Shakespeare Company, the Royal Court, the Donmar and anywhere else you care to mention. Of course it's painful. What was it Jesus said? "You can't be a prophet in your own country". Maybe that's the case.

AS: You're prolific as always. We have in front of us three recent books that you've published. Could you say a bit about them please?

HB: *The Ecstatic Bible*, which Oberon have just published – in a very handsome edition, it must be said – was a very, very long play I wrote over two years in 1994–1995, with a cast of about a hundred, and a twelve-hour duration. We did actually perform at the Adelaide Festival in 2000. It was a collaboration between an Australian company [Brink Productions] and The Wrestling School, and it was the success of the Adelaide Festival that year. Now it's got into print, but I doubt anyone's going to perform it, as such, for a long time.

   It's divided into parables, which is the sense in which it is a Bible: amoral parables which could be lifted out independently of each other, and could well be interesting for people to perform.

   The second book is the text of *Dead Hands*, which Oberon have also brought out. The third one is Routledge's publication of my theory book *Death, The One and the Art of Theatre*, which is about tragedy, the role of death in tragedy and about the idea of 'The One'. We talk, don't we, about passionate involvement with other people; we say, 'he's The One', 'she's The One'. It's a very interesting notion of the ideal partner. It's about that kind of identifying with and absorbing of another person, but also the fatality that's involved in recognizing the individual who is, in a sense, your destiny. Those three elements are put together in this book in relation to theatre.

This interview was recorded on 11 October 2004 – on the occasion of the premiere of Barker's play Dead Hands *– for broadcast on the website www.theatrevoice.com*

The Ecstatic Bible. Gerrard McArthur (The Priest) and Gerald Lepkowski (Poitier). The Wrestling School & Brink Productions, 2000. Photo credit David Wilson

'Crisis is the essential condition for art forms'

With David Ian Rabey and Karoline Gritzner

David Ian Rabey (DIR)
Howard Barker (HB)
Karoline Gritzner (KG)

DIR: The exordium has become an increasingly important ingredient in your direction: sometimes specified in the text, sometimes not, and sometimes developed differently in rehearsal to the scripted abstract (as for your own production of *He Stumbled*). The exordium is a sequence and proposition combining recorded sound with strong visual images and rhythmic movement, presenting the audience with striking imagery as soon as they enter the space, so that the audience enter the space on the performers' terms, rather than on those of their own daily routines and discourses of 'sense'. These images then resolve into a narrative when the performers are released into language. *Found in the Ground* begins with a scripted exordium, but in this play more than any other of yours to date, the aesthetic drive and rhythm of the exordium seems extended into the scenographic propositions and drive of the entire play, and we lose any Interlude (such as we formerly encountered in *The Bite of the Night*, *Rome* or *The Last Supper*). In *Found in the Ground* you seem to invoke and orchestrate an opera for a moving landscape, in a way which is perhaps only comparable to Robert Wilson's scenographic direction.

HB: The exordium is my substitute for properly possessing the performance space. I have often said that the foyer is an obstacle to a spiritual experience, an area of trivia littered with the distractive detritus of entertainment. I cannot own a theatre, so I am compelled to create the conditions for my work in that critical time lapse between the auditorium doors being opened and the beginning of the performance. Naturally the audience are not expecting this environment as they take their seats – they may even resent it – but it is a necessary break with the normal continuum of street-foyer-performance-street, an admonition that they will not be seeing or hearing according to the conventional rules of social realist theatre, comedy or what is routinely on offer.

The routine of the exordium has to be repetitive, however complex it can sometimes appear, partly for practical reasons, such as its late arrival in the rehearsal, when the actors are already fully occupied with the technical, so it cannot be too demanding of their time and resources [...] an example might be provided by the Wedding Machine in my 2003 production for The Wrestling School of *13 Objects*: as a simple fulcrum rises and falls, lifted on a pulley by a seated, visible actor, one end plunging a collection of objects – lilies, a clock, a trowel – into a tank of fluid, and the other simultaneously lifts a framed wedding photograph high, away from a half-naked bride who is contemplating it [...] she rises to follow it and turns to accuse another seated bride [...] as her gesture is completed a shriek comes from the sound system (pre-recorded of course) [...] it's a simple rhythm [...] but I have to say actors lack physical training and often cannot do it [...] Victoria Wicks is exemplary but she has a dancer's rhythms [...] in *A House of Correction* an actress doing a similar series of movements never got over an innate feeling that it was 'silly', and one failed element sinks the whole thing [...] again and again you are brought back to the value of the ensemble [...] you have to recruit people who want your sort of aesthetic and believe in it.

You are right to observe that in *Found in the Ground* some of the choreographic features of my exordia remain [...] the choruses of nurses with trays [...] the march of the headless victims [...] the racing approach of the dogs. Perhaps I was thinking here of sustaining the musical nature of the exordium [...] so that the play is like a string quartet by Bartok [...] the themes keep returning always developed and furthered, the torsion increased [...].

DIR: You often use sound as an invasive force and factor, in your exordia and subsequently.

HB: I have nearly eliminated music from my theatre but instead use drones or reassembled cuts from a small number of modern composers, or recorded cries and breaths. I use the cries to punctuate the image.

DIR: Your use of costume has become increasingly distinctive and important, through realizations of the designs of Billie Kaiser. They are often simple, blending the modern with the classical or 1940s/1950s monochrome features combining with set and lighting in a highly painterly stage image.

HB: The Barker/Kaiser designs are part of an overall vision of the stage, part of the denaturalizing imagery. For one thing, they tend to be monochromatic, as the sets do, creating a flat plane for voice to dominate [...] the costumes are beautiful and as you have observed owe a great deal to classic haute couture of the 1930s, 1940s and 1950s, not least in their hats. They are intended to raise the status of the female characters both socially and sexually, hence the common use of the half-veil and high heels. They have a profound relationship with the naked body because, in some sense, they almost command their own desecration, the unveiling of the female characters. Of course, here again the designs make demands on the actors; you have to know how to walk in these costumes. Wicks, Jessop, Bertish know how to walk and the sound of the heel on the floor is critical. The use of the narrow range of shades in the clothing of the performers asserts the non-naturalism of the production, and obviously the eruption of one colour becomes powerfully suggestive: I'm thinking of Gertrude's sudden appearance in yellow in *Gertrude – The Cry*. Inversely, the collapse of a character's moral status might show itself in the poverty of a garment, as at Doorway's dying speech in *The Fence*.

DIR: In *The Fence,* Photo is blind, as are his father and sister, a recurrent motif in your work to suggest a particularly thin-skinned character (such as Isonzo in *The Twelfth Battle*, Smith in *Rome* [...]); paradoxically, you create increasingly visual landscapes in production, through which these blind characters must move [...].

HB: Blindness in my plays has something intensely and fundamentally *of theatre* about it [...] it has an irresistible moral value, which is nothing to do with pitying blind people; I mean a moral aesthetic. It has its supreme moments in *Isonzo* and *The Fence* in a similar context, when a loved woman is exposed in her nakedness to eyes that cannot see. It is densely metaphorical in *The Fence* when Istoria goes to her friend and undresses her for the sightless eyes of Photo, a gesture of sexual possession, and, of course, the triangularity between what the audience *can* see and what the character *cannot* is full of exquisite contradictions. In *Isonzo*, the old man's entire store of sexuality is invested in sound or in his imagined ability to hear what the sighted cannot [...] the *interior* of his loved one [...] blindness is licence to penetrate more deeply than the sighted might require.

DIR: You have spoken of your aesthetic objective being anxiety, rather than more conventional theatrical forms of pleasure. The audience encounter a spare, often monochromatic, energetically costumed production, with excessive language at the core of the event, and focus shifted onto the actor's body as an instrument of speech and movement, with sound (rather than music) cues adding a further processed, spatial quality to create a soundscape to stress the audience, rather than comfort them or create an emotional climate within which to engage sympathetically. As Chris Corner has observed, this is an aesthetic density, rather than an opulence or richness of detail, a richness which does not overwhelm the actors. As you have said, this is work which offers an obligation rather than a conventionally recognizable pleasure, presenting extreme situations which can answer a boredom with the status quo and recognize a hunger to search.

HB: Beauty and anxiety are not strangers to one another, and because beauty is something of a privilege, it is privileged in my *mise-en-scène* also, where the effects are most carefully prepared, and – might I say – the result of a single vision and not a compromise of competing imaginations, however 'collaborative' they might seem to be. I am attempting two things simultaneously: to draw the audience into a relationship with the stage which eradicates sympathy at the outset as a prime condition and replaces it with an obsessive gaze and its audial equivalent, both overwhelming and both a plethora. If the exordium announces new terms of seeing and hearing, the play confirms it, and, for those who are willing, frees them of the common expectations of 'understanding' and replaces these with a hypnotic regard. The anxiety comes from what's said and what's done, because they are profoundly resistant to conventional morality, obviously. This moral refusal has produced a wall of resistance to my work in the critical and theatre worlds; [which is] revealing, in itself, of the collusive nature of these bodies, but has also made it painfully (once) and luxuriously (now) clear that "I do not know the theatre and the theatre does not know me".

DIR: However, it also strikes me that the invocations and manipulations of anxiety are very much the currency of recent reactionary politics associated with the so-called 'War on Terror', in which political leaders of various ideologies seek to 'bind' their subjects 'with fear', to recall a resonant phrase from your 1980 play *The Loud Boy's Life*. This political climate, with its ideal of an impossible 'security', makes it particularly difficult to advance the offer and characterization of anxiety as exhilarating – difficult, but perhaps particularly necessary, to unlock prevalent associations. How would you distinguish your ideal form (and sensation) of anxiety from indiscriminate fearfulness and contraction?

HB: Let us not confuse fear with anxiety. Fear exists between men in all social situations, and politics sometimes manipulates it. Social democracies like ours create fear whilst attempting to ameliorate pain, a dazzling contradiction. Fear of sickness and death is obsessive here, and the State, in its medicalization of all human experience, makes itself a body-snatching agency in the process. Organ removal, an extreme form of the impertinence of the *demos* and the eradication of the private, is justified only by dread of death. But I think of anxiety in my theatre as a state quite different to fear […] rather it is a troubling of the fixed strata of moral conventions […] a sort of low quaking that threatens the foundations of the stable personality […] the public doesn't quite know where to place its feet, there is an insecurity, but one which is simultaneously exhilarating – surely the best example is the shock and freedom lent to Katrin by the fall of the social system in *The Europeans*. I think of these plays as types of prayer; they demand something of a world which won't give it, but one does not cease praying […] Isn't one anxious when one prays? Tragedy originates from these same sources.

DIR: As Brendan Kennelly puts it in his version of *Medea*, "Prayer [...] is anger at what is, and a longing for what should be"?

HB: No, I think that would be to reduce prayer to a practical statement of aims and desires. It is without anger; it is uttered without hope, to a wall of silence [...] the cosmological oblivion to which it is addressed does not, however, detract from its passionate need, its value as *expression* [...] I tried to introduce this in *Two Skulls* (Danish radio 2002).

DIR: Nakedness is another recurrent motif in your plays and productions, but you characteristically combine elements of erotic allure with associations and experiences of fear, a horror which may potentially be common to characters, actors and audiences. This is a further feature of your landscape of anxiety, in which (self-)exposure is simultaneously fixing and unsettling.

HB: As Gay says in wonder at the state of nakedness in *The Bite of the Night*, to be naked is to be weak in some ways, but potentially powerful in others. For example, the authority of the final naked moment in *The Fence* isn't simply erotic. In that final image, Algeria's nakedness is a supreme rebuke to the forces that overthrew her regime; it is a triumphant reversal of the sordid nakedness of the dead dictator, as when Mussolini and his mistress were suspended upside down and humiliated in 1944. It is such a mobile surface of concepts, the unclothed body, a surface which, no matter how overwritten, still has the power to be discovered *differently* [...] it mocks pornography, which plays with the secret, by being authentically secret.

DIR: However, there is a powerful element of eroticism in the mesmerism of your plays in performance, though this eroticism may be more to do with the sense of anticipation, which can prolong excitement or "stretch pleasures [...] to their breaking point" (to use a phrase from *Isonza*). Perhaps there is here an unconventional acknowledgement of the *instability* of eroticism: a staged awareness of how easily it can turn into, and back from, its opposite.

HB: I should not want to suggest that I don't employ the erotic in the naked. Obviously in *Gertrude – The Cry* the triangular agony of the opening scene is deeply erotic: two lovers kill for passion and find deeper desire through their own cruelty, and a victim must watch the taking of his own sexual property by another (and I say "property" here deliberately [...] the Queen is the property of the King, primarily for procreating the line of dynasty; see *The Gaolers Ache*) [...] hence the three cries, each one musically distinct for the emotion it contains. Nakedness was critical in this scene, and when I saw the play in Vienna, in a good production, much was forfeited because the actress declined to be naked but wore underwear to protect her modesty, and I don't criticize – the stage is terribly revealing – but I must also praise Victoria Wicks in The Wrestling School premiere production, for her phenomenal bravery in her playing of the sexual moment and its complete success. And yes, she wore high heels throughout; I was constructing a sexual moment of intensity which necessarily employed the erotic conventions of its day. What I did not want to do was to imitate a sexual act naturalistically [...] it was an exquisite metaphor made vivid by the language spoken. You are right to suggest that such scenes always risk bathos [...] it is in the actor's power, if she trusts the director's concepts, to keep that at bay.

DIR: In the context of eroticism, I am also interested in allusions you have made to sex as a potential basis for religion, or neo-religious beliefs, and also in your developing sense of 'the religious' in your work, which seems neither institutional nor conventional, but a passionate rejection of conventional worldliness.

HB: Why do I sometimes speak of the religious aspect of sexuality? I think because religion shares its ecstatic potential, but more, because religion is the study of secrets, and the secret retreats always before knowledge and takes up residence somewhere else [...] so does sexuality; it is self-inventing; it has its great books, its great testaments; perhaps I have written one or two myself, and it is also irreducible to anything else [...] look how pitiful the sex manual is [...] the scientific is abolished here [...] and it entails the prayer [...] what lover has not looked on the nakedness of his/her desired one without uttering a prayer of devotion? What is the demand in that prayer? The hope that this is the doorway to some other truth [...].

KG: The catastrophes of the twentieth century feature strongly in your work. Many of your protagonists devise precarious ways of stepping out of their historical moments. Social context does not seem to restrict the possibilities of their actions.

HB: Yes, the world wars are in The Love of a Good Man and The Power of the Dog. In the latter the two egoists, the beautiful fashion model and the dreamy philosopher, try to escape the elimination of the individual by faceless bureaucrats and policemen in Stalin's Europe. The protagonists are discriminating in their unconscious. Suicide is a way of avoiding the historical moment: you might say most of my protagonists are suicides, even if they don't perform it. Their absolute solitude is probably a form of suicide also. I write plays in which the social context is diminished but not overcome – hence the absence of authentic victims from my work. The social context might be oppressive or catastrophic, but few of the protagonists allow that to extirpate their spiritual or erotic ambition. It is this resistance to the moral and political climate that might be said to constitute the milieu of the action, and whilst I deny the value of terms like optimism or pessimism with regard to tragedy, this self-assertion is clearly a moral confidence and not a nihilism.

KG: Would you agree that there is an underlying tension or contradiction between intellectual argument and emotional response in much of your work?

HB: I don't think ideas are the material of my plays or poems, though characters ponder their circumstances at length, they are meditative, even in surroundings that abhor meditation. But this exercise, startling though it is in some instances, only thinly disguises the crucial operation of instinct, the all-powerful coercion of desire. The twin poles of my 'realism' are coercion and decay. Between these absolutes, men and women struggle to find love and meaning.

KG: Many of your characters are involved in complex processes of self-exploration and self-definition which, in a cultural context of postmodernity, could almost appear anachronistic.

HB: The self is a vital component of culture, and to talk of dissolving the self is to usher in a terrible nihilism masquerading as popular democracy. Perhaps the dubious aspect of the self is the idea of the 'authentic' self – rather we can evolve and invent ourselves from a disparate store of private sources, which to me are sacred. Everything tends to violate these, now more than ever.

KG: Do you perceive a crisis of theatre in the current political and cultural climate?

HB: Yes, but crisis is the essential condition for art forms; without crisis they are unlikely to reinvent themselves spontaneously, that much goes without saying. But this particular crisis? It's a transitional moment, because there is a dominant theatre ideology which is decayed. This is social realism, with all its political ambitions, its projects of Enlightenment (i.e. social control) and so on. It's very close to the functioning of Socialist Realism in the Stalin era and has the same kind of critical police working it up all the time. The 'crisis' in this is manifold, but perhaps the worst aspect is that the decline of a theatre language and form has done deep damage to acting training, so skills in voice and body, on which it is necessary to build the new forms, are being lost. We know how voice and its trained modulations are now persecuted as 'elitist'. This is sham democracy, with Robespierrist rhetorics, but no one much notices it. One has to note also that the function of the writer in all this continues to decay [...] what he had, which is imagination, is the very thing *the theatre* most likes to stamp on; after all, imagination is never *relevant*, and relevance is the slogan of a people's society [...] ask any dramaturg [...] it's his favourite word [...] and meaningless.

KG: What does it mean to be 'European'?

HB: To be European is to hold to opposites and live, if not rejoice, in the contradictions. Read [Louis-Ferdinand] **Céline**, and read Thomas Mann. Look at Bosch, and look at Rembrandt. Read Voltaire and [Joseph] de Maistre, or place [Albert] Camus beside [Emil] Cioran. What is more, migrate from one to the other, for it's impossible to extend one's treasured *tolerance* to all of these. The individual and the collective are never more embattled than they are here, and reconciliation is impossible given the now ancestral nature of the conflict. It is perpetual oscillation, and all talk of harmony is false, a self-deception. Further, whether or not Europeans invented beauty, they have argued beauty to an extreme; it dominates every street in an old city, and we sense the agony of these streets; that also is our way [...] if you cannot relate pain to beauty, I think you are not a European in your soul.

This interview was originally published in the collection Theatre of Catastrophe: New Essays on Howard Barker *(London: Oberon, 2006), edited by Karoline Gritzner and David Ian Rabey.*

'Not what is, but what is possible'

With Thierry Dubost

Thierry Dubost (TB)
Howard Barker (HB)

TD: Yesterday was the world premiere of *Révélations*, the French title of your play *The Dying of Today* [which was translated into French by Isabelle Famchon]. How significant is it for you – an English playwright – to see the premiere of your play staged in France?

HB: You will know I am quite a prolific writer of plays, which means that – given my situation in England – it's impossible that all these plays will be staged in England. Recently, my own theatre company, The Wrestling School, was defunded by the government – it lost its grant – so from now on it will be even more difficult for my work to be staged in England. So, in this regard, it's excellent for me to have a country and a theatre which is prepared to produce my work. *The Dying of Today* is perhaps two years old, and this production by Guillaume Dujardin's company is the first opportunity I have had to see it performed. As a matter of fact, I have recently tried to have it produced on BBC radio, where I have a history of productions. So, that may happen, but I don't know yet.

TD: Before the interview, you mentioned the defunding of your company, and you were quite critical of the National Theatre in England. I guess it is part of [any country's] traditions to have national theatres whose dramatic approach is somewhat obsolete – so does the problem lie in the National Theatre, or does it lie elsewhere?

HB: It lies in the whole concept of a national theatre, I think – and they would certainly not regard themselves as archaic in their taste. On the contrary, they would think of themselves as being extremely modern, or contemporary. The question really is how they regard their idea of the contemporary or the relevant play in society. So, the management of the National Theatre produces a range of styles of work, but its primary function – and these bureaucrats carry the function out very well – is to reproduce a kind of political ideology of the time. Of course, 50 years ago, the National Theatre would have been a patriotic establishment involved in the support of the Royal family or the support of the government, or saying how excellent modern democracy was. Of course, that's changed. What happens now is that the theatre becomes almost a factory, a factory of critical texts. These texts appear to examine and criticize society, hence this constant emphasis on the relevant, but we all know that every self-evidently revolutionary form degenerates into a convention, and now the relevant is the conventional.

As a consequence, the management of these theatres in certain cases, and for no reason that they will adequately explain, choose not to perform plays (which break with the convention); the treatment of my work is certainly one of the most egregious examples of this. One of the grounds on which they will say they don't wish to perform these plays is that don't seem to be what they call 'relevant'. This 'relevance' would reside in there being, self-evidently, a certain sociological background to the work – if it seemed to reflect contemporary problems, these sorts of things. I suppose you could say a writer like David Hare would exemplify that, continually using theatre to debate the ever shrinking subject of the political system. My work does not do that. It eschews that, it abandons that. So, I can't expect really – realistically – to find a place there.

TD: This is interesting because in *Arguments for a Theatre* you wrote that you have shunned relevance in every play you have written; to a certain extent, however, I find it difficult to avoid relevance, because the play which we saw yesterday was relevant – maybe not at an obvious level – but it connects to society.

HB: I don't think of myself as a fantasist. My plays may not be naturalistic representations of the real world – whatever that is – but they are not fantasies. I always argue that my plays are not about what is but what is possible, and nothing that occurs on my stages is ever impossible to imagine. But the key word is 'imagine'. It must be imagined. The description of the destruction of the soldiers and the sailors in *The Dying of Today* is pretty well exactly as described by Thucydides, in that part of the Peloponnesian wars dealing with the Syracuse expedition, which was one of the great military disasters of European history. So, in that sense, and because we fight wars – as indeed we fight them in Iraq and so on – you could say that might be an image. However, that is not really what is regarded as relevant by the dramaturgy of relevance. The dramaturgy of relevance would say: 'no, we don't want a metaphor, we must have the thing itself. We must show. If you want to write about Iraq, you write about Iraq; you show the contemporary situation'. So, yes, I don't say for a moment my plays make no comment on the contemporary world; they can be interpreted as doing so, but without a political message, I would add.

TD: My next question is a follow-up to the previous one. Thinking about the title of your book *Arguments for a Theatre*, how possible is it to argue for a different kind of theatre in England today?

HB: About arguments, and the need to argue, I say in the preface to *Arguments for a Theatre* that, in a way, argument is not quite the word, because I am not arguing. I am just stating. I would never have written that book – nor any of the subsequent books I have written about theatre – had I not been so isolated in the contemporary English theatre scene, under constant attacks from press critics, though with some friends in academia, I must say, loyal friends in the academic world. Because I was not defended, I had to speak for myself, and I began with a piece in the *Guardian* newspaper called 'Forty-nine asides for a tragic theatre'. Subsequently, I continued to do it, and defined my position, refined my position over and over again. I was trying to defend something that no one else at the time was very interested in defending, which is a poetic discourse, a form of language specially designed and constructed for the theatre; this, in itself, demands a form of performance, which not all actors can or will do any more.

  We could come onto this question, but actor training in England now – and I am certain it is the same in France – is devoted to the televisual style. Consequently, it's a naturalistic training, and one can audition young actors, and very few of them really have the habit of taking a speech of twenty lines and delivering it in a way which, for me, should mesmerize the audience. Because I am not interested in arguments – to come back to this – I am not interested in arguing with the audience. I am not interested in debating with the audience. I am interested in the actor fascinating the audience, rather in the way that I have always argued, rightly or wrongly, that somehow the medieval priest speaking Latin discourse could nevertheless fascinate a congregation who knew no Latin at all. Just as in Shakespeare – we can no longer keep up with the Shakespearean speeches, it's too difficult for us – but in the hands of a trained voice and a body – the voice and the body in collaboration – we could create something extremely fascinating.

TD: This is what you mean by, "the actor is different in kind".

HB: Absolutely. This is a gift. It's a peculiar gift, but it's a training, and then – I use the word elite quite freely in my argument – it is an elite function in the theatre. You and I, the public, cannot transpose ourselves for the actor. Whereas in naturalism, almost by definition, you or I can go onto the stage and play a role – because it requires no training to be naturalistic.

TD: Yes, and there is something else which is difficult for the audience in *The Dying of Today*: the cynical views of the messenger who brings bad news. I saw that as an inverted picture of the pseudo-compassion of what I would call – alluding to one of your expressions – the "daily theatre of catastrophe", that is what we see on television. We are expected to sympathize, but this expectation is superficial, because journalists do not really care about what is taking place. Your play provides an inverted picture of that. My question is how can the audience associate with that, knowing that they are trained to sympathize? It's a form of political correctness. You are expected to sympathize.

HB: This is how the plays work, I think, if they work at all. We know that, as you said, televisual reportage has a spurious relationship with pain and cruelty, in which we are invited to sympathize, but in fact it becomes a form of drug. We are now fascinated by it, by suffering. This brings us very much back to the Roman Empire and the games, the spectacle of the games. We're not so far away from this now, but in portraying a character who luxuriates in and makes a passion of delivering bad news, purely to examine the effect of news on a suffering person. It's as if one has microscopically bought up the experience of bad news in a society like ours, which now – in a sense – thrives on bad news. It goes further psychologically, however, in suggesting that, in a way, we welcome bad news; not that we just enjoy the spectacle of it, but we wait for it to affect our private lives. We long secretly to be devastated. That is the argument which, of course, an audience would recoil from, as a concept, but my work doesn't happen at the moment of the stage. You don't say to your neighbour in the theatre, 'I know what he's saying'. No, it's impossible, because you can't say what I'm saying. I don't know myself. But, I can assure you that, with the passage of time, these questions begin to operate within sensitive minds, and the phenomenon of people returning to see my plays several times is not unknown, actually.

TD: The paradox of the play is that one gains access to the intimacy of the characters who are, in fact, denying the intimate feature of their tragedy. I felt that was part of the power of the play, different from a more common feature of tragedy, where you expect characters to show their grief.

HB: There's a key line in it, which comes from the bad news man. He says, "I loved you". He says to the barber, "I loved you because I saw you were in pain, I saw you control your pain, and then I saw the pain coming through the control. The three stages of the beauty of the human soul". And he then says very near the end, "Don't tidy up your shop. Just suffer, be suffering, let me enjoy the beauty of your suffering".

I suppose, in a way, one has to say modern society, with its medical obsessions, wishes to eliminate suffering from every moment of your life – even sexuality is now called recreation. The BBC has a programme on sex now, and it's called 'Recreation'. Desire has become recreation. So, everywhere, the pain is removed; even death is no longer a significant act.

TD: What about the pain of the artist? I saw *The Dying of Today*, and thinking of the character who brings bad news, I saw it as a veiled portrait of the artist, voicing his anger at society because there was a deep misunderstanding, which prevented the voice of the artist from being heard. Would I be right to say that? Or [...]

HB: I can't answer that one very clearly. Many people have said to me that the artist figure in my work recurs even when he is not an artist. It's a good statement. I don't know. I'm not conscious of it.

TD: About this disconnection, this desire for disconnection – not as such, but in order to provide new aesthetics for theatre – what is the importance of silence in your work?

HB: That's an interesting question, because, as you know, I write profuse text, and there are very few thoughts that occur to the character – or to me, of course – which are not actually on the page. So, rather like Shakespeare, there isn't really a subtext in my plays. If it's thought, it's said. Actors find this quite difficult to deal with sometimes, because they want to play subtext. French actors more, even, than the English, actually. So, the silence is the moment when at last all forms of articulation have failed. The articulation is very, very desperate, but at some point even that fails. And that silence is therefore – I would say – earned, or deserved, in a way that it might not be in Harold Pinter, if I might say so. I don't want to compare or contrast anything, but it's a quite different silence. It's a silence of expressive exhaustion.

TD: Writing about political plays, you said, "it should return the onus to the audience, to the soul". Soul is a religious word. Should one infer that religion has a part to play in your work?

HB: I suppose I think of soul as that part of one's consciousness or unconsciousness which is impenetrable by ideology. In other words, it's very difficult to find, difficult to describe, because ideology by definition leaves no part untouched. But somewhere there is a part that is untouched. That's why I think I write a lot about sexuality, but not in this play, oddly enough. There's hardly any sex mentioned in this play. But generally for me the sexual act, the sexual feeling, the encounter of lovers, is a moment of liberation from the ideological construction of society, even whilst knowing much sexuality is conditioned. So, the soul for me is that part which one can insert – a lever – and open something which is ideologically free. I don't pretend I'm immaculate, of course – I'm a product of my society.

TD: I should like to conclude on sexuality onstage, and nakedness. What is the place of nakedness onstage in your work? How significant is it for you, bearing in mind that, it seems to me that one of the striking features of your work is that you shun that which is easy for the audience? I would not see nakedness as a way of entertaining the audience, but it is there. So, what is the purpose of nakedness onstage in your view?

135

HB: Well, I don't consciously employ it for this purpose. You spoke earlier about the profusion of nakedness in the theatre in France. Nevertheless, I think it remains a shock. I am not one to use shock tactics, though I know my language is very shocking because of its modes. The body unclothed, for me – and I sense from my own productions of my work – has an unsettling effect on an audience, which, at the same time, plays a little with the erotic. But the key point is not so much the nakedness of the actress or the actor, it's the circumstances in which that nakedness is played. Firstly, we never say it's naturalistic. So, if there's an active sexual partnership, I would never direct it as a naturalistic moment. For one thing, the text makes that difficult. The text plays against naturalism all the time. Secondly, in the staging, for example, of an active sexual intercourse, I would never stage it as naturalistic. I would always use metaphorical devices. Or, I would position the actors in positions that would make it clear that nothing sordid – in the sense that naturalism can be sordid – would occur. But, in a funny way – because we've talked about naturalism – this very absence of naturalism makes the thing more disturbing, and not less.

TD: Yes.

HB: I have to assume you believe me saying that.

TD: I do.

HB: There's something about the Royal Court form of naturalism which is full of fucking, full of killing, and wounding, perpetually – it's a relentless diet – which has no value whatsoever. But the moment that you isolate the nakedness of an actor – in a situation which is in fact artificial – it's the theatre.

TD: One could connect that to puppets.

HB: I'm glad you've said puppets. I was about to say that. There's something very moving and uncanny about a puppet's emotions. I sometimes work with actors, and I often tell them exactly where to stand. I say, "you stand there. No, not there, there", and they say, "all right, I'm not a puppet". And I always say, "if you were a puppet, you would have more power than you realize you have". I don't treat actors as puppets, but you understand what I mean; the element of the uncanny is very important in that nakedness.

This previously unpublished interview was conducted in Caen, France in October 2007 on the occasion of the world premiere of Barker's play The Dying of Today *by Guillaume Dujardin's* La Compagnie Mala Noche.

'About things on the stage'

With Elisabeth Angel-Perez et al

Elisabeth Angel-Perez (EAP)
Howard Barker (HB)
Alexandra Poulain (AP)
Sarah Hatchuel (SH)
Magali De Block (MDB)
Vanasay Khamphommala (VK)
François Gallix (FG)
Peter Buse (PB)
Claire Finburgh (CF)

EAP: You have written a number of plays in which objects play a prominent part. Could you explain why objects are of an interest to your theatre?

HB: Well, there's a paradox about the objects in theatre (and it doesn't for example apply to films), which is simply that the object is small. I'll be speaking as a writer and perhaps mostly as a director of plays – the object very often tends to be a small object, and, therefore, to use it in a scene is problematic because, quite simply, the audience cannot always see what is handled. For the making of a film, you would, of course, use a close-up, so you could see the value given the object in the way the object is handled by the actor and, therefore, it would enable it to have a life of its own. It's much harder to achieve this onstage. There's a declining fascination with the object because it's not visible enough. That's a practical problem.

AP: How do you resolve the problem of the visibility, or absence of visibility, of the object on the stage? Are there specific strategies in the writing, in the acting?

HB: Well, I think it's a particular problem for big theatres, for obvious reasons. I don't often direct plays in big theatres; I tend to do studio shows where the visibility problem is less important. But, quite simply, I suppose, on a big stage the strategy would be to direct the eye of the audience to the object by planning the moves and an effect of lighting on the object. For instance, if the thing had huge iconic significance, I would expect the lighting designer to isolate it. But it becomes a problem, a considerable problem, on a big stage. I don't think, for example, that 13 Objects would work anything like as well on the main stage of the Odéon – Théâtre de l'Europe as it would in a studio.

SH: Regarding the stage of the theatre itself or the playing area as objects, when you start writing a play do you have in mind a particular kind of stage? A big venue? An intimate space? A circular stage? Or not at all?

HB: I have to say I've clung to my naivety over the years in thinking that these plays should happen on big stages. I think of the spaces as having no edges, and on very rare occasions in my career I've worked in places where normally you're not supposed to do that; I'm thinking of the castle of Elsinore where we played *Gertrude* or factories and so on. Places where it was possible for the characters to emerge into the light from the dark, which is something that maybe originates from the etchings of Goya, where dark and light make an important *chiaroscuro* effect.

I suppose, in my mind, I've always imagined the significance of light playing on an actor, on the actor being able to move around in that light; and when I direct plays the lighting is very important. So I very rarely think of a small space and I don't think of a theatre as such, but I think of a big playing area. I would prefer not to play in theatres at all, because the theatres have been annexed by the bourgeois and commercial sphere. The foyer is a very destructive place. In the foyer people talk about their cars and their holidays.

You've observed [that] objects appear a lot in my work, but it's not actually because I'm that much fascinated by objects. The human body is vastly more important than any accoutrements or any items attached to it. Speaking as a writer, the beauty of the theatre is the body and the space, and how the body moves in this space and how the body is related to other bodies. But within a more general sense, human beings living in the world, objects carry with them associations, obviously; but, in a sense, they are a surface – a seductive surface – on which social neurosis and individual psychology operate. The character projects onto objects values and, indeed, negativities that wouldn't necessarily be discovered in a normal exchange between living personalities.

They're also, I think, essentially unfaithful – there's a decay concerning the moral value of objects. Let's take *13 Objects*: there's one piece about a painting by Holbein, in which a grotesquely rich character collects pictures and comes home with his unique Holbein portrait, and though he loves it – he adores the beauty of the object and its uniqueness – he decides to set light to it and to destroy it, which is an agony, but, at the same time, a triumph for him. He regards this unique work of art as entirely corrupted by the social system which has put value on the painting. Although he is a millionaire, he despises the concept of value, and it gives him, I suppose, a transgressive triumph to destroy something society places so much value on.

I think what made me write that piece was listening to the BBC reporting the latest sale at Sotheby's of an impressionist painting which was discussed only in terms of its value. So the character decides simply to transgress that kind of reification of a work of art by destroying it. It is an example of what I'm saying: the object exists in its own right but something is laid upon it and the object decays; there's a decay attached to it. Similarly with a soldier's medal (another one of the *13 Objects*). The medal is awarded to the soldier apparently for his bravery, and therefore it has a meaning at that moment. But it immediately begins to decay in a way an object literally decays. It decays morally at the same time. And other people who handle or see the medal reinterpret it for other ends, so one likes the object because it appears not to be plastic. The meanings we attach to objects alter their status continually.

My work is driven by two moral forces: one is coercion; the other is decay – those are the two rules of life, as far as my work is concerned, and the decay is attached both to people's ideals and to the meanings of objects.

EAP: In one of your plays, *Knowledge and a Girl*, we have the impression that the metonymic object defines both the function and the status of the character: "what is a Queen without her shoes?" is the question asked. And shoes are one of the most frequently used props in your plays.

HB: Yes, well, there are shoes and shoes, of course. The high heel shoe is what you're talking about. The high heel shoe has, I suggest, an investment of six hundred years of European culture behind it. I can't think of many easily obtained objects, that you could buy in the street, that have been invested so seriously for six hundred years, and which have developed form after form whilst retaining the whole idea of lifting the woman's body.

I was reading recently about the court of Dionysius in Syracuse in the fourth century BC. This corrupt dictator of Syracuse forced the servants of his household to wear one high heel shoe. This is a very great subtlety of eroticism, because if you're wearing one high heel shoe, it forces your hips to move in a certain way, which has a huge erotic value. It also of course endows the person wearing it with a certain state.

Talking about the Queen, wearing those shoes meant having to look both higher than everybody else and to manoeuvre her body in certain ways.

EAP: You've written about 70 plays, several collections of poems, two important volumes of theatre theory, but you're also a wonderful painter. In your paintings, you do use a number of recurring objects, like tables or trays, and I was wondering how this relates to the use you make of objects and things in your plays. Is there a link at all?

HB: I find it terribly difficult to talk about that but I'll try. I have a great liking for white sheets, for example. But there's a personal origin for that. The women of my family were laundresses. So I saw a lot of sheets as a child. There's also a great beauty in the white sheet – a laundered sheet is strangely disturbing in the milieu of the theatre, because the theatre is a very dirty place. There's dirt and dust everywhere and when actors come to rehearsal they come in dirty clothes, and I always say to actors, "No, would you please try to wear nice clothes in rehearsals because it changes the milieu?" So, if you use pristine sheets as part of the setting design, it produces a shock. It's an enchanting visual image. It's also cheap, which is a very important consideration in theatre as I work in it. Sheets are cheap!

MDB: Talking of the importance of sheets in your work, I noticed handkerchiefs were also quite present in your plays [...] how important are they in your work? Do you see them as a reduced image of sheets?

HB: It's also in Chekhov, I think, "Madam you've dropped your handkerchief. Here it is". So it's a seduction device. If a handkerchief is removed from a pocket it has a small explosive effect. These details are important in productions.

EAP: In your production of *Gertrude – The Cry* at the Riverside Studios in London, you did use quite a good number of sheets [...]

HB: Yes, I did. I also did in a production of *He Stumbled*. The whole business of laundering, washing and arranging sheets – which people don't do much any more – has a great historic function. And it's interesting visually, it is an action. If you have a sheet, you have to perform an action with it. It's in many ways more interesting than a gun. A gun is a cliché in theatre.

EAP: Shoes, handkerchiefs and sheets – things that are related to the human body, obviously. So, what is behind objects in your theatre is the human body.

HB: Yes, there are other plays you mentioned. A one-woman play, I'm thinking, *Und*. There's a Jewish woman who is waiting for the visit of a German officer and pretends she's giving a tea party for the German officer and he never appears, but things keep entering her world and these things are flying on trays. In production, the trays were flying on mechanical swings, and on each tray, kept in a proper horizontal line, is an object which, for her, has a meaning which you can't always work out. It could be a heap of earth, some flowers, a pen, all sorts of things. So, her consciousness is continually being shaken by the appearance of an object which has cultural significance.

EAP: Cultural significance?

HB: Yes. In her case, the pen is not just a pen. If she were to use the pen, how would she use it to create an effect on the man, who's not present, by a certain form of writing? What does the writing mean in such a form, and so on […]?

In 'Cruel Cup, Kind Saucer' (*13 Objects*), the cup is a coffee cup. When the scene is played, it's not simply that the actress plays with the idea of holding a coffee cup, but it's the way in which she handles this object which is very significant, because it has a spoon. And the way in which the actress should deal with the coffee cup and the spoon is extremely important: there's a rhythm to handling of the object. She should stir it a number of times and put the spoon into the cup, and when the spoon falls onto the saucer, there's a certain sound that we all recognize. This gives a sort of discipline to the performance. So, the object can sometimes discipline the actor. The final object is the dead body, because for me the living body is not an object. The dead body is a surface, a permissive surface. Because if we speak of necrophilia for a moment, one can endow the silent cadaver with meaning that no living body could possibly possess. It lends power to the observer.

EAP: Are you thinking of *Judith* – the climax of which precisely revolves around a scene of necrophilia – for instance?

HB: I'm thinking of *Judith*, yes.

EAP: In terms of *13 Objects*: you have selected a number of objects which generate action, is that right?

HB: Or thought, thinking.

EAP: So, objects are the departure point; you chose them for their suggestive power but also for their dynamic power.

VK: One of the objects you chose was a rattle which becomes a substitute for language in *The Talk of a Toy*, and since you're also a poet, I wanted to ask you to what extent language could be compared to an object, or words be compared to objects.

HB: That's a good question and a good example of how an object has a percussive, almost musical action which, in some ways, serves my language. I expect language to be performed in a way that respects the internal rhythms and the rhymes which are inside those lines. I'm not sure whether this works in translation, but in the English original there's a strong rhythm in that speech and in the way the shaking of the rattle commands attention, So, speech delivered by actors in my work is [engaged in] a continued challenge to be heard. I'm not a naturalistic writer, so the actual speech is a deliberate act of the characters in order to provoke

141

a response. Everything is a challenge, and I suppose the rattle is a challenge, to attract attention. So I'd say that it has a linguistic value.

EAP: In this respect, what about the way you organize words on the page?

HB: That commands a certain rhythm. The way in which speech is organized on the page is to direct the actor, to some extent, to obey the rhythms of the speech. It's a suggestive device.

VK: When I was talking of the linguistic value, I was also thinking about the almost iconic value of words and their power to conjure up the image of the object. The first scene of 13 Objects deals with a spade and it acquires a second meaning [...] It seems to me that in your work the words are heavy with history so that they don't just signify for themselves but they also signify a history that is hidden behind.

HB: I don't disagree with what you're saying. I think most of my plays are very heavy with culture or history. Not because they are set in historical periods or imaginary and mythical periods; they can only exist in that form because of my very powerful sense of being a European.
        I suppose the spade is an example of that. But it's also, in a way, about how the individual psyche plays with that very element. The play is about an officer playing with two prisoners whom he wishes to bury alive and then enjoy the spectacle of people dying. He watches them dig. So, he's forever making ethical and personal judgements about the style of dying. The spade becomes a matter of life and death because, if they don't dig properly, they will die. But what it is to dig properly is entirely in the officer's mind. This is getting obscure, isn't it?

FG: Keeping in mind what you said about objects never being innocent, have you found in your plays that objects have different meanings according to the nationality of the audience? You mentioned a cup of tea and stirring the spoon in the cup of tea [...] in an Arabian country, you drink tea and you never stir it. Have you come across some wrong interpretation of an object which was misunderstood because it was translated?

HB: That's a very good point, but the simple answer is no, I haven't. That's because my work is not so much performed outside Europe or America. There have been some Arabian productions of my work, but I'm afraid I have not seen them. But it reminds us of the idea of gesture [...] it's the same thing, I suppose. I'm very interested in gesture onstage and I'm aware that as Europeans, we have a kind of repertoire of gestures, most of which goes back, probably, to ancient Rome and Greece. One has to go to a museum of classical statues to realize that gestures used in classical times still continue in our own time. I suspect, however, if one went to Africa there would be a different set of gestures – that's interesting. I'm very careful not to resort to gestures as such in my work.

VK: You said your relationship to objects was very much defined by the fact that you were a European; was that a major influence in your choice of objects? One of the things that struck me in *13 Objects* is that there seem to be connections within the scene and yet, at the same time, your choice seems arbitrary. It seems that there is a subtle interplay between arbitrariness and causality. Is that possible and how did you choose these thirteen objects?

HB: I hope what you're saying is true, because it's much more interesting if a text consists of both the arbitrary and the intentional. I think as I got to number thirteen, I was running out of objects [...] because I had selected the number thirteen before I started. So, as I got to ten, I was starting to scrape the bottom of the barrel to find the other three. Inevitably in a piece of thirteen, some are going to be more effective than others. The best one in my opinion is the camera. The mystery of the camera has been explored, mostly by French philosophers, but we know that the camera is an amazing and fascinating object, and so is the photograph. Because the boy speculates when the father gives him a camera as a present, he is continually looking the other way round to try and see what's in the back of the camera. In a way, that's quite a primitive reaction but he asks himself all the time, "what has this camera seen? What is the moral value of the experience of the camera? Has it seen a football team? Maybe it has. Has it seen a soldier who is about to be killed in a war? Has it seen an atrocity? Has it seen many endless families portrayed?" and so on. As an object, it has much more detritus inside it than many objects one could think of. We all know when a writer is inspired by something, he writes more fluently, and I think that's the most fluent of them. I like cameras.

PB: I saw *He Stumbled* a few years ago in Salford, and what you have said made me understand better your choice of the surgical instruments, because, of course, they have a reflective value. It seems to me that there's even an element of sadism in them, because I remember being blinded, quite often, by reflections and sonic values – it almost sounded as though these objects had been chosen arbitrarily, but they still retained their meaning within the story about a surgeon, but is that important?

HB: That's a very good point. It's again a decision made after I had written the piece. When I directed this piece, I tried to organize quite a simple, but semi-surreal action between the actors, especially the opening section before the audience comes in and takes its seats. It is an action which is repetitive but also quite intriguing, which I call 'exordium' (in German 'vorspiel'). I had a surgeon's assistant wash all these instruments (scalpels and surgeon's knives) and she picked one, wiped it with a towel and threw it into the bucket. Underneath the bucket was a microphone. So, not only were people performing the actions in various ways, but she was creating this deliberate, slightly sinister sound of a knife falling into a bucket. I think of these things at a later stage, rather than before I write.

EAP: A question about literary objects, such as tales, legends and myths, and the way you manipulate them in your Theatre of Catastrophe, the aim of which, I assume, is to create some kind of disruption from what is expected or dismissed. Can you say a few words about those literary objects that are so well codified?

HB: Because I also paint, I've always been interested in how contemporary artists, and artists throughout time, always go back to the same subjects. There are certain themes which you would find in any provincial gallery in France or Britain, and one of these is Judith and Holofernes. There are thousands of versions of Judith and Holofernes painted between the sixteenth and the twentieth centuries, and, somehow, I'm drawn to do my version of this haunting story. I've also done it with myths, such as Helen of Troy, and The Last Supper, but also canonical works such as *Uncle Vanya*, or *Minna von Barnhelm*, or *King Lear*). I almost feel an obligation, as an artist of my time, to revisit some of the themes of the past, as well as contributing new narratives of my own. In that sense, I feel I'm both in a tradition and outside it.

In retelling those stories I bring a whole different consciousness to the story, not entirely to shock people. To take Chekhov for example, the initial function degenerates or, as time goes by, is perceived differently. *Uncle Vanya*, as a text, is a major work of theatre. It is played continually and always, to me, with the same nauseating pleasure in impotence that lies somewhere in that productive process. It's a celebration of failure. So I ask myself, 'what is the socio-political reason why *Uncle Vanya* has now become so significant in England at this particular moment?' It's as if the culture has innovated, but, at the same time, it is seductive, and we all see the image of innovation as seduction and, therefore, we are all gratified by it. We all leave the theatre thinking, 'Uncle Vanya wanted to seduce Helena, he failed to seduce Helena, but that's alright because seduction is such a hard job anyway'. And there's a sort of decadence in that. So, when I rewrote it, I wrote it from the moment in which Vanya, in Chekhov's version, misses the professor [with a gunshot]. In my version the bullet hits the professor, which, of course, initiates one choice after another. My version is action, whereas I would say that Chekhov's version is inactive. Mine is tragedy and his isn't. That's an example of how I might attack an existing property.

EAP: A word about the object of objects – the Bible in *The Last Supper*.

HB: As I've got older, I've liked the Bible more. I suppose, as a subject of stories, a kind of reservoir of narratives. I was always interested in why Jesus asked God to relieve him of the responsibility of his own mission and how he panics. It makes me convinced that Christ's story is true because Christ panics, and I think that's very human. The humanity of Christ is simultaneously the failure of Christ.

EAP: In the earlier plays, *Wounds to the Face* for instance, plays that you wrote at the end of the 1980s, which, along with all the texts (such as *The Last Supper* and *The Castle*) that consecrated this new theatre – the Theatre of Catastrophe – you came up with a disturbing amount of reified persons, like the dead baby stuck in the back of Skinner in *The Castle*. How does that connect with the reification of human beings? Or does it at all? As a spectator, when I first saw *Wounds to the Face*, I was really struck by the incredible number of objects, like the mirror, which helped the human being to be reified somehow [...] In the Theatre of Catastrophe, is the object summoned so as to facilitate the reification of the human being?

HB: To come back to the culture of Europe, the actual destruction of the human body in the West has been so persistent – not just by having fought two huge wars in the last century, but by having wars constantly since the medieval period – the body becomes a kind of sacred object in terms of its illustrative value, its pornographic value and so on. At the same time, the amount of sheer destruction of the body is drastic.

Let's take the example of Helen of Troy – whose body, according to the legend, produced the Ten Year War. Her body is now, perhaps, regarded as a metaphor for something else, because no one accepts primitive narratives except as metaphors. But I wanted to reverse that and say that, yes, indeed this body had been quite simply the cause of the war; the possession of a woman's body justified a cultural conflict. But, at the same time, it suggests this idea only because her body has reached a point of maturity, and because its meaning has started to change. It is a site, not of adoration, but of punishment. The relics of her flesh continue to exercise a strange and magical authority because, even if Helen is reduced to a trunk and a head in this text, she's still revered because she was a beautiful woman. Then she acquires the additional authority of someone who suffered because, in western culture, the suffering of the body is something immense – it's almost religious. From Christ onwards, the body which suffers acquires this value, and I was trying to put these two aspects together.

EAP: On the reification of the body, a question that is probably very often put to you about the nakedness of women. We've just had this paper (by Claire Finburgh) on your *Judith*, and there was this idea that having a woman naked on the stage was perhaps a way of turning her into a body or a body-thing, an object. I know you're very often asked this type of question about the nakedness of women, but still [...]

HB: Let's go back to the origin; I've been trying to intellectualize what I do a lot, but, in fact, I work for the theatre, so let's go back to basics […] The theatre is a particular space in a dark room in which the human body moves around. To exclude the naked body from that space seems to me, in essence, a strange form of censorship, a meaningless form of censorship.

On the other hand, there was a period in the English, and in the French, theatre now, which has returned to an over-familiarity with the human body; it has almost become stereotypical. For me, it has a great value in creating a moment of shock, but the body also speaks. The naked body which speaks, and speaks in a poetic way about itself, I regard it as a very great moment of the theatrical experience. Not like in a film, this actor or actress is naked in front of you; she's in light, intense light; you're in the dark – you share none of her ordeal. I find it so purely theatrical I know nothing else like this in any other art form. Because that body is alive, it may be beautiful, it may not be beautiful, but in either case it carries a huge status. It then describes itself, speaks about itself, in a particular tongue. I don't know anyone who works as a dramatist who wouldn't want to use those moments, to examine those moments.

To be naked onstage is both to be vulnerable and to be powerful simultaneously. When we take our clothes off in front of somebody else, we are nervous. We experience anxiety, and that anxiety, in the focus of the stage, becomes vastly increased. You then ask your actor to carry that nakedness with confidence, but, at the same time, to bear the tension of it. She can't merely be relaxed with her nakedness. I understand that in some classes you're asked to be naked and relaxed, but I'm saying, 'no, don't be relaxed, otherwise it becomes a cliché', as though you're in your bedroom on your own, and that's not the point.

On the stage you suffer the gaze of another person and you suffer the gaze of the public. That tension must be there; it must be in the body. So, you're an object, but, at the same time, you bear the anxiety of the public. For me, one of the great effects of tragedy, as I write it, as I think of it, is that it should make you anxious. You should leave the auditorium anxious about your life, about their lives. It's not a process of gratification, a process of repetition or a process of massage for your morality. You must leave tensed from what the actors have suffered for you. The actress suffers for the audience.

EAP: It means that your actors undergo some sort of sacrifice?

HB: Yes, they're sacrificed.

CF: About nakedness, it strikes me that we have no problem at all seeing nakedness on the TV or in the cinema; we are desensitized to it, and I think one of the reasons for that, especially regarding the female body, is that it is, on the screen, reduced to a sequence of objects because we never really see the whole of a woman's body. We will see fetishized aspects of that body, generally the face, breasts or genitals. It strikes me that what can potentially be very powerful about nakedness in theatre, from the perspective of a woman, is that the audience is confronted with the whole of the woman's body. I wondered if you'd agree with this idea of objectification of the female body.

HB: I suppose so, because the presentation of the female body in pornography and in commercials tends to be stereotypical. As you say, certain zones of the body are selected for attention. But these are presumably erotic zones. Especially with the living body, one could create some serious psychic damage by reversing some of that, so you would see bits you'd normally not see. It could happen on film, but it would be more powerful onstage because the body is alive.

EAP: With this question of anxiety, and almost angst, we're reaching the very heart of the Theatre of Catastrophe. One of the things that I've noticed in your theatre is that each time you use an object in your catastrophist plays, the use which is made of it never conforms to one's expectations.

HB: I'm not sure that this is particular to my Theatre of Catastrophe. Any artist worth his salt would strain to avoid cliché. He re-stimulates the deadliness [of an object or image].

EAP: Do you see any ethical value in objects?

HB: Maybe, but I don't think I'm an ethical person, so I don't think in those terms. My plays have very little ethics. I don't think of my projects as moral in the least. The theatre is a place where one need not be moral. The pleasure of marginalized theatre evades morals. My theatre company has almost been destroyed by the ethical judgement of the government. Ethics have continually attacked artists, and theatre artists in particular, in their space. The funding of English theatre is based on moral judgements about the content. That's what I call censorship, and that's where we are.

MDB: About the authority of things: *Tin* and *Navy Blue* in *13 Objects*. On the one hand, *Tin* is about the usurpation of the medal as a way to assert the character's poetic authority, whereas *Navy Blue* has a contrapuntal approach, because we don't know to whom the shoes belong. I was wondering if objects could be a way to get rid of ethics and morals, and, pushing this idea further, if things could be a way to assert someone's poetic authority and identity.

HB: The object is essentially neutral. Its meaning comes from the way the actors describe this object and how they manipulate it, and how that contrasts or supports the social value of the object. The medal is a good example: the soldier is awarded a medal because he is said to have been brave, so it has a social value for all of us, but the reinterpretation of that occurs when other characters within the scene deny that meaning; they choose to deny the meaning of the medal. It reverts to being a piece of tin. It is tin because it is emptied of its social value. But then the soldier finally comes back and says to the Old Woman, "I'll have it, after all, because, even if the war was unjust and the King is a fool, nevertheless my action was extraordinary and I shall never repeat it in my life, and for that I should wear the medal". He reinvigorates the medal, not from a social and political point of view, but from a personal point of view. The medal then becomes the locus of the judgement of himself. In other words he personalizes and validates a corrupted symbol. In a very short scene (one page) the meaning of the object changes three times.

VK: I wanted to go back to the idea of the atomized body and the whole body by comparing them to the contrasts between different types of plays in your work, namely your collections of smaller plays and plays which are full narratives. Could you explain the relationship between the two and how you alternate between the two?

HB: When I was very young, I tended to write very small pieces. And then, for some reason, I started to write three-act plays; I don't really know why I did so. Since then, I've always alternated between very long plays (four or five-act plays) and collections of small pieces. One of the joys of small pieces, like *Wounds to the Face*, is that they have a sort of a musical form. I'm a great admirer of Bartok's *Six Strings Quartets*, one of the most important modern European composers. [I'm fascinated by] the ways in which themes are taken, distorted and played against themselves, dropped, lost, revived and brought back in; this dominates my whole approach to *Wounds to the Face*. Pieces like that – whilst they accumulate meaning – don't normally generate intense emotional engagement. I have to say that I don't think the audience of *Wounds to the Face* would be intensely emotionally engaged in the story. Whereas watching *Gertrude*, *He Stumbled* or *The Castle* should, if the acting is operated properly, entail a very painful experience for the public. That's the symphony.

EAP: As opposed to the rhapsody?

HB: Yes.

This interview took place at the University of Paris-Sorbonne (Paris IV), on 12 October 2007. Howard Barker was the keynote speaker of the 'Things on the stage' International conference, co-organized by Texte et Critique du Texte and Société d'Études Anglaises Contemporaines. It has been published in Etudes Britanniques Contemporaines 35 *(Montpellier: Université Paul-Valéry, 2008).*

Transcript: Magali de Block.

13 Objects. Sarah Belcher. The Wrestling School, 2003. Photo credit Robert Day

'Ecstasy and the extremes of emotional life'

With Mark Brown

Mark Brown (MB)
Howard Barker (HB)
Hugh Hodgart (HH)

MB: Your work is very well regarded internationally; we'll come onto the question of England maybe little later. Recently, for example, on a trip to Portugal, I noticed that your reinterpretation of Chekhov's *Uncle Vanya* was being produced in Almada, and it's normal, as you travel around the world, to find Barker productions cropping up here and there. How do you account for your reception internationally?

HB: Well, I could reverse that and say, 'How do you account for the fact that I'm not so celebrated in my own country?', which, I suppose, is the same question in reverse really. I suspect most European theatre activists find these texts open to interpretation, although they're very dense [...] They are open to a range of interpretations, and they don't carry a moral content, at least not a visible one; it's impossible to write a work without it having some kind of moral meaning, simply by virtue of it being a narrative, but it doesn't have an overt message. For the English that's a big problem; I can't speak for the Scots, but I always think of Scotland as a European country, and England as, unfortunately, not one. The prejudice against my work in England is predicated on something that probably goes back to the Reformation, which is the idea of the utility of works of art. These plays have no use.

We could ask these actors [in the Royal Scottish Academy of Music and Drama production of *Wounds to the Face*], 'What is the use of playing this play?', socially – not the use of it for an actor; for an actor it's a pleasure to play, I'm aware of that – but in terms of what it does to an audience, it doesn't have a very ostensible use value. You don't leave the theatre thinking, as Brecht would have liked you to have done, 'time to storm the police station'; it doesn't enable you to do that. In fact, it produces the opposite effect; it produces an effect of some kind of disengagement, I think, of confusion, of moral decay. That's a problem for the English; I don't think it's a problem for the French, Germans, Slovenes and the other people who are kind enough to do my work. In fact, it fits very much into a European tradition.

What makes Europe the greatest culture in history is a conflict between the rational and the irrational that's not represented in any other culture in the world. The obvious examples are Hitler and Stalin, although they meet in the middle in a funny sort of way. But if you go back through European culture, particularly, say, in writing, arguably the greatest novelist of the twentieth century is Louis-Ferdinand Céline, the French writer, who's an outright collaborator with the Nazis, a racist and a right winger without any hesitation, but an incredible writer, a brilliant writer. And you could put opposite him Thomas Mann, a great humanist, wonderful narrative writer as well, with a huge moral impetus. These elements are repeated over and over again in European culture. So, where I'm situated within that spectrum is not a problem for European audiences.

MB: You write in the 'Fortynine asides for a tragic theatre' that tragedy, "dares to be beautiful", and then you ask, "who talks of beauty in the theatre any more? They think it is to do with the costumes". What is the source of beauty in a tragic theatre and, more particularly, in the Theatre of Catastrophe?

HB: Pain itself is beautiful when it's represented dramatically. Tragedy is about pain, and it's about voyeurism, to some extent; it's about watching the pain of a person, or a group of individuals, on the stage. The moment you put an action on the stage, of course, it changes; it's not the same as an action in the street. The theatre of the 1950s, and it still happens at the Royal Court, rather insists that the street and the theatre are the same thing; I would say they were never the same thing: the street is the street, and the theatre is the theatre.

Once you're in a darkened room, it is not the street. The fact is, it completely alters your perception of an event. A murder or a passionate love act committed on the stage is quite different from one committed in the street, and pain, in that context, acquires a certain beauty. It seems to me society requires pain, civility requires pain. We must suffer, we *do* suffer, individually, but also collectively we must suffer. Tragedy makes suffering its business, and it makes it beautiful.

How does it do that? That's a matter for staging, to some extent, but also tragedy makes poetry its discourse. Tragic acting is not about naturalism; it's not like telly – it requires a highly developed skill, and a love of language – if you want to play tragedy, you've got to love language, you've got to want to speak it to people and move them, and hypnotize them with the power of the poetry. You're creating an experience which is, essentially, very beautiful, even though its subject matter is often frightful.

Some critics call this sort of thing 'pessimism' – I don't know why. If there were ever useless terms in criticism they are 'pessimism' and 'optimism'; they're redundant terms. It's not pessimistic to die, you just die. It's got many meanings, but it's not pessimistic, and tragedy knows that, and it brings death to you, and it brings death to the life of the audience. We cannot live without death, it conditions our whole existence. Which is why I argue that tragedy has never been out of date and never will be.

MB: In a sense, you've begun to answer the question I wanted to ask you next. You've spoken of your admiration of a number of modern European poets: Rilke, Apollinaire and so on. Do you feel that the art form to which theatre is closest – or, at least, the art form to which it should be closest – is poetry?

HB: Yes, I do. I think a good writer inevitably develops a voice. If you're a naturalistic writer, you don't need a voice; that's the conundrum of naturalism. In fact, you can't tell one naturalistic play from another.

MB: We know about the hostility with which your work is treated by much of the English theatre establishment, but nonetheless you have had as friends of your work many actors; Ian McDiarmid is an obvious example, and Kenny Ireland, the actor and director, was a founding member of your own company The Wrestling School. How do you account for that strong bond that seems to develop between actors and your work?

HB: Actors like to speak. It's that simple. It's funny, sometimes when you audition young actors, some of them actually don't want to speak. It's an odd experience. You ask a young actor to come in and read a text that has maybe got fifteen or twenty lines in it, and they don't really want to. You know they're not really the kind of actors you want to work with. They may be good on television, they may be good on film, but others want to give you that text, especially if it's got a rhythm in it, which good writing has. They really want to deliver that text to the public, to you. And it becomes erotic, the whole experience of a great performance. Ian McDiarmid, who you mentioned, and Juliet Stevenson, another actress I've worked with a great deal, have an immaculate ability to lift meaning off the line immediately and to find the rhythm in that line. They react to it viscerally, sexually even, I think.

There's a very good quote from Friedrich Nietzsche, who knew a great deal about drama, although he was not a dramatist, who said – and it should be written on the wall in a room like this (a studio theatre at the Royal Scottish Academy of Music and Drama) – "if you don't know the rhythm of a sentence, you don't know the meaning of it". That's why an actor doesn't have to be an intellectual. An actor can play the most complex meanings within a speech without actually knowing what the writer thought, what the writer's intentions were, and all this stuff, it's not important. What *is* important is that they pick up the rhythm and deliver the rhythm, and then instinctively they know what they're saying. You can always tell in rehearsals, I think, when someone doesn't know what they're saying, because they can't get the rhythm right, and you think, 'that sentence is wrong, it's not in balance'. And you ask them what they think they're saying, and suddenly it's revealed, they didn't know what they were saying, because they haven't got the rhythm. The rhythm's critical. And my writing does that [provides meaning through rhythm] for them; it gives them a great experience in that way.

Also, it's constantly about confrontation. It's obvious in *Wounds to the Face*, people are always up against each other, they're at the extremes of their emotional life, and there's some ecstasy at play.

MB: My next question is in respect of your writing – whether it is your plays or your writing about theatre – and your speaking about theatre in forums like this. At all times you seem extremely self-assured, and sometimes you've observed that others may consider that to be an arrogance; I don't [perceive an arrogance], but I do perceive a profound sense of self-assuredness. So, I suppose the question is do you agree that you are a particularly self-assured writer? [Barker laughs, audience laughs]. And secondly, within that, does that assuredness come from having found your own artistic voice?

HB: I wrote my first play and had it performed when I was about 25, at the Royal Court, and it has to be said I've had a pretty dire time in English theatre since 1971, or whenever it was. If I hadn't developed some carapace in which to conceal myself I'd probably have committed suicide; and I don't mean to self-dramatize, but you know I've had a bad time in England. So, you have to find ways of solving that problem.

One of those was to write theory. You talk about my theory books; having been under sustained attack from the English [theatre] establishment for a very long time, over the last fifteen years or so, I thought if no one else would speak on my behalf, I ought to do it, [addressing Mark Brown] because you weren't around then [audience laughs]. So my first book [of theory] was an *apologia pro vita sua* [defence of my life]; I was trying to defend what I was doing. I had to find a critical framework in which to justify instinct, because a good writer is, first and foremost, instinctive; you do it because you have to do it. Then, afterwards, you look for a way of describing what you've done. If *Wounds to the Face* were a new play that hadn't been performed before, I couldn't have talked about it. When I'd seen it, then I'd be able to talk about it.

Having been able to write some theory, I felt a bit protected from the hounding I was getting. If I sound self-pitying, I'm not; that's how it goes. People have hard times, and some of the writers I most admire in the world have suffered vastly more persecution than I have [he laughs], and, as you pointed out, in other countries things are a lot better.

So, yes, self-assurance is a way of protecting myself against the pain of some pretty awful reviewing.

MB: You've written plays for the radio, and you've spoken very warmly of radio drama as a neglected art form. I have to say, it's probably [BBC] Radio 4's fault, but I personally have a prejudice against radio drama, but I'm interested in your liking for this genre, particularly as the body appears to play such an important part in your stage drama. What's the basis of your attraction to radio drama?

HB: It's loyalty, in one way, because the BBC did my first plays – in fact, my work was presented on radio before it was first put on stage.[5] But, then, I'm not a very loyal person, so that probably isn't the key to that.

I know no one listens to radio in a darkened room any more – but that's how I used to listen to it as a kid, when my parents would turn the lights out. What I like about [radio drama] is that the actors, with the very few effects that are available – which are very primitive on radio – are obliged to create visuality from invisibility. That's rather exciting, I think. That [excitement] still lingers. Recently, because it was my sixtieth birthday, the BBC did a play of mine on Radio 4, for once – normally I'm consigned to Radio 3, which is the obscure bit.

I wrote a play about a sixteenth-century humanist scholar who was secretly a murderer. We got into this tiny room – radio studios are getting smaller all the time; technically you can do it in a bedroom now, which you couldn't do fifteen years ago – and I sat there with Michael Pennington, who was playing this scholar, who was meant to be walking down a muddy road in Eastern Poland in the rain. He just walked in a tray of earth while speaking the lines from the text. It's primitive and rather extraordinary. It sounded wonderful when he heard it. I'll always feel a certain affection for radio drama.

But, yes, the body's important to me onstage, absolutely.

HH: You were saying earlier, Howard, that the thing about radio [drama] is that it's done very quickly.

HB: You have to take it off, the actor has to get it right first time. There's no rehearsal in radio, frankly. You cast it correctly or you fail.

MB: In a sense the final question I was going to ask you has already been answered. I wanted to keep the question of England to last, because it's very easy, certainly for English journalists, to present you as an oppositionist playwright, and I wanted to talk positively about your theatre, rather than discuss it in the negative.

It seems to me quite clear that in Scotland your work is more widely and broadly supported than it is in England. You only have to look at the work here at the Academy, and also to recent productions at the Lyceum in Edinburgh, Dundee Rep and Strathclyde Theatre Group here in Glasgow – a semi-professional company which did a very good production of A Hard Heart a couple of years ago. To the hilarity of myself, I have to say, and I'm sure of some other people, Pitlochry Festival Theatre – arguably Scotland's most conservative theatre– has actually put The Castle on its shortlist for next year; whether it actually makes the six [plays] that go on the programme is another matter, but [it's] very interesting to see a theatre of the nature of Pitlochry Festival Theatre actually broaching the possibility of staging your work.[6]

In a sense, you've already partly answered this question, in terms of your belief that Scotland is more of a European nation [than England]. Is that really what it comes down to?

HB: I don't know. There's a Ph.D. to be written, perhaps several, on why my work evidently cannot ever be staged in the National Theatre in England. It is a place that's got huge resources, huge stages; I write big plays. If anyone should have plays in the National Theatre, it should be me. Except, of course, for the key point, which is that ideologically I don't fit.

I don't want to get into the big debate about national theatres – you've got your own arguments about that here [in Scotland] as well – but it seems to me that the national theatre does speak the national ideology, otherwise it wouldn't be a national theatre; that's one of its defining characteristics, presumably. Its remit is to produce the best work of its time, but, in effect, it must carry the burden of contemporary thinking, or perhaps one should say contemporary prejudice. The National Theatre of England doesn't celebrate the Queen or the Empire any more, obviously, so what does it represent? It represents the consensus of a broadly liberal humanist society, one of the pretentions of which is that it's critical, it criticizes society, rather like the *Guardian* newspaper pretends to criticize society. So, the writers they [the National Theatre in London] will employ will appear to be serving the critical agenda.

Those who know *Wounds to the Face* know it's not a critical play. A poor soldier comes home with half his face missing, but it's not a pacifist play, I'm not a pacifist. If it was a pacifist play, it probably would have been put on at the National Theatre. Do you see the difference?

You have to fit these criteria – as you do for the Arts Council if you want funding, although that's another story – but there are criteria. At the National Theatre they are hidden criteria, but they nevertheless exist, and if you don't match them, you probably won't be performed.

MB: I don't want to lobby too publicly, but I do hope it's not too long before we see the National Theatre of Scotland producing Howard's work, but that's a matter for the current directors of the NTS […] but I know that it's been broached [audience laughs].

This interview was conducted as part of the symposium on 'The Theatre of Howard Barker' at the Royal Scottish Academy of Music and Drama, Glasgow, on 24 May 2008. The symposium was held on the occasion of Hugh Hodgart's Royal Scottish Academy of Music and Drama production of Barker's Wounds to the Face. *An audio recording of the interview was first made available on the website www.theatrevoice.com.*

'A rupture to the moral curve'

With Elizabeth Sakellaridou

Elizabeth Sakellaridou (ES)
Howard Barker (HB)

ES: You haven't dealt much with classical material. In *The Dying of Today* what was it that drew you to ancient history, the particular event of the Sicilian war and the particular historian, Thucydides?

HB: Of course I dealt with classical material. Remember I did *The Bite of the Night* around the myth of the Trojan War, which was a pretty long tragedy. And I know a lot about Greek history. We did it at school. I read it as a boy. Thucydides is one of my favourite writers and I know about the Sicilian expedition from him and from other historians who refer to it.

ES: Did Plutarch's story about the barber and the stranger come to you as a separate source or in combination with Thucydides' history, which, by the way, does not mention the incident?

HB: It came separately. Concerning the barber incident, you are quite right. It is in Plutarch. I quite like Plutarch, he is in my library. So I must have read the story there and then lost it in my memory. I must also say that I like messengers, I am fascinated by the news they bring. But I also like barbers myself. I have very good relations with barbers, such as my own barber, whom I have had for over ten years. I like old barbers' shops, with all the items they have around. They are nothing like modern hairdressers' shops. Those old shops tend to disappear, you hardly see them any longer. I have been drawn to barbers since I was a child. I had my hair cut as a child by two barbers and they had both lost their legs in the First World War. I have written a poem on this. You will find it in my prose book *A Style and Its Origins.*[7]

ES: I must say that I was struck and amused by another extended reference to barbers in another play, *Dead Hands*. Is this a coincidence? I think you were writing these two plays around the same time?

HB: There is no connection between the two plays, certainly not a conscious one.

ES: Given that the two protagonists create a strong dialectical relationship in the play, would you say that your sympathies lie equally with both or is Dneister the one you would identify with as a character?

HB: I suppose I would identify with him. Dneister is an artist because he is interested in how people are affected and he is the one who manipulates the other. What many people miss in the play is that Dneister does not tell the story himself. He has the barber tell it. How? This is a mystery. By instinct he tells things he does not know, yet the fact that they have happened he deduces by his own experience in the army.

ES: Something like a divination?

HB: Yes, that's the word, divination.

ES: So you have no sympathy for the barber as a character?

HB: Sympathy? No. I do not have sympathy. This is not how I write, with sympathy for the characters. I simply expose them as they are.

ES: What I mean by sympathy with the barber is, 'are you are interested in him as a character?'

HB: No, I am not. I think sadists, who draw pleasure from manipulating other people, are more interesting than victims.

ES: At the closure of the play, when the barber gives this extraordinary line, "Goodbye, I said", whose is the greater tragedy, I wonder, the barber's, who has lost everything, or Dneister's, who has nowhere to go? It seems to me that, when the narrative – which kept them both constituted and in context – is over, they are both utterly dislocated and they disintegrate.

HB: I think Dneister is in worse trouble. The barber will be killed. As Strabo says, "culture disappears, civilisation dies", and the barber will go down with it. He is happy to do this. The barber has loyalty to the city and he is willing to die for it. Dneister has no loyalty. He is a mere witness. And the boat is gone. He has missed it.

ES: Certainly, after the storytelling is over, it would take him a while to create another context for himself and find another victim.

HB: Yes, but one has to think of the realistic facts as well. The boat has gone. Perhaps missing the boat was a deliberate decision for Dneister.

ES: It is my impression that this play, *The Dying of Today*, is one of the most controlled, balanced, precise and complete tragedies you have written; it is austere and orchestrated, like a musical piece or a choreography. I can only compare it to another two plays I love equally, *Judith* and *Und*. There is something classical about them all, though I find this one the best of all in terms of tragic achievement. In your other plays there is a baroque element that gives them a different character. What is your attitude to all this?

HB: Yes, I quite agree. I see your point. On the whole I don't like small theatre. My instinct as an artist is not to work with known territory. I don't like domestic places. I want ideas to burst out. It's the act of diffusion I admire in things.

ES: Precisely. Even *The Dying of Today* or the other two plays I mentioned are not about domestic places. They open up to the world, to greater issues.

HB: Quite right. As to what you said about music; take Bartok, for instance. What I like about Bartok, as a string quartet composer, is that a theme, an idea, comes in again and again, [and] it keeps returning and developing.

ES: What is your definition of modern tragedy and, if you have one, does it align you at all with any identifiable tragic tradition – either the classical or a later European one – or would you consider your Theatre of Catastrophe a completely iconoclastic one?

HB: It is not iconoclastic. It has to do with tradition, though I do not know which tradition. The Greek? The Shakespearean? But it does not seek retribution; there is no punishment, no catharsis; the characters go like that, there is no payment.

ES: Your theatre has often been compared to Jacobean tragedy, which is dark, full of crime and transgression.

HB: But there is severe punishment in it. The characters pay strongly for it. What I am trying to do is to bring a rupture to the moral curve.

ES: Surely it is very difficult to find a general formula for tragedy, concerning morality, even between the three Greek tragedians. Aeschylus, Sophocles and Euripides are so different from each other. Euripides' Medea, for instance, is not punished for her crime at the end of the play. A chariot comes down and she is lifted to the skies. Euripides is a very subversive writer on issues of order and catharsis.

HB: Perhaps there is something in common between me and Euripides.

ES: I am glad you are saying this. I have always thought you share something in common with Euripides.

       Now, let me ask you a more general question. You are both a myth-maker and a myth-revisionist. Which way of writing is more delightful to you and in which do you think you can handle characters and situations more fully and more solidly?

HB: I feel as free with an existent myth as with one I construct totally on my own. Of course there is an obligation to deal with existing myths. We all feel that. But I feel very free with it. Take for example the new play I have written, which is called *Four Chinese Women*, which is based on a very brief story narrated by a colonial officer, Admiral Sir Roger Keyes. It is only this far that the influence goes. Then I develop my own story.

ES: What I meant by my question was whether, having a story or a myth already there, it is easier for you to structure the plot more fully and develop the characters more deeply.

HB: Shakespeare would always depend on stories told by other people. He would take them over and work on them. I take great pleasure in inventing my own stories, something totally new, things that people do not talk about. Take, for instance, *He Stumbled* or *I Saw Myself*. They are totally new, I invented them.

ES: Yes, I find them both strong, fascinating plays. They are original and convincing new myths.

HB: I am very proud when I do this.

This interview took place at Barker's home in Brighton on 16 July 2009 ahead of the Greek premiere of The Dying of Today. *It was originally published in the programme for that production, by the Nea Skini company at Cycladon Theatre, Athens in November 2009, directed by Lefteris Voyatzis.*

'On Shakespeare'

With Vanasay Khamphommala

Vanasay Khamphommala (VK)
Howard Barker (HB)

VK: How did you first come into contact with Shakespeare?

HB: My mother used to walk about the house reciting this one speech. She was from a very poor family and left school at fourteen, but she had done a Shakespeare play at school when she was a child in the 1920s and she remembered this one speech [From *King John*, Act IV, Scene I]:

[…] when I strike my foot
Upon the bosom of the ground, rush forth,
And bind the boy which you shall find with me […]

I've never traced it, but looking back, she used to walk around the house just saying this, because she liked the sound of it. She didn't know more than that […]
      Then, at school, we probably read *King Lear* and a comedy. I don't remember which one. Every schoolboy then – I don't know about now – did a Shakespeare play at about the age of fourteen.

VK: What did you think of it? Did it appeal to you in any particular way?

HB: I don't know, I think not. I was never involved in theatre either at school or in university. Not that I found it difficult or that I resented it, but it didn't particularly move me as a schoolboy.

VK: When *did* it start to move you, then?

HB: I'm not sure it did, and I'm not sure it does now. It's easy to rehearse the conventional wisdom about Shakespeare, and of course I feel that, namely that he was a man of fairly humble origins who did a great deal with the English language and played with the rhythms of the people, mixed in with alliterative speech form. This is what I do, this is what I have in common with him; whether I got it from him I don't know. As I said, my mother spoke urban argot, London slang, and I know I could hear words from the seventeenth century in her speech. It was a popular language with intense rhythmic quality. When my mother was abusive, which she often was, she almost sang with the abuse, and this meant a lot to me. A woman who is very angry, from a proletarian background which is not inhibited, actually speaks poetry, in my opinion. Shakespeare probably had a similar background.

VK: Then, you wouldn't say that Shakespeare belongs among your favourite authors, would you?

HB: No I wouldn't. My favourite authors are of eccentric tastes. I read Shakespeare rarely, and the reason I don't read it is probably because I find it a little impenetrable. On the other hand, I enjoy Orson Welles's *Chimes at Midnight*. And when I hear that and look at it, I'm intrigued because I hear some implied political statements made by Shakespeare which one wouldn't notice, except in the mouth of an actor. For instance, at one moment, Henry IV reproaches Hal that he has become, "sick and blunted with *community*" [Barker's emphasis; *Henry IV*, Act III, Scene II]. And I realized that Shakespeare here used the word *community* with absolute contempt: the community is debased, vulgar, worthless. Today, we have reversed this, and we use the word community as the highest form of praise. Political things in Shakespeare sometimes reveal themselves to me like that.

VK: Do you think that Shakespeare has become politically controversial, then?

HB: He can be.

VK: Do you have an interest in academic criticism about Shakespeare?

HB: Not in the least.

VK: You once said that, "Shakespeare was the last English writer who was not a moralist". Would you still agree with that statement?

HB: Yes, but I have to refine it. What Shakespeare is able to do is to allow his instinct as an artist to eclipse morality. It's always been my sense that he found evil vastly more interesting than good, even when he indulges moral conventions. I also find this fascination for evil in Goya. Everyone likes Goya because he appears to criticize inhumanity. I'm convinced Goya is inhuman himself. These figures who were annexed by the radical left or the critical left are in fact more ambiguous.

VK: Another Renaissance playwright on whom you have worked is Middleton. How does Middleton differ from Shakespeare, according to you?

HB: I think he is similar, perhaps more conventional. I sense that the organization of the text is a bit more classical and less anarchic. Like so many of the other Jacobeans, he also has what appears to us now as these slightly absurd endings, where everybody dies. It's a solution to dramatic problems, but a cheap one. I'm interested in death onstage, but not so much in mass slaughter.

VK: Why did you choose to work on *Women Beware Women*, then?

HB: The Royal Court Theatre, which is a left-wing theatre, commissioned it. They wanted me to write a criticism of money and the Stock Exchange. There is something of that in there, of course. But the way I did it was not to just modernize it and put it in modern banks. Instead, I offered to write my own ending. But the director, William Gaskill, one of the most famous directors in this country – very left wing, very good with actors – didn't know what to do with it. He told me, "You did a marvellous editing job on part one, but I don't understand part two. I don't believe it". This was Stanislavsky speaking: he couldn't believe it, and as a result he couldn't direct the actors. But art is speculation, it is not relation. So Maggie Steed, the main actress, playing the part of Livia, told him, "I don't see what the problem is, Bill, I can do this!" And they ended up doing it themselves. Because to them, it was not intellectual, it was visceral.

VK: What plays by Shakespeare do you find particularly interesting, or particularly uninteresting?

HB: I don't care much for the comedies, although this is a generalization I shouldn't make, since I haven't seen many of them. The ones I find interesting are *Hamlet* and *King Lear*, of course, and also *Macbeth*. I suppose I find them interesting because of what I have referred to before as their absences, their silences.

VK: Do they appeal to you as cultural emblems, too?

HB: Not that I am aware of. You might find it odd, but I'm not an iconoclast. I was one as a young man: *The Love of a Good Man* is a very iconoclastic play. But this is not how I behave with a classical text.

VK: So would you say that you work around the text rather than destroy it?

HB: Because the plays are so well known, there must be some degree to which I try to disturb that. But I wouldn't recognize it as iconoclasm. What I am trying to do is to expose something that convention has made too solid. The conventional treatment of Gertrude, for instance, dismisses her as an oversexed bad mother. Something in me wanted to pose an alternative, to refocus, to put the light on different areas. And, obviously, I don't like Hamlet as a character. But you're right, I wouldn't do that if the play was not known, would I?

VK: But it's difficult to genuinely like *Hamlet* as a play, isn't it? It has almost become an obligation.

HB: That's the trouble with the whole canon. When I wrote *Gertrude – The Cry*, many Oxford-educated people were profoundly outraged and tried to ridicule my project, and I couldn't understand why. This has to do with the canon. I was also detested, unforgiven, for rewriting *Uncle Vanya*.

But many young actors now are willing to challenge the canon, and also the tradition of naturalism. Why would you want to go to the stage to speak naturally? The problem is that actors don't have the training for anything else. I was at Royal Academy of Dramatic Art to see a student production of my play *Crimes in Hot Countries*. The students came to me and told me, as if they were a conspiracy or a trade union, "We so like this play, but we didn't feel we were able to do it because we're not properly trained".

VK: You mentioned that you were not particularly interested in Shakespeare's comedies. What about the histories and their relation to historical truth?

HB: I don't know them very well. We often mention that they were based on Holinshed. But how accurate was Holinshed? To me history is a fluid and nearly absurd concept, not because facts don't happen – I'm not a surrealist, I know they happen – but because history is *interpretation*, it cannot be anything but interpretation; it's never just a narrative or an objective account. So I'm not surprised that Shakespeare wanted to play with it the way I play with it.

Thucydides – from whom I took the account on which *The Dying of Today* is based – has a section on the Corcyran mutiny, a proletarian uprising in Corfu. It's a wonderful piece of writing, very lyrical, but it is clearly informed by Thucydides' political position, his standing within the political system of Athens at the time. And the biggest joke of all is Stalin. Stalin painted himself *out* of pictures or painted himself *in* pictures. I find it quite amusing, I don't even object to it because I find that to be the truth of the discipline, in essence.

VK: This is very much what the dictator in *Wounds to the Face* is doing too […]

HB: Absolutely.

VK: So would it be accurate then to say that speaking about historical facts, rather than confirming them, makes them all the more questionable, because subjective? That the only facts that exist for sure are the ones that are never reported?

HB: It's an interesting proposition. But sometimes also, fictionalizing something makes it more telling than any authentic version. The American movie will convince more people than a scholarly work. The problem is that it applies to good work as well as bad work. It's also true of literary memoirs. If you take as an example Ernst Jüngers' *Storm of Steel*, he tells his own story, but he does it in a lyrical way which is so poetic and so driven by its own poetry that, as he commits the act, he convinces himself that it is poetic even if it is simultaneously sordid. It becomes compelling by the telling.

VK: You referred to *Victory* as a semi-history. Do you think that it relates in form to a history play by Shakespeare, for instance?

HB: I shouldn't think so. You might say it is more Brechtian in form, because it is picaresque. You also have scenes which are laid one against the other which appear to have no connection for a long time. The interlude, for instance, has always troubled directors, as if it were extraneous, but it's not. It's very much of the world. But I suppose you could find these juxtapositions in Shakespeare and in Marlowe too.

VK: You could. *Doctor Faustus*, for instance, is a succession of episodes. I also sense a kinship between the myth of Faustus and your work: a man, having attained the limits of knowledge, decides to resort to the dark arts, of which the theatre could be a metaphor [...]

HB: Theatre is a dark art, or at least it should be. The fact that it ceased to be one is very worrying. When we do plays like mine, we are playing with the dark arts, and I know that because these plays work viscerally, they work on instincts, not through the rational, the critical or the objective.

VK: And do you think it's dangerous?

HB: It might be. But one couldn't worry about that; you can't let it inhibit you that it might be dangerous. It's not socially dangerous (I'm not a revolutionary): it's not so much about what is shown, whether it's desirable, and hence whether or not it might be imitated. This is always possible. It's about the fact that it takes place in this space called theatre, and there's something about that space, because it is not the street, and this is why I always insist that the theatre and the street must be differentiated, in fact *and* theory. When you cross that threshold, you enter a space which declares itself independent of the world. That means that whatever happens in this space is not infectious, because it is not in the world. The theatre immunizes the action against imitation. If I thought by showing a scene somebody might imitate it, I would judge that a poor result.

My theatre can be unsettling, but I could never intend that. I have no intentions; this is the fundamental difference between me and Brecht, Shaw, Bond [...]. And it's probably because I have no intention that I am able to go freely where I wish to go, and maybe entrap odd individuals on the way. But it's never intended. As I have often said, artists have no responsibilities but to themselves.

VK: Critics have often called your work Shakespearean. Why do you think that is?

HB: I think it is sheer ignorance. It's presumably because my plays are wide in scope, because they usually have a large cast, because the language is not social realism, and because they're pseudo-historical or mythical. So critics put these things together, and think, 'Who else does that? Oh, it's Shakespeare'. I can't see what else it could be. The critical class knows nothing about creativity as such, and so what they look for is identification. I am not an imitator of Shakespeare and I don't particularly like the assumption that I could be.

VK: What would be your definition of the word *Shakespearean*?

HB: It's about crisis, it's about moral dilemma, power, not much about sex in my opinion, and it's expressed in a narrative form which is entirely free. It's also characterized, as I said, by a superficial moral attitude within the poetry. That, of course, is so much of its charm: it plays with the illegitimate thought. Shakespeare himself is seduced by that, and it's good to see a man seduced away from his purpose. That's what a great artist is: someone who allows himself to be diverted from his course. If he stays on the course, he's dull.

You can see Shakespeare drawn away by Edmund in *King Lear*, for instance. He likes Edmund, whom he finds sexy, saturnine and good with women. And yet he insists that Edmund issues a grovelling apology at the end. That's the annoying thing about Shakespeare. He denies his characters the integrity they deserve. Why should Edmund apologize? Why should Macbeth apologize? That's ridiculous. Do you know any evil men who apologize? I was once persuaded to work in a prison with a group of murderers. They were routinely insincere. They were self-pitying. They had killed people in the most appalling ways. And they felt sorry for themselves, they did not feel sorry for the people they had injured. Apology? There was none at all.

VK: Aside from the fact that your characters don't apologize, how else are your tragedies different from Shakespeare's?

HB: In my plays, the tragedy goes on. It doesn't end. It could, with death, but it doesn't. If you take *The Europeans* as an example, what Katrin is going through goes on. She becomes an outsider, she wills herself to be an outcast, she won't accept the conventional wisdom of apology and forgiveness, and this condemns her to a life of pain, but she still won't stop it. She's not educable. Edmund is, it appears. Lear is. I always speak about anxiety, and I insist that some people want anxiety. In my plays, that anxiety is continuous and people must take it away with them.

VK: Could you describe more specifically the relationship between *Hamlet* and *Gertrude – The Cry*? Should we look for similarities between the two?

HB: *Gertrude* is neither a sequel, nor a prequel to *Hamlet* (whereas *Seven Lears* is a prequel to *King Lear*). It is a rewriting of the story of Hamlet and his mother, which is not Shakespeare's – Shakespeare never thought up a story in his life; in this sense I am vastly his superior. He took the story from somebody else, and in this instance, I did the same, even if I took it from him. So it is simply a retelling.

VK: And would you describe Ragusa as pure invention on your part or as manipulation of pre-extent material?

HB: I didn't think of Ophelia at all. And Cascan is there because of my love of servants. It may make me sound naïve, but it was not a conscious decision.

VK: But it's probably impossible for the audience not to try and pinpoint the links between the two plays […]

HB: I suppose you're right, but that's not my problem.

VK: Do you think that "rewriting" is the appropriate word to describe *Gertrude* in relation to *Hamlet*?

HB: You could say it's an annexation, but it wouldn't be an annexation of Shakespeare: as I said, it's from the original story. It's not an interrogation either, in the way that *Seven Lears* is an interrogation of *King Lear*. *Seven Lears* comes out of the question why there is no queen. It's a startling absence, because *Lear* is a family tragedy, with this absence that is so obvious that you scarcely think of it. I tried to invent the pretext for her absence, and in my version she is killed because she is morally pure. That's not what happened in *Gertrude*. *Gertrude* is just my question: why is that woman rendered so horrific, when she is driven by love? That was my intervention.

VK: You still consider *Gertrude* to be one of your best plays, don't you?

HB: I do. I also wrote the part for an actress with whom I was very much in love when the play was written, for whom it all made sense, and who, in my opinion, could play it better than anyone else. There is always a private investment in those things.

VK: Aside from the more explicit engagement with the Shakespearean canon, would you say that some of your plays are written under the influence of Shakespeare?

HB: Positively or negatively?

VK: Both.

HB: I can't think of these influences, but this author sets a framework of ambition in all English theatre that can't be ignored.

VK: Do you think you are influenced by any other authors in your writing?

HB: Of course, I can't speak of unconscious influences, can I? Consciously, not at all, and I have to say, not ever. Even as a very young writer, I don't think I was. Now if you ask me if there are authors I like, of course, I can answer that question. But being consciously aware of imitating another writer, or even sensing their presence, no, I can't say that.

VK: Would it make sense then to ask you if you think you might be under the unconscious influence of someone?

HB: [Louis-Ferdinand] Céline, perhaps, as an after-effect. What I have always tried to achieve in some of the very long speeches I write is the way the authorial identity wanders in and out of the character's voice. Also the way the mind is diverted. This is difficult to do for actors, because they're trained, in a Stanislavskian manner, to follow a line. When I started to read Céline, I realized that he does the same thing – he talks to the reader – he says, "Oh listen, I suppose you're getting fed up with this story, well I'll shorten it for you, anyway, along came these Germans, and then a bomb came, and then the RAF came by and blew the place up, oh you're bored, now? No you're not. I said to my partner [...]" This is how he writes. This is the most extraordinary invention in fiction, it influenced generations of American novelists. Also, I hear music in his texts. Of course, Céline's work is based on a poetic manipulation of argot, even if this is something difficult to realize in the English translation.

VK: About that, do you think that the music of your text can be recaptured in translation?

HB: Well, it's difficult for me to say. But some of it comes through, I'd say.

VK: Coming back to Céline, would it be right then to say that you strive to achieve the same effect with your own means?

HB: If I was to just imitate Céline's means, I would use his famous dots, and sometimes I've used dots, but it's just a writing technique that he took to a very high point […] I sometimes now work, and I'm doing it with the play I am now working on [*Nausicaa at 50*], with oblique lines so that the actors are not taught by conventional punctuation what the rhythm of the text is. It started in *Albertina* and *Deep Wives/ Shallow Animals*. I remember saying to Juliet Stevenson, "Are you troubled by these obliques? If you prefer, you can get a pen out and put in commas and full stops". And she said, "No, this makes life easy for me". So, I'll probably use some more of that in the future.

VK: You have an elaborate system of punctuation […]

HB: It relates to periods in my life. Sometimes there is no punctuation at all, it just runs on. Sometimes there are simply dots, and now I use obliques. I don't use dashes. What I'm always trying to do is to establish a rhythm. I try to find ways to oblige the actors to follow the rhythm. And in the new play I am [currently] working on, *Nausicaa at 50*, a very long play with a dense text, I use the oblique, because there are pages and pages of speech, with simultaneous speaking, and this requires something like musical notation.

VK: Is the increasing proportion of verse, as opposed to prose, in your texts another aspect of this musical writing?

HB: The practical reason is that I write much more poetry now than I did. And what I have allowed myself to do is to let the poetry flow back into the plays. So now I spend quite a long time on a speech, even though I've acquired a voice now that is fluent, in finding *le mot juste* [the right word], which will be a rhyme or a half-rhyme in the middle of a speech, in which a sound will echo throughout the speech. The major problem with all innovation is to find the actors who are able to perform them.

VK: Does this interest in sound patterns and rhythm pertain to classical poetry, or to the influence of other poets?

HB: Not that I am aware of. There are poets of course whom I respect, whether or not I regard their poetry as great, and Eliot is one of them, of course: *The Wasteland* is a great poem. There is also the American poet George Oppen, whom I like very much, but that's about it, in English. I don't read much poetry.

The play I'm writing at the moment, however, is about two poets, one of which is slightly influenced by the life of François Villon: he's a criminal, he's a murderer, and a poet. The despot of the regime in which he lives, a woman, continually refuses to acknowledge publicly what a great poet he is, and awards prizes, over and over again, to an inferior poet. He is in misery, can barely survive, but she knows that to reward him would destroy him, so she perpetually deprives him. He has to live in the wretchedness of his art form, but it is enhanced by his ordeal.

VK: Are there any other specific stylistic traits which you would identify as being idiosyncratic of your style?

HB: There must be some. Sometimes it's simultaneous speaking, but this is a more recent development. There is also repetition; it's musical, but I can't think of the origin of it.

VK: When you say it's musical, do you have any specific music in mind?

HB: I love Bartok. I try to write the way he composes. In the string quartets, for instance, there is continual returning. Having gone off somewhere, he manages to come back seamlessly into the form again. I find that intellectual management of spontaneity magnificent.

There is an example in the play I am working on at the moment. I knew that I was coming towards the end of it; like a breath, it was running out, of its own accord. For some reason, I flew in a tree over a dead man. I didn't know why, I just thought, 'I'll have a tree fly in'. And I wrote on without thinking too much about it. Then the heroine, Nausicaa, enters holding a chair, and she doesn't know why she's holding a chair (and I don't either). She talks to her lover, and I just knew I needed this moment of redundancy. And then I had this rope ladder falling out of the tree, with no one on it. The main character, the poet, is filled with dread at the sight of the ladder. They then see feet coming down the ladder, which, when they get to the bottom rung, cannot proceed, because the ladder is not long enough. The woman now understands why she carries the chair. The poet tries to stop her, telling her that if she enables the stranger to descend, it will be the end of him, obliging her to choose between him and her inclination to help strangers. She goes then to the ladder, places the chair so the man can get off the ladder, onto the chair, then onto the ground. I didn't know who it was. And then I deduced it was the character whom we had seen ever so briefly in the beginning of the play, a gun-hirer who comes back to deliver the gun with which the poet can kill himself. I don't plan such things: it appears arbitrary.

It's almost uncanny, the way something like that works. On the last play, I was struggling with a difficult scene, but it was coffee time, and I was desperate for coffee, and so I thought, 'Oh, I'll just have somebody come in'. And so I typed, "A man enters, holding a spade". I went down to make myself some coffee, and while the water was boiling, I thought, 'The postman has probably arrived'. And as I opened the door to get my mail, a man walked past with a spade on his shoulder. I am not trying to mystify my life, but only saying this also describes the way things happen in the plays.

VK: It's almost as if your imagination had its own coherence that you weren't aware of [...]

HB: Yes, it's not governed by anything logical.

VK: Your writing is very precise and yet very abundant. Do you consider yourself a spontaneous writer, or do you tend to go back to what you've already written and rework it?

HB: It's spontaneous. But with these complicated poetic speeches, I will look back at yesterday's page, and I may see that a single word is not the best, and I may change it, but it is unusual. Fluency is very important and I have been doing this for 40 years, so that, to some extent, I can trust the fluency itself. I now have experience and a voice. A young writer takes more time to write a page.

VK: You once called yourself a "contemporary classic". Would you care to explain what you meant by that?

HB: I'm not sure what I meant. I was probably talking about my belief in the value of certain traditions in literature. I believe that theatre is a natural place for invented language, I believe in the high acting style, and so on. I'm not a revolutionary writer at all. I never thought of myself as one.

　　　If I had worked in the theatre, as you will, starting quite young, going to it as a director, seeing a lot of work, knowing my Shakespeare, knowing my Racine, knowing everything else, maybe I would never have been what I am, the sort of writer I am. I come from a background of ignorance. There are many texts I don't know. It took years before I saw *Hamlet*. So in a way, to think of myself in radical terms is not possible, because I'm not familiar with the formal normality. So, whatever I do that is unusual is accidental.

VK: On a more conscious and traditional level, are there any poetic traditions that you identify with?

HB: No, but probably I would only know that watching an actor when I direct him. The acting question is crucial. We're talking about my own writing, but the biggest conundrum after that is how you stage it. I don't know where my aesthetic values come from. I'm not a theatre-goer. I don't see plays, I don't read plays. I'm quite bored by the theatre. But I paint and know European painting quite thoroughly. Hence the origin of *Judith*, for example, but my way of staging it was not *pictorial*.

VK: So would it be right then to say that your plays are informed by material that is not theatrical?

HB: Yes. Certainly.

VK: But also by philosophy? Nietzsche, Adorno [...]

HB: How can you not like Nietzsche if you like theatre? He's not a dramatist, but he knows about acting. The more you read Nietzsche, the more you understand what an actor is. "If you do not understand the rhythm of a sentence, you cannot understand the meaning". This paradox should be written over the door of every drama school. Let's not argue about the meaning of a sentence: just speak it. And when you speak it, I will know if you know what it means. I think that sound and rhythm can communicate as much to the public as if they were listening to an argument. The possibility exists of a text that is entirely sound, and yet conveys meaning.

VK: Hence your interest in soundscapes in your productions?

HB: Yes, not music as such, but sounds, pastiches, altered phrases, and the voices. I've always described my company as an orchestra of various voices and pitches.

VK: What about contemporary writers and playwrights? Do you feel any kinship, any affinity to any of them? To Sarah Kane, for instance?

HB: I don't know her. I had people say to me, in Vienna, for instance, "That play was surely influenced by Sarah Kane". She was half my age! I am not being disingenuous: I haven't seen or read her plays.

   However, what interests me is why she was adopted by the theatre – what made it possible for someone who was superficially problematic, anarchic, violent and cruel to be embraced by the system, in a way that Galactia's work is finally contained by the State in *Scenes from an Execution*. Why were they prepared to contain Kane? The reason must be that her plays can be read as critiques of contemporary life, and the modern theatre is obsessive about critiquing contemporary life. So I could cut your throat, rape you and set light to you, but it's tolerable; we'll all watch it as long as it's perceived as a humanist document, i.e. the origin of it is your profound humanistic concern for the social order. This is why Sarah Kane was permitted. There was an original frisson, but it was suitably bourgeois in the end. For to call a work bourgeois can only mean that it gratifies the bourgeoisie – what else? Just as Beckett is bourgeois. People coming to my plays in search of a critique of society are not going to get it: it's not there. This humanism explains why I'm on the outside and will die on the outside of the theatre – I cannot satisfy the criteria.

VK: But the plays themselves are less bourgeois than their cultural appropriation […]

HB: Perhaps […] It's hard to be certain of the author's intentions, isn't it? I was reflecting on having seen *Waiting for Godot* recently and finding it very ordinary, poetry apart, in terms of its narrative. It also does that thing which nauseates me so with Chekhov, of making failure and misery the norm. 'Haha!' we go, as Uncle Vanya fails and becomes impotent. 'Haha!' as Lucky trips again. Theatre might be affirmative without *reconciling*, you know.

VK: Are you at peace now with the place that you occupy in the theatre in England?

HB: I'm never at peace. But I'm not complaining that I'm not in the National Theatre. It's not clear to me, if the National Theatre offered to do a season of my work, [that] they would know how to do it.

VK: If you had another 'conversation with a dead poet' and could meet Shakespeare to ask him a single question, what would it be?

HB: I would turn down the invitation.

VK: Do you like the fact that people applaud at the end of your plays?

HB: Yes, because they must thank the actors for the ordeal the actors have been through. In my plays, actors are sacrifices; they suffer, and you must thank them for that. I don't even mind an actor smiling because, even if he thought he wouldn't get through it, he did and he smiles with relief. What I don't particularly like is a buzz in the audience. But I'm a civil person, I like manners, and I think it is good manners to applaud.

This previously unpublished interview – which appears in Vanasay Khamphommala's doctoral thesis, 'Spectres of Shakespeare in Howard Barker's work' (Université Paris-Sorbonne) – was conducted in Brighton on 11 February 2010.

'An education in living poetry, vivid and violent'

With Nina Rapi

Nina Rapi (NR)
Howard Barker (HB)

NR: There is an element of spirituality in your work, in its intensity, precision and use of ritual, reminiscent of Genet. Do you see theatre as a potentially spiritual space?

HB: Entirely. I see no other pretext for its existence. Such is the plethora of communication, both in entertainment and so-called information, it is wilful suicide for theatre to permit itself to be annexed to functional ends. I have a compulsion to stage theatre, just as actors suffer the same compulsion to utter and move. These rhythms in a fixed space immediately call up certain ritual processes. If, furthermore, your concerns are with death and how we arrive at it, you have to say yes, we make spiritual life our concern. That a public hardly exists for such theatre detracts not at all from the desire to create it. There is something of the secret in all spiritual processes, I would suggest. And my work's a rumour, essentially.

NR: What is your creative impulse when you write a play?

HB: I would describe it as an impatience. When I am not engaged in a creative act I experience time as loss. To write is the precondition of any other form of activity, personal or public. It is therefore a process of keeping equilibrium, a sort of health. What I am writing I rarely know. I have said frequently that ignorance is a precious gift for artists, a profoundly rewarding point of departure.

NR: So how do you construct a play? Your structures are to die for!

HB: Yes, I have an innate sense of stage dynamics. I can't deny it.

NR: Power and sexuality seem to be your core, recurrent themes. They have also been classic themes in theatre from Greek tragedy to Sartre and Genet to Caryl Churchill, Phillip Ridley, Anthony Neilson and Sarah Kane. What is your particular fascination with the subjects?

HB: I have written long and agonizingly about sexual love. And sexual seduction is manifestly an exercise of power, exquisitely irresponsible, and socially disruptive. But it's necessary to admit the symbolic nature of sexuality, both in its essence and in its changing social manifestations. When one writes of sexuality one writes of the body but not only the body. What does the body represent as longed for, possessed, entered, maimed? The theft of the body, the annexation of the body, has interested me since my earliest plays: Lenin in the mausoleum; the Unknown Warrior; the fetishism of clothing. Its metaphorical reach is huge.

NR: And what about State power? In *Scenes from an Execution*, for example, the focus seems to be State power.

HB: State power figured in a number of my plays around 1980–1985, [and] in *The Europeans* also. At a certain point, the sexual body and State power coincide appallingly, as in *Judith*. But in *The Europeans* Katrin's half-butchered body also becomes a ground for struggle between State and private will.

NR: In *Found in the Ground*, your latest play, the main character is a figure of authority, but, at the same time, he is also the most vulnerable. Power here is shown as non-monolithic, which is appealing.

HB: Toonelhuis is a nihilist, having been a moralist. His literal hunger to digest the remains of war criminals is perhaps the sort of destiny that unites apparent oppositions. In burning his library he mimics Hitler's abnegation of culture in the ruins of Berlin.

NR: The representation of sex onstage is very tricky. But I find the representation of sex in *Found in the Ground* and your other plays effective: it's both stylized and convincing. Do you stylize deliberately in order to create distance?

HB: My way as a director is to emphasize the separation between stage and the so-called 'realistic' media, like film and television. Theatre is body-in-space, and it calls up from the psyche of its public imaginative resources the so-called realists don't demand. It doesn't *require* mimetic fastidiousness. And anyway, who really believes the dead character is dead, or the sexual character is engaged in a sexual act? It's infantile to pretend like this. My obligation as director is to create metaphorical truth. For me, theatre is about suggesting things, not about telling everything.

NR: You rarely speak of your working-class background and people assume you are middle class. How much, if at all, has your class influenced your take on reality and your aesthetics?

HB: My mother sent me for lessons in elocution. She loved me and thought I might emerge from my background with the help of a 'nice' accent. How mistaken she was. How was she to guess the convolutions of modern snobbery? For some years I was conscious of the class struggle and described it. What I did not do – however much I might have believed I did – was to write the political play. The left had no time for me. The seat of Marxist theatre, the Royal Court, rejected *Claw*, *Victory* and much else. Already tragedy was coming through these narratives, and that doesn't serve the left's agenda.

In terms of my method in dialogue, my background has been deeply significant. The rhythm and pulse of my mother's and grandfather's speech can be heard in my own texts. It was an education in living poetry, vivid and violent. And the vocabulary – especially when anger informed it – was replete with words from the seventeenth century. When my mother was abusive, it was musical. The mix of this ancient argot with the cultivated phrasing I acquired through literature creates a distinctive voice. No other writer sounds like me.

NR: How do your characters differ from those of the dominant genres?

HB: The characters speak not only in a fashioned way characteristic of me, but also *fully* in a way that is impossible in naturalism. They have excess articulation, no matter what their class or education. I aim deliberately at plethora, knowing full well the public can't keep up. The speeches are broken, themes dropped and recovered again, strange, swift perceptions suddenly described, then buried under a coarse banality. That's their pattern of speaking. In terms of their motivation, I'm unconstrained by Stanislavskian or Brechtian ideas of truth. Since I have nothing to *tell*, I don't need to adhere to laws of theatre that are primarily to do with telling. And is the chaos in the minds of my characters less authentic? Hardly, I think.

NR: You've written against "clarity" in theatre. But I personally find your plays attractive because of their clarity of conception and execution. Do you feel there is a contradiction in this?

HB: The conception is actually not at all clear. I never set out with an idea or any intention. The attraction and, indeed, the spiritual element of the artistic experience is its ignorance, its blindness. The execution is different. Here I have an intention. I want to work with actors whose clarity of articulation is simply abnormal. I want to create images of beauty and this entails rigour and discipline. I direct actors. I rarely listen to them, and they understand this. They bring their gifts to the service of the vision I try to impart. Everything contributes: set, costume, sound, light is under this degree of control.

The theatre suffers from a numbing aesthetic of solidarity, elucidation, clarity and so on, a sort of debased democracy that insists on shared values and enlightenment. It is as if the culture was in dread of dissonance. Personally, dissonance is where I feel at home. Now, what is the consequence of this? It makes the public anxious. Some of it wants to get out as fast as possible. I don't stop them. But some sense the pleasures of anxiety in the dramatic space. Possibly they sense discipline in the cultural field is unhealthy. Perhaps they feel manipulated when they enter the Royal Court Theatre, or the National. If they don't, they should do.

NR: And perhaps this connection with dissonance is what marks you as different. You've written, too, that the differences between us, "might be sources of hope, discovery and creativity", not just what we have in common. Is this notion of difference at the heart of your theatre project?

HB: In my plays you don't see the world as you know it, but you see a world which has a point of contact with the world you do know. This culture is obsessed with the real world in a way that has never been before. All young writers are encouraged to write about themselves, about what they know or experienced. A lot of this goes back to a movement coming from what the Royal Court thought it was doing in the 1950s. It thought it was liberating the theatre into the world of reality and, therefore, it would bring the pain and problems of contemporary life into the stage. If that was a revolution at the time, it has now become concretized and sterile.

For me this is the dead end for theatre; it's a cul-de-sac. You have this extraordinary medium, which is 6000 years old, in which you have an actor and a body and a voice in this particular space. It's a situation that calls out for invention and imagination. The advice to the theatre to bring the real world into the stage is now reactionary in my opinion. Are we then making the social issue the substance of a democratic discourse? Well, this is clearly circular. And I think the hostility I have experienced in the past 30 years in this country from dramaturgs, critics and theatre managements is because I'm not and cannot be associated with that process.

NR: What keeps you going in the face of such hostility to your work?

HB: I have to say I'm not greatly injured by it.

NR: I have a feeling you thrive on it.

HB: It would be a sort of corruption to enjoy a marginal position in theatre for its own sake. I would not resist the staging of my plays (which are frequently large in scale) by large companies with resources. The question is, are these national institutions even capable of presenting them, given the political and social prejudices that dominate their aesthetic *attitudes* – we cannot call it theory? Probably this will never be tested. But I have to say, the ensemble is the only significant practise in theatre, and there are virtually none. The Wrestling School is exceptional, and, of course, looks exceptional.

NR: But you used to be produced by the Royal Court, the Almeida and the Royal Shakespeare Company. What happened?

HB: At a rather early stage in my career I was nauseated by social realism. Nietzsche suggests we sense the death of an idea by its corrupt odour before we identify it intellectually. This was my experience. But what is peculiar is that the corpse lives on, and expands, as I suppose a bloated corpse expands. I also wanted theatre to be a place for a poet. But the Royal Court and the rest squirm at poetic discourse, as they squirm at tragedy, which must also be poetic. They want to laugh at everything, because they are in the grip of a neurosis, as society is here. Whilst laughing, they think they can get the audience to swallow a few political ideas without noticing. It's a sordid practice, and infantilizes the public. Does the public resent being infantilized? That's the question.

NR: A part of it surely does. What would you say the duty of the artist is, if such a thing exists?

HB: It may sound, from what I say, as if I believed in moral responsibility in artists, but I don't, and it is, anyway, a false dichotomy. The artist has no duty except to himself, by which I mean to say, to his instinct (not his *conscience*[...]). If he obeys this injunction to speak his darkness, he will – inevitably – serve a public, for theatre speaks what is not spoken elsewhere, [that] is its supreme beauty.

This interview was first published in the sixth edition (Spring/Summer 2010) of the literary magazine BRAND.

Found in the Ground. Suzy Cooper (Burgteata). The Wrestling School, 2009. Photo credit Robert Workman.

'On The Wrestling School'

With Duška Radosavljević

Duška Radosavljević (DR)
Howard Barker (HB)

DR: The Wrestling School has recently had its 21st anniversary as a theatre company. When you look back on this period, what would you say have been the most significant stages of the company's development?

HB: The most significant stage without question was my assumption of the role of director with *Judith* in 1995. This remains one of the company's outstanding productions. It was as if all my frustration at the aesthetic cul-de-sac into which my work had been driven initiated this new style. Much of this can be seen in Ivan Kyncl's memorable photography. It was rich in images. The performances were first rate, also. Everything came together. Other stages reflect alterations in my ambitions as a writer, the assumption of control of the whole visual aspect (excluding the lighting), and the aural aspect [and my melding them] into a whole. But all this was pretty well there in *Judith*.

DR: Could you name the key members of the company (past and present) and what they have individually brought to the evolution of The Wrestling School as an entity and an ensemble?

HB: The three members of the *Judith* cast remain deeply embedded in the company, Melanie Jessop and Jane Bertish particularly. Jane had worked with Kenny Ireland on my plays before. Few of the actors of that phase came into my period, but for these two women. The major figures that followed were Victoria Wicks, Sean O'Callaghan, Julia Tarnoky and Justin Avoth. More recently, Suzy Cooper has entered to play leading and less-leading roles. They bring a quality of perfect diction, perfect rhythm, perfect physical balance, all vital to me. They could each follow the syntactical and emotional complications of the later work. They master it by instinct. Instinct is everything, training rather little, I now think.

DR: How are new collaborators and members of the company selected and initiated into the working/creative process?

HB: I prefer to work always with the core ensemble, adding new individuals, usually in minor roles to begin with. Interesting young actors appear, some of whom go on to huge reputation. We employed Tom Burke and Philip Cumbus directly from drama school in *Gertrude* and *The Fence in its Thousandth Year*, respectively. They wanted to work with The Wrestling School. Many, many people do. For a company with no State finance, which is constantly ignored or attacked, this is remarkable. We are, as I have said before, a rumour. We are immune to hostility. But I have to say, I look for qualities in actors, and these qualities of precision, of presence, of joy in articulation, are rare.

DR: How has the Arts Council funding cut in December 2007 affected the present operation of the company?

HB: The brutally political decision made by the drama panel of the Arts Council to eradicate the company failed. It was a political decision; I am not indulging in hyperbole. The criteria for funding grants are nakedly sociological, and Soviet in content (benefit to community, raising community involvement, addressing gender or race issues etc […]). Quality was not identified as a reason for subsidy; this alone makes my point succinctly. We were out of action for a year, and in that year, following a reading of *I Saw Myself*, an individual unknown to us came forward, invited me to breakfast, and provided funding at an enhanced level for three years.

DR: What plans are in place for the near future?

HB: This funding runs out after the 2010 season. I am, however, ready to initiate the 2011 season with new work: *The Forty*, *Wonder and Worship in the Dying Ward* and, our first film, *A Dead Man's Blessing*.

DR: The recent memoir authored by yourself and an alter ego highlights a very interesting model of authorship that has emerged around your own work more recently – i.e. the idea of crediting imaginary artists with various aspects of each production (costume and set design etc.). Could you explain how and why this has come about? Does Howard Barker ever come into conflict with Thomas Leipzig or Billie Kaiser?

HB: Heteronymity isn't unknown in artistic careers. But there are good reasons why my set and costume design integrate the style of The Wrestling School. I am a painter and photographer. I have learned what kind of decor suits my texts (not entirely a matter of economy), and provides both a setting for voice (the chief factor) and also a distinct statement of non-realism. The images are by Eduardo Houth, another alias. In all this, a single eye on the production creates the distinctive mode for which we are now known. When I speak of 'we', I talk first of myself and the actors, but I also talk of the assistant directors, the lighting designers and the financial manager. On certain occasions, directors are used who have (1) been actors deeply involved in the company's work, e.g. Gerrard McArthur, or (2) assistants I feel have come close to my sense of values.

DR: In the book you confess to a "dread of the collective" and yet your work (like most theatre work) is produced collectively. You often write epic plays for big casts. What challenges do you encounter in this way and how do you resolve them?

HB: The Wrestling School, let me state clearly, is not, and has never been, a collective, nor is it an actors' company, as some mistakenly believe. It is a company for one writer/director. Decisions rest with me, the texts are mine, and the artistic policy is my own. Naturally, there is discussion, but rather little. We are peculiarly efficient and our long history proves how much can be done with a small amount of bureaucratic equipment. Furthermore, given the huge ambition of these plays (think of *Found in the Ground*), it is unimaginable that such things could be created by any other body in four weeks with such poor financial resources. If there was friction, factionalism, sub-division, it could never be achieved.

DR: In the conversation we had last year you mentioned the analogy of working with the ensemble as if it were an orchestra. You also discuss the idea of "text as music" in your book. Could you say a bit more about the importance of rhythm in relation to meaning which you attributed to Nietzsche on that occasion?

HB: Nietzsche's insight that meaning and rhythm were synonymous is borne out by all my experience with actors. When an actor is bluffing, i.e. saying something the meaning of which he has not got, it is immediately obvious in the handling of the inner pace of the speech – we are talking of a highly developed and poetic form here. You [as an actor] are born with this sense of rhythm. It is a gift of God. The overall meanings of plays are unknown to the actors because they are unknown to me. All they require to know is their emotional condition in each scene.

DR: You have noted that one characteristic of Howard Barker's work is that it keeps changing and the style keeps developing. Could you pinpoint its evolutionary stages and the direction it is moving in at the moment?

HB: Here are some stages: *Victory*, a semi-political picaresque history play, with a language metaphorical and coarse. *The Possibilities*, a string quartet of related but separate stories mythical and semi-historical. *The Last Supper*, a revisiting of a religious story broken up by parables acted by the company. *Seven Lears*, a speculation on a Shakespeare classic, as is *Gertrude – The Cry. Found in the Ground*, a balletic, imagistic, anti-linear series of dreams and chorus. *The Forty*, forty scenes of despair with only one sentence in each, entirely dependent on its spatial organization.

DR: Could you describe any rehearsal room rituals that may have emerged with The Wrestling School way of working? Or, alternatively, what kind of a spiritual experience does the work aim to invoke between the actors and the audience members?

HB: There are no rituals, or any methods peculiar to us. I spend no time at all at a table but begin moving the actors in space immediately. I discourage discussion of meaning or purpose, nor do I permit political argument, or newspapers, in the space. While I do not make a fetish of it, I regard [the space] as sacred to the work, and want to exclude extraneous influences. We work amicably; I mean by this [that] there is tremendous respect for one another's talent. But the director must direct. I cannot work with people who want to *collaborate*, they must – and do – give themselves over to my direction because, quite simply, they trust me. This trust works both ways. I know their powers, or they would not be here. And we do no research whatsoever. The very idea is anathema to me. As for the audience, it does not enter into my calculations. I aim for the realization of the text. The spiritual value of theatre relies on its absolute integrity. This integrity means, frankly, ignoring what might please or reward the public. This is not contempt for the public, but the opposite.

DR: Last year Gerrard McArthur directed one of the two annual Wrestling School works. This year he has been given another directorial opportunity while the companion piece has been entrusted to Hanna Berrigan. Considering that, as directors, they would bring their own collaborators into the process, this seems like a significant departure from the previously established – distinctly monolithic – way of working. Could you say a bit about why this has come about and what it means for the further development of The Wrestling School?

HB: These directors do not bring their own collaborators – as you persist in calling them – into the work. They use our existing people, i.e. Tomas Leipzig, Billie Kaiser, Ace McCarron, a long-time lighting designer. Nothing is altered in the fundamentals; how else could we be a school? It's not a free-for-all. The style is not up for negotiation. Hanna Berrigan has assisted me three times and is ready to do her own play. I wrote this short piece for her. She understands the demands of the work. Am I saying there is only one way to do Barker? No. But in The Wrestling School, we have one style, and this develops organically. As for your remark about the company being monolithic – an implied criticism, I think – it is a company created and developed out of one writer's distinctive work. This work has very particular demands, which must be realized. Where these demands are not realized, the productions have been imperfect (we see this all over the world). In other words, we have set a very high standard for presenting Barker texts.

DR: Are you pleased with how the '21 for 21' initiative has gone, and has this created any new, interesting opportunities for the internationalization of the company's or your own work?

HB: My work has always been international, at least since the 1980s, and this has coincided with the attempts made to eliminate me here (successful attempts, it must be said). The situation in which I find myself – and the company finds itself – is unprecedented in theatre. We persist in spite of vicious journalistic reviewing, a collective (yes, here there is a collective) decision by all the national companies to cease performing my plays (new and old) but yet we enjoy a powerful subterranean reputation. In May there is a major conference in New York devoted to Barker studies. If you can think of any artist who has undergone such a strange fortune, I should like to hear of him/her. But it's not important. The fact is, *no one* in the National Theatre, the Royal Court or the RSC would know *how* to direct a play like *Gertrude – The Cry* or *The Fence in its Thousandth Year*, nor could I – without the company – have ever written them. It works out in the end.

This interview was conducted in the Spring of 2010. It was first published in Western European Stages, *Volume 22, Number 2/3 (City University of New York, Autumn 2010).*

'Art is about going into the dark'

With Mark Brown

Mark Brown (MB)
Howard Barker (HB)

MB: In your recent play *Hurts Given and Received* the character of Bach is very singular in his pursuit of his art. I wonder if you see a parallel between this and Loftus's seduction of God in the play *The Seduction of Almighty God*. These characters seem, to me, to share both a destructiveness and a narcissism.

HB: It's a very interesting question. They are two young protagonists; I don't often write young protagonists. *Claw* was one, back in 1975. What Loftus does is to try to recover, to recuperate faith in a form in which he thinks it's been abolished; he's the only serious person within the monastery, in fact. Faith in an age of unfaith is always very exciting, dramatically. He's taking up the teaching, I suppose. Therefore, he's not as solitary as Bach is.

   In terms of degrees of solitude, no one is lonelier than Bach. That is self-inflicted; it's a decision; it's an aesthetic, rather than a moral, decision to remove himself not only from others, but from human feelings as such, at least from conventional human feelings. He deliberately eliminates such feelings in himself; which is why the stage direction often says, after he's damaged someone profoundly, "he exults", because he knows he's trespassed. Loftus doesn't have to do that, because he's the keeper of the truth, so his experiences are less wounding to him.

MB: Yet there is a destructiveness on the part of both of them, is there not?

HB: Yes, but I suppose Loftus has a pretext, in that he's protecting something against its corruption. Everyone he destroys could be identified as corrupt.

MB: Doesn't Bach believe that he's defending his art?

HB: No, I don't think so. That certainly wasn't my intention. He chooses to transgress against his own moral values, as well as the collective ones. He's continually cutting away, and hence he says, in effect, 'I can't view the world unless I'm completely outside it'. If you're in society, if you share its values, then you can't really criticize it. You must discard everything you've been encouraged to believe in order to gain a perspective that others can't have.

MB: Isn't there a narcissism in that?

HB: I can't think of an artist who's not a narcissist. It comes with the profession.

MB: In terms of *Hurts Given and Received* and the issue of moral ambiguity in your work. The character of the schoolgirl Sadovee One has a precocious intelligence and self-awareness. Does that undermine a conventional sympathy for her, which, in a sentimental theatre, you would automatically have for her because she's a child?

HB: She's not only self-aware, she also has a death wish. In a sense, therefore, she is hugely sophisticated, more by instinct than education. And it isn't Bach who murders her, even if she had selected him to do precisely that. Bach's narcissism – if we are going to so describe it (his introversion is, of course, immensely painful) – obstructs him from comprehending her intention to go out in search of her own destruction. Does one sympathize *ever* with extraordinary people? It becomes a redundant category in my theatre.

MB: It seems to me that in a naturalistic/sentimental theatre you would be asked overwhelmingly to sympathize with this young girl.

HB: Yes you would, especially in a society which, at the moment, is obsessed with paedophilia. However, she rejects that victim status.

MB: In your latest play, *Wonder and Worship in the Dying Ward*, I make an observation about images. People talk often about the linguistic density and richness of your work, but it's important, I think, not to forget how imagistic it also is. When one thinks of the dead animals which fall to the ground at the end of *Wonder and Worship*, it's striking that you are still creating powerful images, images which are not necessarily easy to represent onstage. One is reminded of Scrope's lips being ripped from his mouth in *Victory* or Skinner having the carcass chained to her in *The Castle*.

HB: I create visual images because I have always thought visually, and I have never let the material conditions of the stage obstruct this. I don't feel confined by the stage. I am also certain of theatre's intrinsic ability to *show* and not merely to tell.

It would be absurd to try to show naturalistically. I hold such efforts in contempt. But to show by strictly theatrical methods, it's the test of the great director. As writer, I write without inhibition. As director, I come back to the dilemma of representation and try to solve it. Always I know it can be solved.

MB: You haven't, over time, lost your appetite for the theatrical image?

HB: Not at all. I have many books with paintings which I make while I'm writing. So, I'm always referring back to the visual. I can't really understand a theatre that doesn't include that.

MB: Allow me to come onto the question of humanism. Contrarily, I perceive there to be a grain of it in your work.

HB: There's lots of it.

MB: I see it in relation to *Slowly*, in terms of the final princess, Calf, who chooses to subject herself to atrocity. When we have her moment of terror, the source of the terror is not the oncoming atrocity that she will suffer, but the fact that she has to suffer it alone. That seems to me to have a profound implication, and a humanistic one, in the broadest sense of the word. Is that something you perceive?

HB: I do. But it's also interesting, when she repeats the word "someone". The first time she says it is a cry of fear, as one might for another hand to hold. Then she says it a different way: she demands it as a scream. Then she makes a very critical movement with her hands; she places one hand over the other; she tranquillizes that sort of panic which says, 'I need another'. She then accepts her total solitude and the confrontation that awaits her, and she says the last "someone" almost ironically.

MB: I'm interested in the fact that her terror doesn't come from the oncoming atrocity itself.

HB: All through the piece, almost from the top, she's planning that death; she's concluding that's the way to do it. In that sense, her imagination is huge. It's the other remaining character, Sign, who interprets it; of course, she interprets what her game is, that the atrocity will weigh on the consciences of the invader and, eventually, destroy them. As you might say, the destruction of the European ideality has been caused by the workings of European conscience. The shame that attaches to all European peoples, which is a problem for them, is caused by the recollection of imperialism. The fact that all great States are imperialist – inevitably so – doesn't relieve this peculiar condition.

MB: My next question is prompted by a conversation I had with my friend, the Portuguese scholar and Barker translator Paulo Eduardo Carvalho, in the cathedral in Santiago de Compostela in Galicia, northern Spain. He, coming from a southern European, Catholic background, was complaining that the cathedral was not ornate enough, whereas I, a northern European Protestant by background, was offended by how ornate it was by comparison with the Dutch Protestant churches that I admire. We concluded that, whether or not one is an atheist, one's sense of aesthetics is still very much informed by one's religious heritage. We found that this related, somehow, to your own work.

I perceive that there is an austerity in your work which can be said to be beautiful, which is not to say your visual aesthetic lacks opulence – something can be simultaneously austere and opulent. Is there an aspect of your aesthetic that is informed by something essentially Protestant?

HB: No, I suspect not. Let's talk about the design for *Slowly*, though. It's austere in the sense that its fundamentals are relatively simple. For example, the costumes are completely black, and quite enveloping. Within the concept of the costume is a deliberate attempt to invoke, however dismal it is in our minds, the seventeenth century's association of a small colour palate and physical immobility with high status. There's only one place to go for that, and it's seventeenth-century Spain. The etiquette of the court of Philip IV was characterized by absolute stillness. And also the cost of the material is very high.

So, you might see combinations of styles and manners. Not *all* austerity is a northern, post-reformation characteristic. But, to talk specifically of what I always attempt with The Wrestling School, my method is not to overwhelm the actors – and, significantly, the speech – with visuality. The intention is to focus. I have to say, however, that even with a play which purported to be contemporary – say, *Wonder and Worship* – I'd always avoid commonplace costume design. I'd want to announce, in costume, this isn't the world as you know it.

MB: So, when I say "austerity", would you prefer 'simplicity'?

HB: I suppose so. You invoked northern Protestantism. I'm very drawn to Baroque southern Germany, Spain and so on, but I don't try to replicate that. There's very little gold in my productions. Monochrome is dominant. It has something to do with the relationship between the visual and the voice. I don't know why, but it's my sense that an over-elaborate colour range and too much stuff, literally, on the stage diminish the status of the voice in that context. If you have that much voice to get over, you can't start blinding the audience with diversions.

MB: Let's come onto silence, which, again, becomes an issue in your most recent shows. Calf, the final princess in *Slowly*, for instance – her choice is articulated by Sign. Calf remains entirely silent. Then, in *Hurts Given and Received*, you have

Bach's silence. This interests me, because you're known for the richness of your language, yet you seem to have a great respect for silence.

HB: I sometimes wish there was more of it. It's such a powerful thing when speech stops. When very highly wrought speaking stops, the power of the silence is huge. So, probably I might have benefited from using that device a little bit more. I can certainly see that it can be quite chilling.

I don't use silence in the way that Harold Pinter used it, to mean that there's something going on in those silences. I'm not interested in anything going on in the silence; it's just literally a stop, a stop of the flow. Technically, sometimes, I think an audience sometimes requires room to breathe.

MB: In *Slowly*, Calf's silence has ramifications. It has an effect upon Sign. The tumult of emotions within Sign, as she realizes that, actually, Calf is more admirable than she herself is, that is a catastrophic moment for her. It's also, in a curious way, a euphoric moment for her. The more Calf's silence continues, the more Sign's euphoria is enhanced. Sign is more deeply impressed the longer Calf maintains her silence.

HB: Yes, and that comes partly from the fact that these four women split into two pairs. Having thought how alone she was in declaring that it's better to die than be conquered, Sign now realizes that Calf has worked this out further, and can see the ramifications. So, there's a profound admiration for her intellect.

MB: Her speechlessness is confirmation. I'm fascinated by your capacity to create a silence which is affirmative in this context, because there's no gesture either. Calf is without gesture and without speech, but the very fact that she does not engage in any negative gesture confirms for Sign that what she's saying is true. With each statement Sign makes about Calf's motivations, the speechlessness and the lack of gesture acts as a confirmation. That's very powerful.

HB: Watching the production the other night, I thought she becomes a mummy, in effect – the way the light falls on her, the way she's costumed and so on. She has no need for speech. She's mummified. She's waiting to be discovered.

MB: This brings me onto the subject of the sacred. Correct me if I'm wrong, but I assume that you're an atheist.

HB: Yes, probably, although the word 'atheist' worries me because it implies a conscious hostility to religion which I don't have.

MB: The sacred, as it exists in death, in desire, in love, in art and, in particular, within those realms in your theatre, is it partly prompted by a nausea at the denigration of the sacred within what I would call late capitalist society, where hyper-commercialism precisely denigrates the sacred?

HB: Individualism is the triumph and disaster of the West, a typical contradiction arriving with the deepest range of experience ever encountered in human society. The individual is the focus of profit-making, gratification, consumption and so on, but, at the same time, the receptacle for scarcely tolerable 'rights', all legally enforceable.

So, where has the sacred migrated to, if it exists at all? Is it in private life, in what is effectively a religion of sexuality? It's possible. I have contemplated this in *Gertrude – The Cry*. But it's a sacred place that is routinely violated. What I think of as sacred is the unconscious and the instinctual, places society and its coercive mechanisms are forever attempting to invade. Here, in the uncivilized and uneducated aspect of human nature, is where I place my theatre, and it's here you might find the ecstasy of tragedy, I suggest.

MB: Whether one likes it or not, that ends up having political ramifications, I think. In the sense that late capitalism, hyper-commercialism, secular democracy, whatever you want to call it, does rob the individual of a sense of something beyond her or himself. It is also hostile to death; it attempts to pretend that death doesn't exist.

HB: Yes, it tries to abolish death, at least to medicalize it. The hospital – scarcely a caring environment – becomes the prison of the population, with its false promises of rejuvenation and hypotheses about 'collective responsibility'. Most political programmes in western societies are designed around health and education. What chimera lies behind all this? It's the idea of the 'good life', I suppose, a sort of utilitarian notion of generalized happiness. It can't cope with pain, either physical or moral. None of the *soi-disant* 'progressive' societies, from Robespierre's secular religion, through Leninism, into Welfare State paternalism, even understood suffering or death except as a malformation, a sort of diabolical distortion. As for sacrifice, that's a thing inscribed on war memorials.

MB: How far does the Nazi Holocaust impact upon the Theatre of Catastrophe?

HB: I'm not aware of such an impact. Have I written about it?

MB: No. Hitler makes an appearance in *Found in the Ground* but […]

HB: But only to talk about painting.

MB: Quite. I'm not suggesting there's a conscious reference to the Holocaust as a subject. What I'm suggesting is a connection between the Theatre of Catastrophe and something Primo Levi wrote in his book *Moments of Reprieve*, where he's talking about morality within the death camps, and the fact that you cannot apply the morality of bourgeois democracy to the death camps. In other words, one's moral compass is changed profoundly. That's where I see the connection: in situations of catastrophe, one's motivations and morality change.

HB: Yes, all breakdowns in collective discipline are likely to induce catastrophe, aren't they? Interesting speculations surround the recovery of certain spontaneous emotional impulses which are normally submerged. Are these inevitably appalling? I'm not certain. In *The Europeans*, the protagonist has suffered an atrocity, and is invited – in the interests of harmony – to forgive. She declines to do so. She even constructs her life around this unforgiving. We are conventionally urged to abolish anger, but perhaps we forfeit something in doing so. I'm not sure.

In a more recent work, *Wonder and Worship in the Dying Ward*, a transgressive mother refuses to apologize for the act that unintentionally disfigured her child. She senses that to do so would damage her sense of herself – it's a powerful intuition. Of course, it's always easy to say sorry when one sees the consequences of an action. But perhaps it's induced, even insincere, in many cases, rather as criminals are sorry when they are caught.

But to look further than that, there is the integrity in an act which might define the self, and to save this self from annihilation, another might need to be sacrificed. How can one actually argue for this? It's impossible. It's the *tragic sense* […] always, one sees why society hates tragedy.

MB: Of course, the catastrophic experience need not be as extreme as the Nazi Holocaust. However, I wonder to what extent the infantilizing of culture in liberal humanist democracy is a response to its inability to come to terms with a Holocaust which occurred only 65 years ago.

HB: Yes, there's a constant propaganda that, if you're not self-policing, as a human being, you might commit the kind of atrocities committed by the Nazis. I don't know how it works in Germany, where there's a huge amount of investment in controlling the minds of the young, but lying behind it must be the idea – and the Holocaust must be crucial in this – that we all have the capacity to participate in mass murder.

MB: I'm very aware and respectful of your suspicion of politics and of a political motive being assigned to your work. Thirty years ago you observed that you had lost the support of critics on the left, because you had moved away from a straightforward satirical theatre. However, I observe that your theatre stands against the denigration of the body and desire, and against the denial of death, both of which are important aspects of our prevailing culture. It also defies the commercial imperative to a theatre of entertainment. Doesn't that, in a sense, make your drama among the most radical of theatres?

HB: I think it's impossible to make any art that doesn't have a political implication somewhere inside it. Certainly, you're right in identifying the governing obsessions of the work. My theatre is concerned deeply with the sacredness of the body, particularly in its sexual life, and what that releases through passion, which society would prefer to govern through pornography. There is also a reconciliation with death, which, I completely agree with you, is deliberately occluded by welfare culture.

   As things stand, I sense from the rhetoric of our time, the old are now going to be picked out as a group to be persecuted over their consumption of resources. This is very much a Brave New World. So, death, I think, will be re-examined, only as an element of the economy, but not as experience; it won't have any spiritual meaning.

MB: On this question of your earlier work where the expression was more easily defined as being political and of the left. It seems to me that you were defined as being an 'angry young man', and part of a left group of writers. Do you think you were perceived to have defected or, at least, to have betrayed that? Is that part of the hostility you still face from the English theatre establishment?

HB: I think I was never at the service of an idea. The idea is, for me, always oscillating, and the theatre is a poor device for instruction in any case. In plays I wrote about the contemporary world and its politics, the tragic instinct – in a rudimentary form – came through the narrative, and this must explain my estrangement from left theatres. The Royal Court rejected *Claw*, *Victory* and *The Castle*. This seems scandalous, even inexplicable. But it's not surprising. The Brechtian theatre – of which the Royal Court was a vigorous child – insists on clarity and enlightenment. This can't be got from me.

MB: Do you think that the perception the left critics had that you'd betrayed them was part of their hostility?

HB: I'd already stopped listening to them by then, so I couldn't tell you what they were thinking.

MB: It seems to me that the London critics see themselves as the defenders of the castle that is London theatre. They boycott you, but they attack you in passing; Michael Billington, for example, manages to attack you while reviewing Torben Betts, who, of course, wrote under the patronage of Alan Ayckbourn, but has, more recently, expressed himself to be influenced by your work. I find Billington's comment quite sinister as it seems to be saying to Betts, 'if you continue your considerable journey from Ayckbourn to Barker, your fate will be the same as Barker's'. The London critics seem to see themselves as protecting the gates of the castle from catastrophism, from whichever quarter it comes.

HB: I have to agree with that. I deepened my menace, didn't I?; because not only did I adopt tragedy, as an opponent of any systematized, comforting theatre, but I then went on to do something that I think caused graver offence, which was to appear to attack the pantheon. I rewrote Shakespeare and, above all, Chekhov – as I've always said, I think Chekhov is the national dramatist in England, not Shakespeare. The critical response that I got for my (Uncle) Vanya was bitter. It was the last time they ever bothered to turn out for my work in any numbers. They considered that I was attacking the whole pantheon structure of art, the major artist, the genius, and belittling it. Of course, I wasn't; I have certain respect for Chekhov, but the way that Chekhov is used here offended me. In articulating this dramatically, I effectively banished myself.

MB: There are two modern tragedians, yourself and Arthur Miller, who undermine central pillars of the Aristotelian model of tragedy. One the London critics are prepared to accept and the other they are not. I think the reason for that is that what you say implicitly in your work is more threatening than what Miller says. Miller says that the tragic hero need not be high born, the tragic hero can be working class. Whereas what you say is more profound, which is that the fatal flaw is not necessarily the driving force of tragedy, that the driving force of tragedy is the connection between sexual desire and death, which is more difficult for the critics to accept. They can handle Miller because, at least, he accepts the notion of the fatal flaw. Whilst you do reference antiquity, you don't feel the need to hold Aristotle's hand as you do so.

HB: No, and I've never comprehended catharsis either, as an aesthetic theory. I can't see the point of creating a work of art which enables a public to discharge some anxiety in order to leave the theatre in a healthier condition than when it came in. I don't ask that of the public or of the actors. If good art wounds you, I want that wound to be experienced continuously, not resolved. So, the play has no utilitarian function at all.

It is not a problem for the liberal establishment to swallow a Marxist thesis, for the idea that money is evil has such a pedigree, and originates in antiquity. More recently (though it's scarcely *modern*), the theatre applauds itself for its responsibility in issuing social critiques (entertaining ones, preferably). No one's soul is much damaged by this exercise. Nor nourished, I think.

MB: Clearly it is difficult for young playwrights coming after you who are attracted to the Theatre of Catastrophe. Do you perceive there to be any discernible strand of catastrophism after you?

HB: Oh, I think so. I don't go to the theatre. I'm not a visitor of the theatre, so I can't claim to know what's going on, but, from individuals I know and meet, and from those who've done my work, and students especially, there's a growing sense that naturalism is defunct. At RADA this year they performed my play *Crimes in Hot Countries*. At the end, a group of students came up to me, modestly and seriously, like a delegation, and declared they were sorry they hadn't done the play justice. I said, "I rather enjoyed it, I thought it was good". They replied, "we just know we're not being taught properly, we're not being equipped to play this work". They seemed to be looking to me to do something about it. Of course, I have no influence over drama teaching. This was a sign, I think, that the complete triumph of naturalism in every quarter – which obviously has political implications – is creating an unease among young people in the theatre.

MB: I'm intrigued by the relationship between your theatre and the drama of Sarah Kane, who spoke very warmly of your work. I perceive in *Blasted* an attempt to create a Theatre of Catastrophe, to consciously set up a realistic situation, and then explode it. She was turned upon ferociously by the London critical establishment – albeit that some people, notably Billington, recanted their original position after dramatists such as Harold Pinter and Caryl Churchill came to the play's defence.

HB: I can only think this was made possible by the incorporation of the text or the writer into the project of liberal humanist culture. If you can interpret the text as an attack on, or a critique of, contemporary culture, especially capitalism, nationalism or any of the bête noires of the liberal establishment, you can be included. It doesn't matter at all what the plasticity of the work is, or its value in metaphor, language, obscenity or image; none of that matters at all to this question, 'can the work be brought within?' Everything must be included.

MB: Allow me to ask you about your relationship with modernism. I perceive you to have one foot in antiquity and the other in modernity. There's something about your approach to antiquity which bears the hallmark of what I would describe as the 'liberation of modernism', in terms of what modernism allowed writers to do in relation to the naturalism that preceded it. Your *Vanya* is a prime example of this. It relates, I think, to Pinter's comment that, in the theatre, something can be simultaneously "true and untrue". That's something that Ibsen and Chekhov would have disagreed with; for them there had to be a consistency in chronology, in setting, in time and place, which you breach, and early modernism also breaches it. Do you perceive yourself to have that relationship with the 'liberation of modernity'?

HB: No.

MB: So where does that breach in naturalistic consistency in your work come from?

HB: I really don't know where it comes from. There is no serious passage of time in my work. In *Hurts Given and Received*, for example, there's no moment consecutive to another. I can't identify the origin of that sense of freedom I have.

MB: You're not aware of any relationship to modernism at all?

HB: No, I'm not aware of it. Is Kafka a modernist?

MB: Yes.

HB: In an artist like Kafka, I sense a predecessor. The extreme imaginative licence – above all, the freedom from mimetic discipline. The absence of ideology. The random nature of the event.

MB: When people choose to theorize that your work has a complex interrelationship with certain forms of modernism does that offend you?

HB: Not at all, since I don't understand it.

MB: You've talked about how your theatre creates in the individual audience member an opposite effect to that intended by Brecht, that individually it creates a sense of moral, emotional and psychological isolation, and even decay, this as opposed to the solidarity intended by Brecht. I agree with that, but I perceive there to be a relationship nevertheless. Brecht re-imagines history, and you do also. Brecht alienates, and I would suggest you do too; albeit in a different way, to a different end. So, rather than your theatre being merely very distinct from Brecht's, does it bear an antithetical relationship to it? In other words, would your theatre be different if Brecht had never existed? Is it in part a reaction, consciously or subconsciously, against Brecht?

HB: I can only say I'm not aware of that. But I am aware, and I've stated this before, that nausea is a vitally important aspect of artistic development and artistic change. If I hadn't entered the Royal Court in the 1970s and encountered so much middle-class Marxist theatre, I probably would never have moved so violently towards tragedy and tragedy's ambiguity. I experienced this nausea in the sheer amount of propaganda that that place was issuing out, in the name of the working class, with whom the directors had no relationship whatsoever. As a working-class youth, which I was, I observed that there were few others, mostly actors. From the model of the Berliner Ensemble, they thought they would educate an entirely imaginary working-class audience in virtue. To sit around in that environment made me very uncomfortable. In this state of nausea, I moved, rather desperately, first clutching at satire and then, finding that extremely pernicious and narrow, I tried to discover a tragedy for myself.

Brecht was much greater than anything that went on in his name at the Royal Court, of course. Whether I included a reaction against Brecht in my revulsion, I can't be sure. But the Enlightenment project appals me. I encountered it at the Royal Court, and, as much as Brecht is part of the Enlightenment, which I believe he is, I repudiated that, and I still repudiate it.

The hardest thing – from a technical point of view – in all this is to undo without replacing, without attempting to replace. Simply to cut the Gordian knot of superimposed moral values is enough. To cut through that or, at least, to damage it in a work of art is the first stage. I don't need to talk about anything more than that.

MB: I don't know if you have any knowledge of Maurice Maeterlinck's play *The Blind*, but I perceive a similarity between the blind themselves in Maeterlinck's play and your chorus of terminally ill people in *Wonder and Worship*. It seemed to me almost as if you and Maeterlinck had written it together as an extrapolation from his play.

HB: Another artist I'm not familiar with. But *Wonder and Worship* is not the first of my plays which features a chorus, of course. I used it in *The Last Supper* and *Seven Lears*, precisely as a dislocation, a public disclaimer of naturalism. These choruses are not, however, a sort of public; they are without virtue.

MB: Allow me to come onto the subject of high heels in your work.

HB: [Laughs]. About which things have been written.

MB: I'm intrigued by the use of high heels in much of your work. It subverts the vapid use of them as a mere fetish. It elevates physically, of course, and enhances, for many actresses, their capacity for elegance.

HB: There are two stage aspects to this garment. One is that it gives height, obviously, and posture, because it alters a woman's shape profoundly. Women have been wearing high heels since at least the third century BC; it's well recorded. So, they're inherent in European culture; there's something profoundly historic about this garment.

You might say it has a symbolic relation with sexuality and its opposite, appearing and disappearing with climates of erotic expression and repression. Also – speaking purely artistically, purely of the stage or film – heels have a tremendous sonic value. The actress appearing and disappearing – announced and then the sound slowly decaying – must recall every child's memory of the passage of women on the pavement, one of the deep resonances of infancy, and embedded in the sexual imagination.

MB: Some actresses seem to grasp this from your work, almost instinctively. I discovered this recently, whilst working on the Royal Scottish Academy of Music and Drama's performed reading of your *(Uncle) Vanya*. The young actress Nicola Daley – although she was, in fact, playing Chekhov – talked about her sense that she required high heels. Even playing a male role, she sensed from the play the need for her, as a woman on the stage, to have that elevation and authority. It wasn't being required of her; she herself suggested it.

HB: There's been a generation change here, I think. There was a generation of feminists who regarded high heels as the purest manifestation of enslavement to a sexual stereotype. These ideas seem less influential now. A new generation of women just sees them as part of the great cultural tradition of being a woman, which, first and foremost, elevates your arse.

MB: I discern a connection between the tragic aesthetic of The Wrestling School and the work of the Grotowskian Polish company Teatr Pieśń Kozła (Song of the Goat Theatre). Are you aware of such a connection?

HB: Recently I read some Grotowski. He talks a lot about the theatre as collaborative. There's very little collaboration in my work, with anybody. The Wrestling School is not a collaborative company. It's often misunderstood as being an actors' company, which it's not.

    Of course, the actors serve the work, and in this sense, any production in theatre is a collaboration. But I wish to emphasize that – for all my profound respect for the actor – I do not require his opinion as a means of arriving at some sort of agreement on how he might address the role. I rely entirely on his skill and sensibility. Otherwise, as the writer of the piece, I know not only what is written, but also what I require from its playing. The absence of the collaborative will in the company – I detect no demand for it – both defines it and, perhaps, renders the experience of it luxurious. It must be said, in audition I am as clear as I can be about this. No one wants friction on the rehearsal floor.

MB: Reading your recently published poetry collection *Sheer Detachment*, I experienced it almost as one long poem, rather than as a series of poems, and I experienced it as a landscape. It's a landscape with character voices, which links it to theatre, but experiencing it as a landscape obviously connects it to painting. Your play *Found in the Ground* is a theatrical landscape. I experienced them in a very similar way.

HB: I think that is a proper response. When I talk about *Found in the Ground* – which I find it very hard to do, because it's so disordered, it doesn't have a spinal structure really at all – I have to think of it as an accumulation; it only works by accumulation, not by narrative. That's true of the poems too, as you suggest.

Although they're meaningful individually, really they need to be accumulated to acquire – what? – not *meaning*, but a sense […]

MB: I've suggested a connection, too, with painting. Is the painter in you influential in this?

HB: Probably, yes. My pictures show a landscape that is almost anonymous in its lack of character, in which figures are placed who are engaged in extraordinary activities, illicit activities, criminal activities and so on. They're situated in a hostile, arid place. That is how I approach theatre too, actually. I don't really do detailed sets. *Found in the Ground* didn't have a set; it had mechanical animals manoeuvred on a rusty deck, and the figures came in bringing their cultural history with them. So, yes, it is a point at which all three of my practices seem to come together. It didn't come easily.

MB: If I can turn to your 2005 play *The Fence in its Thousandth Year*. Your resistance to clear, political intentions being ascribed to your work notwithstanding, I wonder to what extent you're prepared to accept that, among its many possibilities, it contains a potential allegory about current politics, in particular the so-called Israeli 'security fence'. I'm not suggesting that you wrote the play as a direct allegory of that, but, rather, that in a profound, philosophical sense, the play suggests that these sorts of physical structures within human societies sow the seeds of their own destruction; the very transgression they are supposed to prevent, they exactly promote.

HB: I'm not sure that the Israeli fence had anything much to do it with it, but the history of fences erected between societies is so long, going back to and beyond Hadrian, that I didn't contemplate writing something that simply criticized the concept of the fence. The historian in me, what's left of it, suspects that sometimes walls are very good things. We've lived through an era, throughout my whole lifetime, in which separation has been regarded as an offence to the human spirit. The view has been that no man should ever be separated from another. Something more brutal in me tells me that it's not a bad thing to be separated from another people sometimes, especially if you have an intransigent loathing or fear of them.

In *The Fence in its Thousandth Year* the wall will always be literally decaying from the moment it is erected, as any structure does. However, that isn't to say that it doesn't serve a purpose at any given time. It may serve to privilege one group over another, but it may also serve to preserve one group against the inveterate hostility of another. Its ambiguity is what makes the fence fascinating to me.

That said, you're quite right, the psychology of the fence, i.e. the psychology of the forbidden that lies beyond the fence, produces strange, irrational and, in the case of this play, sexual mysteries that are objectively invalid, but nevertheless play an active part in the life of that society.

MB: It interests me that these ambiguities are not constructed over time in the play; they emanate from a very unambiguous, very powerful, visual and sexual moment at the very beginning. All of the moral and political ambiguities flow from a moment in which there is no ambiguity.

HB: The opening picture *is*, I think, ambiguous – not in terms of the act, the copulation of a wealthy woman with a crowd of poor men – but in the way the barrier between them emphasizes the erotic investment in *the stranger*, a thing later revealed to be chimerical.

But this is a play without victims, and, I would suggest, without guilty parties either (I think neither of these categories can be discovered in my work). It is deeply rewarding to write of the excesses of the privileged without the obligation to humiliate them. Victoria Wicks' duchess suffers and is never ashamed. This instinct is not available to all actors in a moral age like this.

MB: Although you were brought up by a communist father, and described yourself as a socialist in your youth, you've said on numerous occasions that the extent to which you continue to have political convictions of your own is almost irrelevant to your theatre. Yet, you choose, now and again, perhaps mischievously, to make a statement of your own politics publicly; I'm thinking particularly about the occasion last year (2009) when you suddenly announced yourself to be a monarchist, which will have surprised some people. Regardless of whether or not you consider them to be relevant to your work, how would you describe your personal politics now?

HB: I would not want to suggest I am somehow immune to opinion. I have opinions on most subjects, probably too many. I try, however, not to contaminate my writing with them. Having declared this, I am not so foolish as to assume none of my attitudes have ever permeated my work. But I am essentially reactive in my way with social upheavals; I sense above all the contradictions, and, along with that, I feel the pulse of the past, which cannot be asphyxiated and yet may also threaten. I am a European, and we are made of our past like few other cultures.

MB: You have a number of allies of your work in the United States. How do you view that relationship?

HB: Artistically, it's been peculiar, because there's no subsidized theatre in America. If I've been presented there, it's nearly always been a collaboration between professional actors and academe, which is their equivalent of subsidized theatre, I suppose. I've never sensed that I've actually made much impact in America, but it's hard to say where I have made an impact, frankly. There's a slow turning-over of the work; I don't know how they do it; I've not seen it; I was there in 1975 to see *Claw*, but that's a long time ago. I don't know what they bring to it. I have a sense they are looking for a moral content in it all the time, which is why I tend to get the earlier work done there. No one's done *Gertrude,* no one's done *The Fence.* I shall be surprised if they do these recent plays. They want a theatre that has some kind, earnest, ethical value to it. So, it's not a natural territory for me at the moment.

MB: Which of your many dramas do you feel most satisfied with?

HB: I always refer to *Gertrude* as the major work, but that is, perhaps, because the production realized it so well. It was immaculately cast and performed. By contrast, I have seen brutal and clumsy productions of it also, and had to look away. I also recall with some satisfaction the structure and ethical paradoxes of *The Last Supper.*

MB: How do you foresee the future development of The Wrestling School?

HB: I have often said The Wrestling School is first and foremost a rumour, and it's not easy to speculate on the future of a rumour. Circumstances – financial and cultural – have never favoured it, but, had they done so, it could never have been what it is, in many ways a phenomenon defined by marginality.

The form of the private funding that replaced the Arts Council subsidy is going to alter. We will certainly perform in New York now, a thing unthinkable a decade ago. Also, the terms of my fellowship at Exeter University include a full-scale production of a very large play, *Nausicaa at 50,* in the Northcott Theatre, Exeter. So, some strategy exists. We will adapt to circumstances. The important thing is that it serves as a definition of theory-in-practice, as I've articulated it. This can be managed on an even-further reduced scale, if necessary.

This interview was conducted, exclusively for this book, at Howard Barker's home in Brighton on 3 May 2010. It took place on the day after The Wrestling School presented three Barker plays – a performed reading of Wonder and Worship in the Dying Ward *and full productions of* Slowly *and* Hurts Given and Received *– at Riverside Studios in London.*

Notes

1. *Cheek* at the Royal Court Theatre, London.
2. Howard Barker, *Death, The One and the Art of Theatre* (London: Routledge, 2005), p. 1.
3. Howard Barker, 'Fortynine asides for a tragic theatre' in *Arguments for a Theatre*, (Manchester: Manchester University Press, 1997 [1989]), p. 18.
4. The 1976 screenplay entitled *All Bleeding* was never produced on television. Rewritten for the stage in 1980 as *No End of Blame*, it made its theatre premiere at the Royal Court Theatre, London in 1981.
5. *One Afternoon on the 63rd Level of the North Face of the Pyramid of Cheops the Great* was presented by BBC Radio in 1970.
6. Pitlochry Festival Theatre did not stage *The Castle* in its 2010 season.
7. Howard Barker/Eduardo Houth, *A Style and its Origins* (London: Oberon, 2007), p.92.
8. Howard Barker, *Arguments for a Theatre* (Manchester: Manchester University Press, 1997 [1989]), p. 19.

A Note on Howard Barker

Howard Barker is a unique voice in world theatre. Through his 'Theatre of Catastrophe', exemplified by such plays as *The Europeans, Gertrude – The Cry* and *Slowly*, he has forged his own distinct form of modern tragedy.

For Barker the theatre is a place for imagination and moral speculation, not constrained by the demands of realism or any ideology. "It is not", he argues, "to insult an audience to offer it ambiguity".[8]

Barker's early work was staged by such companies as the Royal Court Theatre, the Royal Shakespeare Company, the Open Space Theatre, Sheffield Crucible and the Almeida. His work is played extensively, in translation, throughout Europe, and in the United States and Australia.

In recent years his work has been staged, to critical acclaim, at both the Royal Lyceum Theatre, Edinburgh and Dundee Rep. No fewer than twelve of his plays (eleven of them directed by Hugh Hodgart, currently Dean of Drama) have been presented at Scotland's conservatoire, the Royal Scottish Academy of Music and Drama.

He writes regularly for radio, both in the UK and Europe. He is the author of plays for marionettes and has written three librettos for opera.

He is currently Artistic Director of The Wrestling School, a company established to disseminate his works and develop his theory of production. In 2009, an international Barker festival, entitled '21 for 21' was held, in celebration of the twenty-first anniversary of the company. Barker's work was presented in seven languages on four continents.

Barker is the author of three works of theory, and seven volumes of poetry. He is also a painter; his paintings are held in national collections in England (V&A, London) and Europe.

A Note on the Editor

Mark Brown has been a professional theatre critic and arts writer for seventeen years. He is currently theatre critic for the Scottish national newspaper the *Sunday Herald*. He is also a contributor to the arts pages of the *Daily Telegraph*. His work has appeared in a wide variety of newspapers and magazines, including *The Guardian*, the *Sunday Times*, the *New Statesman*, *The Herald*, *The Scotsman*, *Scotland on Sunday*, *Sunday Business*, *Business AM*, *The List*, the *Toronto Star* and *Inside Film* (Australia). In 1999 he received the Edinburgh Fringe Society's *Allen Wright Award* for young arts journalists. He is currently a member of the executive committee of the International Association of Theatre Critics (IATC).

As a broadcaster on the arts, he has appeared on BBC television programmes *The Culture Show* and *Newsnight Scotland*, and has made numerous appearances on arts programmes on BBC Radio 3 and BBC Radio Scotland.

He teaches at the University of Strathclyde and the Royal Scottish Academy of Music and Drama (RSAMD). He holds a Master of Research degree (on the contemporary, United States-based theatre company The Riot Group) from Strathclyde.

He has presented public papers on theatre in Poland, Portugal, the Czech Republic, England, Wales and Scotland. His theoretical and critical work has appeared in numerous journals, including *New Theatre Quarterly* (Cambridge University Press); *Sinais de cena* [*Signs of the Stage*] (Portuguese Association of Theatre Critics / University of Lisbon); *Critical Stages* (IATC); and the Czech journal *Svět a divadlo* [*World and Theatre*]. He was recently commissioned to write an article, on the National Theatre of Scotland, for publication in a Farsi-language collection in Iran.

As part of the '21 for 21' festival, he worked as dramaturg on the RSAMD's staged reading of Barker's *(Uncle) Vanya*, directed by Neil Doherty. He has two pieces, 'Barker, criticism and the philosophy of "the Art of Theatre"' and 'Twenty-one Asides on Theatre Criticism', due for publication in the forthcoming collection *Howard Barker's Art of Theatre* (Manchester University Press), edited by David Ian Rabey and Sarah Goldingay.

Notes on Contributors

Elisabeth Angel-Perez is Professor of English Literature at the University of Paris-Sorbonne (Paris IV). She is a specialist in contemporary British theatre. Her recent publications include *Howard Barker et le Théâtre de la Catastrophe* (Paris: Editions Théâtrales, 2006) and, *Voyages au bout du possible: les théâtres du traumatisme de Samuel Beckett à Sarah Kane* (Paris: Klincksieck, 2006) and, with Alexandra Poulain, *Endgame ou le théâtre mis en pièces* (Paris: PUF, cned, 2009). She also translates into French plays and theoretical writings by Howard Barker, Martin Crimp and Caryl Churchill.

Thierry Dubost is a Professor of English and Irish literature at the University of Caen, France. His numerous books include *Struggle, Defeat or Rebirth: Eugene O'Neill's Vision of Humanity* (Jefferson: McFarland, 1997) and *The Plays of Thomas Kilroy* (Jefferson: McFarland, 2007).

Penny Francis MBE is a writer, editor and lecturer, active in the promotion and development of the arts of puppetry, especially puppetry in contemporary theatre, for half a century. She co-founded the Puppet Centre Trust in 1974 and is international consultant to the Central School of Speech and Drama, University of London, where she has taught since 1992.

Karoline Gritzner is Lecturer in Drama and Theatre Studies at Aberystwyth University. She is co-editor (with David Ian Rabey) of *Theatre of Catastrophe: New Essays on Howard Barker* (London: Oberon, 2006). She has written on contemporary British drama and on the connections between Theodor Adorno's critical theory and performance. She is editor of a collection of essays, *Eroticism and Death in Theatre and Performance* (Hatfield: University of Hertfordshire Press, 2010), which includes a contribution from Howard Barker.

Malcolm Hay retired as comedy editor of *Time Out - London* in 2007, after 20 years in the post. His diverse career has ranged from play writing and freelance journalism, to periods teaching at the University of Massachusetts and the University of East London, and employment as a script reader for the National Theatre and the Royal Shakespeare Company. He was a member of the editorial board of *Theatre Quarterly* and was co-editor, with Philip Roberts, of the book *Edward Bond: A Companion to the Plays* (London: Theatre Quarterly Publications, 1978).

Dan Hefko is a teacher of theatre, film, and world literature at Hanover High School in Mechanicsville, Virginia, USA. In 1995 he directed a production of Howard Barker's *All He Fears* at Ripon College, Wisconsin. His poetry has been published in a number of national literary journals including *Threepenny Review*, *River Styx*, and *New York Quarterly*.

Vanasay Khamphommala (Université Paris-Sorbonne) is currently completing his PhD., entitled 'Spectres of Shakespeare in Howard Barker's work'. He is also a director and translates Barker into French for publication (*Death, the One and the Art of Theatre,* in collaboration with Elisabeth Angel-Perez).

Charles Lamb teaches in theatre at the University of Winchester. He is also a director of contemporary theatre. He is author of *The Theatre of Howard Barker* (London: Routledge, [1997] 2005), and an associate of Barker's theatre company The Wrestling School.

David Ian Rabey is Professor of Drama and Theatre Studies at Aberystwyth University. He is the author of numerous critical works, including *English Drama Since 1940* (2003), *Howard Barker: Politics and Desire* ([1989] 2009), and *Howard Barker: Ecstasy and Death* (2009). He is co-editor (with Karoline Gritzner) of *Theatre of Catastrophe: New Essays on Howard Barker* (2006) and is currently preparing a new collection, *Howard Barker's Art of Theatre* (co-edited with Sarah Goldingay). He has directed and/or acted in twelve Barker plays to date, including performing in Barker's own production of *The Twelfth Battle of Isonzo,* and is an associate of The Wrestling School.

Duška Radosavljević is a lecturer in Drama and Theatre Studies at the University of Kent. She also reviews for the newspaper *The Stage.* She has previously worked as a dramaturg and theatre practitioner. Her current research is in the area of ensemble theatre.

Nina Rapi is a dramatist and fiction writer. Her plays – which include *Kiss the Shadow; Reasons to Hide; Angelstate; Edgewise; Lovers;* and *Ithaka* – have been seen in various London venues, such as the Gielgud, the Gate, the Lyric, the Soho, and the Royal Festival Hall. Her work has also been staged at the National Theatre of Greece. Essays on her work have been published in the UK, the USA and Italy. Her short stories have been published in the UK, the USA and Greece. She is also founding editor of *BRAND* literary magazine.

Elizabeth Sakellaridou is Professor of Theatre Studies at the School of English of Aristotle University in Thessaloniki, Greece. She has written extensively on various contemporary British dramatists and on theoretical issues of the contemporary stage (including phenomenology and performativity, gender and culture). Her special interest in Barker has yielded four published essays, one published interview, two more papers under publication and a book project dealing with the discourse of melancholia in Barker's tragic theatre.

Aleks Sierz is Visiting Professor at Rose Bruford College, and author of *In-Yer-Face Theatre: British Drama Today* (London: Faber, 2001), *The Theatre of Martin Crimp* (Methuen Drama, 2006) and *John Osborne's Look Back in Anger* (London: Continuum, 2008). He is currently writing a study of contemporary new writing entitled *Rewriting the Nation: British Theatre Today,* to be published by Methuen in 2011. He also works as a journalist, broadcaster, lecturer and theatre critic.

Simon Trussler was founding editor of *Theatre Quarterly* and is co-editor of *New Theatre Quarterly.* His many books include the award-winning *Cambridge Illustrated History of British Theatre* (1993), *The Faber Guide to Elizabethan and Jacobean Drama* (2006) and *Will's Will* (2007). Formerly Reader in Drama in the University of London, he is now Professor and Senior Research Fellow at Rose Bruford College.

Notes on Additional Questioners

Peter Buse is Senior Lecturer in English at the University of Salford (England).

Magali De Block is a Ph.D. student, under the supervision of Elisabeth Angel-Perez at Paris-Sorbonne (France).

Clare Finburgh is a lecturer at the University of Essex (England).

François Gallix is Emeritus Professor of English Literature at Paris-Sorbonne.

Sarah Hatchuel is Professor of English Literature at the University of Le Havre (France).

Hugh Hodgart is Dean of Drama at the Royal Scottish Academy of Music and Drama. He has directed eleven Barker plays at the Academy.

Alexandra Poulain is Professor of Irish Literature (theatre) at the University of Lille 3 (France).

A Barker Reading List

Plays
The following are published by Oberon (London):

Plays One: *Victory; The Europeans; The Possibilities; Scenes from an Execution* (2006).
Plays Two: *The Castle; Gertrude – The Cry; Animals in Paradise; 13 Objects* (2006).
Plays Three: *Claw; Ursula; He Stumbled; The Love of a Good Man* (2007).
Plays Four: *I Saw Myself; The Dying of Today; Found in the Ground; The Road, the House, the Road* (2008).
Plays Five: *The Last Supper; Seven Lears; Hated Nightfall; Wounds to the Face* (2009).
Plays Six: *Judith; (Uncle) Vanya; A House of Correction; Hurts Given and Received* (2010).
Dead Hands (2004).
The Ecstatic Bible (2004).
The Fence in its Thousandth Year (2005).
The Seduction of Almighty God (by the Boy Priest Loftus in the Abbey of Calcetto, 1539) (2006).
Slowly/Hurts Given and Received (2010).

Theory
Arguments for a Theatre, Manchester: Manchester University Press ([1989] [1993] 1997).
Death, The One and the Art of Theatre, London: Routledge ([2004] 2007).
A Style and its Origins, with Eduardo Houth, London: Oberon (2007).

Poetry
The following are published by Calder (London):

Don't Exaggerate: Desire and Abuse (1985).
The Breath of the Crowd (1986).
Gary the Thief/Gary Upright (1987).
Lullabies for the Impatient (1988).
The Ascent of Monte Grappa (1991).
The Tortmann Diaries (1996).

From Salt Publishing (Cambridge):
Sheer Detachment (2009).

A selection of further critical reading on Barker

In English: *Full-length studies*

Gambit 41(London: John Calder, 1984) (contains text of Pity in History, interview with Barker by Tony Dunn, and articles by Eric Mottram, Tony Dunn, Ian McDiarmid and Ruth Shade).

Gritzner, Karoline and Rabey, David Ian (eds) (2006), *Theatre of Catastrophe: New Essays on Howard Barker*, London: Oberon Books.

Lamb, Charles (1997), *Howard Barker's Theatre of Seduction*, London: Harwood Academic Press/Routledge.

—— (2005), *The Theatre of Howard Barker*, London: Routledge.

Rabey, David Ian ([1989] 2009), *Howard Barker: Politics and Desire: An Expository Study of his Drama and Poetry, 1969–1987*, London: Macmillan.

—— (2009), *Howard Barker: Ecstasy and Death: An Expository Study of His Plays and Production Work, 1988–2008*, London: Palgrave Macmillan.

Articles and essays on Barker

Barnett, David (2001), 'Howard Barker: Polemic Theatre and Dramatic Practice, Nietzsche, Metatheatre and the play The Europeans', *Modern Drama*, 44:4 (Winter), pp. 458–75.

Bas, Georges (1996), 'The Cunts, the Knobs and the Corpse: Obscenity and Horror in Howard Barker's Victory', *Contemporary Theatre Review*, 5:1&2, pp. 33–50.

Barker, Howard, 'On The Love of a Good Man' (RSC Publication, undated [probably 1978]).

——, 'On The Hang of the Gaol' (Warehouse Writers 1, RSC Publication, undated [probably 1978]).

——, 'On The Loud Boy's Life' (Warehouse Writers 9, RSC Publication, undated [probably 1980]).

—— (2007), 'On Naturalism and its Pretensions', *Studies in Theatre and Performance*, 27:3, pp. 289–293.

Barker, Howard and McDiarmid, Ian (1985), 'Barker + McDiarmid', joint interview in City Limits, 18 October 1985, pp. 78–9.

Cornforth, Andy and Rabey, David Ian (1999), 'Kissing Holes for the Bullets: Consciousness in Directing and Playing Barker's (Uncle) Vanya', *Performance and Consciousness*, 1:4, pp. 25–45.

Gallant, Desmond (1997), 'Brechtian Sexual Politics in the Plays of Howard Barker', *Modern Drama*, 40, pp. 403–413.

Gritzner, Karoline (2006), 'Catastrophic Sexualities in Howard Barker's Theatre of Transgression', in M. Sönser Breenand F. Peters (eds), *Genealogies of Identity: Interdisciplinary Readings on Sex and Sexuality*, Amsterdam and New York: Rodopi.

—— (2007), 'Adorno on Tragedy: Reading Catastrophe in Late Capitalist Culture', *Critical Engagements*, 1:2 (Autumn/Winter), pp. 25–52.

Hammond, Brean (2007), 'Is Everything History? Churchill, Barker and the Modern History Play', *Comparative Drama*, 41:1 (Winter), pp. 1–23.

Kilpatrick, David (2003), 'The Myth's the Thing: Barker's Revision of Elsinore in Gertrude – The Cry', *Text and Presentation* 24, New York: McFarland.

Klotz, Günther (1991), 'Howard Barker: Paradigm of Postmodernism', *New Theatre Quarterly*, 7:25 (February), pp. 20–26.

Megson, Chris (2006), 'Howard Barker and the Theatre of Catastrophe', in Mary Luckhurst (ed.), *A Companion to Modern British and Irish Drama*, Oxford: Blackwells.

Neubert, Isolde (1996), 'The Doorman of the Century is a Transient Phenomenon: The Symbolism of Dancer in Howard Barker's Hated Nightfall', in Bernhard Reitz (ed.), *Drama and Reality: Contemporary Drama in English 3*, Trier: Wissenschaftlicher Verlag Trier, pp. 145–153.

Rabey, David Ian (1991), 'For the Absent Truth Erect: Impotence and Potency in Howard Barker's Recent Drama', *Essays in Theatre/Études théâtrales*, 10:1, pp. 31–37.

—— (1992), 'What Do You See ?': Howard Barker's The Europeans', *Studies in Theatre Production*, 6 (December), pp. 23–34.

—— (1996), 'Howard Barker', in W. W. Demastes (ed.), *British Playwrights, 1956–1995: A Research and Production Sourcebook*, London: Greenwood Press, pp. 28–38.

—— (2005), 'Two Against Nature: Rehearsing and Performing Howard Barker's Production of his play The Twelfth Battle of Isonzo', *Theatre Research International*, 30:2 (July), pp. 175–189.

Sakellaridou, Elizabeth (2003), 'A Lover's Discourse – But Whose? Inversions of the Fascist Aesthetic in Howard Barker's Und and Other Recent English Plays', *European Journal of English Studies*, 7:1 (April), pp. 87–108.

Saunders, Graham (1999), 'Missing Mothers and Absent Fathers': Howard Barker's Seven Lears and Elaine Feinstein's Lear's Daughters', *Modern Drama*, 42, pp. 401–410.

Tomlin, Liz (2000), 'The Politics of Catastrophe', *Modern Drama*, 43:1, pp. 66–77.

—— (2001), 'Howard Barker', in John Bull (ed.), *Dictionary of Literary Biography, Volume 233: British and Irish Dramatists Since World War II, Second Series*, New York: Buccoli Clark, pp. 9–21.

Wilcher, Robert (1993), 'Honoring the Audience: the Theatre of Howard Barker', in James Acheson (ed.), *British and Irish Drama Since 1960*, Basingstoke: Macmillan, pp. 176–189.

Zimmermann, Heiner (1999), 'Howard Barker's Appropriation of Classical Tragedy', in Savas Patsalidis and Elizabeth Sakellaridou (eds), *(Dis)Placing Classical Tragedy*, Thessaloniki: University Studio Press, pp. 359–73.

—— (2001), 'Howard Barker's Brecht or Brecht as Whipping Boy', in Bernhard Reitz and Heiko Stahl (eds), *What Revels Are in Hand (Essays in Honour of Wolfgang Lippke)*, CDEStudies 8. Trier: Wissenschaftlicher Verlag Trier, pp. 221–26.

—— (2002), 'Howard Barker in the Nineties', in Bernhard Reitz and Mark Berninger (eds), *British Drama of the 1990s*, Anglistik & Englischunterricht 64. Heidelberg: Carl Winter, pp. 181–201.

A selective bibliography of other material pertaining to Barker

Bell, Leslie (ed.) (1984), *Contradictory Theatres*, Colchester: Essex University Press.

Craig, Sandy (ed.) (1980), *Dreams and Deconstructions*, London: Amber Lane Press.

Hay, Malcolm and Trussler, Simon (1981), 'The Small Discovery of Dignity' (interview), in Trussler, Simon (ed.), *New Theatre Voices of the Seventies*, London: Eyre Methuen.

Itzin, Catherine (1980), *Stages in the Revolution*, London: Methuen.

Kerensky, Oleg (1977), *The New British Drama*, London: Hamish Hamilton.

Rabey, David Ian (1986), *British and Irish Political Drama in the Twentieth Century*, London: Macmillan.

—— (2003), 'Barker: Appalling Enhancements', in *English Drama Since 1940*, London: Longman Literature in English series, Pearson Education, pp. 182–190.

In French:

Alternatives Théâtrales 57 (mai 1998). Numéro spécial Howard Barker, coordonné par Mike Sens, Bruxelles: Alternatives Théâtrales.

Angel-Perez, Elisabeth (ed.) (2006), *Howard Barker et le Théâtre de la Catastrophe*, Paris: Editions Théâtrales.

(1995), « L'espace de la catastrophe ». Éd. Geneviève Chevallier. Cycnos 12:1, Nice: Université Nice-Sophia Antipolis. (1999), « Pour un théâtre de la barbarie: Peter Barnes et Howard Barker ». Éd. É. Angel-Perez et Nicole Boireau. Études anglaises 52, n° 2 (avril–juin 1999): 198–210. Rééd. in Le Théâtre anglais contemporain (1985–2005), Paris: Klincksieck, 2006.

2000-2009Préfaces aux volumes 1–5 et 7 des Howard Barker: Œuvres choisies, Paris: éditions Théâtrales.

(2003), *Notice sur Howard Barker de l'Encyclopédie Universalis*, Paris: Encyclopædia Universalis.

(2006), « Howard Barker : de la catastrophe à l'épiphanie » in E. Angel-Perez (ed.), *Voyages au bout du possible. Les théâtres du traumatisme*, Paris: Klincksieck.

(2007) « Les *7 Lears* de Barker : pour une Généalogie de la Catastrophe », avec Vanasay Khamphommala, in Pascale Drouet, dir., « Réécritures de King Lear » La Licorne, Cahiers Shakespeare en devenir n°1, Poitiers: Université de Poitiers.

Boireau, Nicole (1999), « Le paysage dramatique en Angleterre : consensus et transgression », Alternatives Théâtrales 61, pp. 8–10, Bruxelles: Alternatives Théâtrales.

(2000), « Dystopies » in N. Boireau (ed.), *Théâtre et société en Angleterre des années 1950 à nos jours*, Paris: PUPS.

Hirschmuller, Sarah (2002), « Howard Barker ou la déconsécration du sens. À propos de Maudit crépuscule. » Jean-Marc Lantéri(ed.), Écritures contemporaines 5, pp. 25–42, Caen: Lettres modernes Minard.

Morel, Michel (2001), « La "catastrophe" selon Barker », Geneviève Chevallier (ed.), Cycnos 18, n°1, pp. 65–76, Nice: Université Nice-Sophia Antipolis.

The editor would like to thank David Ian Rabey and Elisabeth Angel-Perez for their assistance in compiling this reading list.